American Statesmen

EDITED BY

JOHN T. MORSE, JR.

CHARLES FRANCIS ADAMS

BY HIS SON

CHARLES FRANCIS ADAMS

BOSTON AND NEW YORK
HOUGHTON, MIFFLIN AND COMPANY
The Riverside Press, Cambridge
1900

Copyright, 1900,
By CHARLES FRANCIS ADAMS.

cessary to connect the narrative, and to throw
light upon it by means of developments since
made, explaining much which was to him at the
time he wrote obscure or deceptive.

C. F. A.

November 11, 1899.

CONTENTS

CHARLES FRANCIS ADAMS

CHAPTER I

BIRTH AND EDUCATION

THOUGH born in Boston, and, until he was over fifty, passing all his maturer life under New England influences, Charles Francis Adams was of mixed Northern and Southern descent. Pure English on both sides, without a trace, so far as can be ascertained, of Scotch or Irish, much less of continental ancestry, race characteristics went with him in the blood, — a factor of no inconsiderable moment in his public life. But while through his father he came of the genuine New England stock, — the Aldens of Plymouth, and the Shepards, Quincys, Nortons, Boylstons, and Basses of the Massachusetts Bay, — on the maternal side he was a Johnson of Maryland. Of this family Governor Thomas Johnson was, in Revolutionary times, the head. An ardent patriot and close personal friend of Washington, he was afterwards not only ap-

pointed by the first President an associate justice of the Supreme Court, but later was tendered the chief justiceship; which position he
declined. A large family, during Revolutionary
times the Maryland Johnsons were well represented in the Continental army; but one brother,
Joshua, twelve years the junior of Governor
Thomas, had in early life established himself
as a merchant in London. When the trans-
Atlantic troubles broke out Joshua Johnson
removed to France, taking up his abode at
Nantes, where he acted as agent of the Maryland colony. After the peace of 1783 he went
back to England; and, in 1785, under the Confederation, was appointed American consul at
London, being the first to hold that office. He
lived in a house near Tower Hill; and J. Q.
Adams, then representing the United States at
the Hague, though recently appointed and confirmed as minister to Prussia, records in his
diary that, at 9 o'clock on the morning of July
26, 1797, he went " to Mr. Johnson's, and thence
to the Church of the parish of All Hallows
Barking, where I was married. . . . We were
married before eleven in the morning, and immediately after went out to see Tilney House."
Louisa Catherine, the second of Mr. Johnson's
five daughters, was, on this occasion, the other
party to the ceremony.

In 1801 J. Q. Adams returned to America. Settling in Boston, he began, rather than resumed, the practice of his profession as a lawyer; and, in February, 1803, being then a member of the Massachusetts State Senate, he was chosen by the legislature United States senator. In 1806 he was further appointed the first Boylston Professor of Rhetoric and Oratory at Harvard. Holding these two positions, now so curiously incompatible, he lived, in 1807, in a frame house which long stood opposite the Common, on the southwest corner of Tremont and Nassau, as Boylston Street was then called, being on part of the present site of the Hotel Touraine. Here, on Tuesday, August 18, 1807, his third child, a son, was born; and nearly four weeks later, on Sunday, September 13th, the father wrote: " My child, born the 18th of last month, was this afternoon baptized by Mr. Emerson, and received the name of Charles Francis, — the first of which I gave him in remembrance of my deceased brother, and the second as a token of honour to my old friend and patron, Judge Dana." The Mr. Emerson here mentioned was then the settled minister of the First Church of Boston, and father of Ralph Waldo Emerson, at the time a child of four years. The " deceased brother," Charles, a third son of John Adams, had died in New York in December,

1801. The connection with "Judge Dana"
was more remote, and there was about it a pleasant sentimental significance. In 1807 Chief
Justice Dana had, only about a year before, retired from the Supreme Court of Massachusetts;
but twenty-seven years earlier J. Q. Adams,
then a boy still in his fourteenth year, had accompanied him on a futile diplomatic errand
to Russia, acting as his secretary and French
interpreter. This remote Revolutionary recollection now bore fruit in a family name.

On August 10, 1809, two years after the
diary entry above referred to was made, John
Quincy Adams, having in 1808 resigned his seat
in the Senate and shortly after been appointed
by President Madison first minister of the
United States to Russia, left Boston, and, driving "over Charles River Bridge to Mr. William
Gray's wharf in Charlestown, there went on
board his ship Horace, Captain Beckford, fitted
out on a voyage to St. Petersburg direct."
With him went the young Charles Francis, a
child not yet two; and "eight full and eventful
years" were to elapse before, a lad of ten, he
was again to see his native town. His education during those years was of a very desultory
character, first in his father's house at St.
Petersburg and later in an English boarding-
school. In Russia, French was not only the

court language, but the language of society; and, curiously enough in the case of Americans at that time, both Mr. and Mrs. Adams had passed much of their childhood in France, — he at Paris, she at Nantes. They, therefore, enjoyed the inestimable advantage, placed as they then were, of perfect familiarity with French; and French thus became the child's native tongue, that which he talked in preference to any other. After his return home, in 1817, close upon forty-four years were to elapse before he was again in Europe; but when, in 1871–72, he served on the Geneva Arbitration, he had occasion to appreciate at its full value that childish familiarity with French acquired more than half a century before.

At the close of April, 1814, J. Q. Adams left St. Petersburg, under instructions from his government to take part in the peace negotiations with Great Britain, shortly afterwards entered upon at Ghent. Mrs. Adams remained, with her child, in Russia until the following winter, awaiting instructions from her husband. The correspondence between father and son, which was to continue until the death of the former, now began, and has still an interest, revealing, as it does, the kindlier, more domestic, and less austere features of the older man's character. For instance, from Amsterdam in June, 1814, he writes to the child, not yet seven, describing how much he had wished his three boys with him in his travels of late, and adding this graphic little pen-and-ink *genre* sketch of Holland : —

" It is a very curious and beautiful country to see, especially at this season. It is all smooth and level as the floor of a house ; a constant succession of green pastures, covered with multitudes of sheep and cattle, and intersected with canals upon which the people travel in large covered boats drawn by horses. I am sure it would be a pleasure to you to see the little boys, in large breeches, big enough to make you two suits of clothes, and wooden shoes, and black round wigs, and pipes of tobacco in their mouths ; and the little girls, with petticoats stuffed out like an umbrella, coming half down their legs, and blue stockings, and slippers without heels, flapping at their feet as they walk along."

Presently it became evident that J. Q. Adams was not to return to St. Petersburg ; so Mrs. Adams, breaking up the establishment there, set out to join her husband somewhere in western Europe, exactly where she did not know ; for the times were troublous, and means of communication poor. Taking with her the boy, now in his eighth year, and accompanied only by a servant, she left St. Petersburg in her traveling carriage, and found her way in midwinter across Europe, then filled with the troops of the allied armies on their way home after the abdication of Napoleon, and finally joined her husband in Paris on March 23, 1815, at the beginning of the famous "Hundred Days." It was a Thursday when she drove up to the hotel in Paris, and Napoleon, fresh from Elba, had on the previous Monday been borne in triumph up the steps of the Tuileries in the arms of his old soldiers, delirious with joy. The journey had been long and trying; but Mrs. Adams was quite equal to the occasion, for she delighted in movement, and never felt so well or so happy as when inside of a traveling carriage. They remained at Paris until the middle of May, when J. Q. Adams, who had then been appointed to the English mission, crossed over with his family to London, arriving there just three weeks before the day of Waterloo. When they started for England, Napoleon had not yet left Paris, and Charles Francis always afterwards had a vivid recollection of looking up, a boy in the surging crowd, and seeing the Emperor as he stood in the familiar clothes on the balcony of the Tuileries, acknowledging the acclamations of the multitude below.

The next two years were passed in England,

where J. Q. Adams was at last rejoined by his two elder sons, from whom he had been six years separated. John, the second, and his young brother Charles were sent to a boarding-school at Ealing, kept by a Dr. Nicholas, where they made a rough and simultaneous acquaintance with English boys and with the Latin grammar, taught, as that grammar in English schools then was, itself in Latin. It was just after the close of the war of 1812–15, — indeed, the battle of New Orleans and the brilliant engagement in which the Constitution captured the Cyane and Levant had occurred only a few months before, and within the year; so it was in no degree to be wondered at that the two young "Yankees" did not find their position peculiarly pleasant. The school was a large one, there being in it some two hundred and fifty boys, and on one occasion at least the two Adamses would seem to have had distinctly the advantage; for, in writing to his mother, J. Q. Adams, referring to the school-life, tells her that Dr. Nicholas was "highly diverted with a repartee of John's to one of the boys, who asked him slyly, whether he had ever been at Washington. No (said John), but I have been at New Orleans." In August, 1815, General Scott, fresh from Niagara and Chippewa, was in London. Of course he visited Mr. Adams; and the old soldier never afterwards forgot the fact that, when he was dining at Mr. Adams's house, young Charles Francis spoke up suddenly, and asked him to tell about his battles in Canada, for use at school. More than twenty years later, while walking with his father through the capitol at Washington, Mr. Adams met General Scott, who recalled the incident, illustrating thereby, as Mr. Adams thought, his well-known personal vanity; though it would have seemed natural enough, and in no way peculiar to Scott, that, within three months after Waterloo, an American officer should feel gratified to find his name and exploits familiar as household words in the mouth of a boy of eight in England.

Singular as it may appear, like the French of his infancy at St. Petersburg, this experience at the Ealing boarding-school was of very appreciable value to Mr. Adams half a century later, indeed was a most important educational factor. It caused him to understand the English character. He had come in contact with it as a child in the absolutely natural life of an English school; and when, as a man, he came in contact with it again, an insight did not have to be acquired. It had, on the contrary, already been bred, probably beaten, into him; and he acted unconsciously upon it. He was in a degree to the manner born; for, though he retained no

pleasant memories of the English character or
of English boys, he and they had been brought
up together in one nursery.

In 1817, at the beginning of the first administration of Monroe, J. Q. Adams, after eight
years' residence in Europe, was recalled to America. Landing in New York with his parents in
August, the young Charles Francis was taken
immediately to Quincy, where, when his father
a month later went to Washington to assume
his duties as secretary of state in the Monroe
cabinet, he remained in charge of his grandmother, Mrs. John Adams. Mrs. Adams was
then in her seventy-third year, and died thirteen months later; but never, to the end of Mr.
Adams's life, did the impression her character
then made on him fade away. Older than he,
and now almost grown up, his two brothers,
during their father's absence in Russia, had
been left under her care ; and in later life Mr.
Adams used to describe his own surprise, shortly
after he got home in 1817, at seeing his big
brothers actually burst into tears as they tried
to exculpate themselves when their grandmother, because of some trifling misconduct, had
occasion to rebuke them. At the time he could
not understand the feeling of affection and rev-
erence with which they regarded her ; though
a little later he himself fully shared in it. Her

death brought with it a change, as complete as it was sad and indescribable, in both the moral atmosphere and the physical surroundings of the house at Quincy; but not until twenty years afterwards did the publication of her letters make apparent to others the cause of the veneration with which her descendants looked up to her, and the grounds of her influence over them.

Immediately after his return to America Mr. Adams entered the Boston Latin School, of which Benjamin Apthorp Gould had then been for three years head master, and came under that teacher's inspiring personal influence. From childhood upwards a matured, self-contained character, he was apparently somewhat a favorite with Mr. Gould, of whom he always afterwards spoke with the utmost respect, while the Latin School and its traditions stood high in his estimation; so high indeed that, as matter of course, he in due time sent to it his own two eldest sons in their turn, with results, to them at least, the reverse of satisfactory. Entering Harvard in 1821, when scarcely fourteen, Mr. Adams graduated in 1825.

CHAPTER II

EARLY LIFE

AFTER graduation, Mr. Adams passed some years at Washington; living in the White House then presided over by his mother, mixing in the society of the place, observing the course of events, and noting down his impressions of the eminent public men of the period, — Randolph, Jackson, Clay, and Webster. In the autumn of 1828, however, Mr. Adams left Washington and went back to Boston, there, as it proved, to take up his residence for the next thirty years. Mr. Webster, in the full swing of his great powers, had advised him that, as things then were, the law was " a man's only course; " and Mr. Adams, reflecting on this advice, made up his mind that " the proper course [for him] to adopt [was] to make the law a profession, so as to rise in character; and, if anything better should present, to take it, provided it [was] really better." So, with this in view, he entered the office of Mr. Webster as a student in November, 1828. His studies do not seem to have been of long continuance, for, on the 6th of the following January, being then in his twenty-second year, he was admitted to practice as an attorney ; and, six months later, on September 5, 1829, he was married, at the family residence in Medford, to Abigail Brown, the youngest child of Peter Chardon Brooks, of Boston, whose other daughters were the wives, the one of Nathaniel L. Frothingham, then and long after, in succession to William Emerson, with one brief intervening ministry, pastor of the First Congregational Church ; the other, of Edward Everett.

Beginning in December, 1859, and closing in November, 1872, the active public life of Mr. Adams was confined to almost exactly thirteen years ; and to the history of those years, and the share he took in their events, this biography will be mainly devoted. Not that the earlier period lacked interest, or interest having an historical bearing, but it was mainly in connection with others, or with great political movements then in the more incipient stage. For instance, between 1830 and 1846, the life of Mr. Adams was inseparably interwoven with the career of his father, and, in reality, not less essential to that career than influenced by it. Indeed, the memorable record made by J. Q. Adams from 1832 to 1846 would not have been possible had it not been for the coöperation and

quiet support he received from his son, whose
own direct influence on public questions was
meanwhile hardly perceptible. Yet at the beginning the son had strenuously opposed the
reëntry of the father into public life.

When, through the election of General Jackson, J. Q. Adams was retired from the presidency, he was in his sixty-second year. According to all precedent he thus found himself, in
the full enjoyment of his great powers, relegated
to what was known as " a dignified retirement."
Meanwhile, adapted to public life, he had an
insatiable craving for it. Accustomed to it,
from it he derived that enjoyment which every
strong man derives from the exercise of his
muscles, intellectual or physical. His son now
wanted J. Q. Adams, with the examples of
Washington, Jefferson, and Madison before him,
quietly to accept the situation, and devote his
remaining years to literary pursuits and philosophical meditation. To the father this prospect was not alluring ; for though, by accident
of birth, some forty years the elder man of the
two, he was in combativeness of disposition considerably the younger, and in feelings the less
mature. Accordingly, on the first opportunity
that offered, he plunged once more into the political current ; nor did he again emerge from it.
As is well known, he sank in the swim.

Meanwhile when in 1830 he, an ex-President, accepted the nomination for Congress tendered him from what was then known as the Plymouth district, he took the chances heavily against himself; for at that juncture he was passing through a severe ordeal. During the previous twenty years his career had been one of almost unbroken success. Minister to Russia during the close of the Napoleonic period, negotiator of the treaty of Ghent, minister to Great Britain after the war of 1812–15, secretary of state for eight years and President for four, he had passed on from one position to another with a regularity and firmness more suggestive of European than American public life. In private, too, he had been sufficiently prosperous. His sons had grown up and chosen their professions; two of them were married; his estate, though not large, sufficed for his needs. Suddenly, beginning with the autumn of 1828, calamity succeeded calamity. Defeated by Jackson in the election of that year, hardly had he been retired from the presidency when he lost his oldest son, suddenly and while on the way to Washington. Five years later another son died. Through the unfortunate business ventures of the latter the father had become pecuniarily involved; and thus, between 1830 and 1835, he was confronted at once by political defeat, domestic affliction, and financial ruin. The situation, in every aspect bad, was made appreciably worse by the fact that the remaining son so disapproved of the father's return to public life that the two were for a time "not upon terms of perfect cordiality."

The elder man, however, bore up bravely; and, from the spring of 1835, affairs gradually assumed a more cheerful aspect. The father's course had then unmistakably vindicated itself. He had demonstrated that he was right, — that he understood himself and the situation. So far as he was concerned, the problem of what we are to do with our ex-Presidents did not call for further consideration. This particular ex-President had developed the capacity to take care of himself; and thenceforth not only did remonstrance cease on the part of the son, but the feeling which gave birth to it changed, as rapidly as silently, into one of pride, loyalty, intense approval, and earnest coöperation. The coöperation, too, was essential. The financial tangle had to be unsnarled; and, while perfectly tractable and quick to adopt any needful measures of economy, J. Q. Adams could not educate himself to business methods or to those details incident to the care of property. One of the commonly whispered charges against him during his later years and after his death was an alleged inclination to parsimony, — a well-developed tendency to New England thrift. The fact was that, by reason of incorrigible carelessness in private monetary matters, he escaped ruin and want — the fate of his predecessor Monroe — only through prudent management on the part of his son, who, in 1835–36, practically, though with that gentleman's consent, put the ex-President under financial guardianship. Though his establishment was a modest one, J. Q. Adams, from that time to the end of his life, rarely lived within his income ; of which his paltry pay of $1500 or $2000 per annum as a member of Congress was an essential part. The increasing value of such real estate as he owned in Boston and Washington gradually relieved him from any pressing embarrassment ; but throughout his congressional career it was solely due to the wholesome oversight thus exercised over him that J. Q. Adams was able to remain in public life. But for it he would have faded out in financial straits.

Thus vicariously doing his share in public life, Mr. Adams turned his attention more and more to literary, historical, and, incidentally, to political topics. The "North American Review" was then the recognized medium through which New England culture found expression ; and towards that medium Mr. Adams naturally turned. Between the years 1829 and 1843 the "North American" was edited first by Alexander H. Everett, a brother of Edward, and then by Dr. John G. Palfrey, subsequently the historian of New England, Dr. Palfrey succeeding Mr. Everett in 1835. The Review was then a vigorous, well-written, high-toned "quarterly," modeled on the "Edinburgh," of which it was an unpartisan and consequently somewhat colorless American echo. In fact, as compared with its great Scotch prototype, it was slightly suggestive of the play of "Hamlet," the part of the Prince of Denmark, in that case personified by Francis Jeffrey, being omitted. To it Mr. Adams, first and last, contributed in all seventeen papers, filling more than four hundred and fifty printed pages, and dealing ordinarily with topics more or less connected with American history, such as the lives of Thomas Hutchinson and Aaron Burr, the Madison Papers and the Northeastern Boundary. Beginning in the January number of 1831, with a review of James Graham's "History of the United States," first published some three years before, and then little known in America, he closed in the number for July, 1846, with an article on the "Letters of the Earl of Chesterfield."

During all these years, as long before, the papers left by John Adams were still lying

bundled up in the boxes to which, in repeated
processes of removals, they had been con-
signed, — a vast, unsorted, miscellaneous accumulation. It was part of the son's plan, only
slowly and very reluctantly abandoned, that
J. Q. Adams should put these papers in order,
and prepare from them a biography of his father ; for, all his life, Mr. Adams labored under
the delusion that J. Q. Adams, preëminent as
a controversialist and for drawing state papers,
had also great literary capacity. Fortunately
J. Q. Adams understood himself much better
than his son understood him ; and, greatly to
the discomfiture of the latter, he evinced the
utmost indisposition to having anything to do
with the John Adams papers or controversies.
His son could not account for this indifference ;
and yet it seems explicable enough when he
records how his father one day, made impatient
by his solicitude, exclaimed upon " the weariness
of raking over a stale political excitement."
There was, in truth, in J. Q. Adams a great
deal of human nature. Yielding to its impulse, he was now again involved in the political movements at Washington, taking, as his
astonished son wrote, " as much interest as if he
was a young man." So, yielding to the influence of the stronger and more active mind, the
son himself next became concerned in questions

of the day, and for a time ceased to occupy himself with the family papers and contributions to the " North American."

Curiously enough, the mutations of " this whimsical world," as he called it, had, during the congressional session of 1835, brought J. Q. Adams into the support, at once vigorous and dramatic, of his victorious rival, now for the second time President. Towards Jackson, personally, his feelings had undergone no amelioration. The Tennessee frontiersman, soldier and politician, offended him from every point of view. " A barbarian and savage, who could scarcely spell his own name," he had, as President, violated both principle and precedent, degrading " the offices of the heads of department into mere instruments of his will." On the other hand, J. Q. Adams entertained deepseated, almost passionate, convictions on certain fundamental points of national policy and constitutional construction ; and upon these points he now found the " barbarian and savage," who had supplanted him, standing forth as the unmistakable champion of the policy for which he had labored and the construction in which he believed, with his own friends and natural allies united in an opposition purely political. The issues were three in number : — South Carolina nullification, known as " Calhounism ; " the complication with France arising out of the non-payment by that country of the indemnity for spoliations provided for in the convention of 1831 between the two countries ; and, finally, the constitutional issue between the President and the Senate over the executive power of appointment to, and removal from, office. As respects these issues J. Q. Adams felt strongly. To quote his own language in a confidential letter to his son : — " I cannot reflect [upon these three subjects] in the aspect which they now bear, and in which they will probably be presented at the ensuing session of Congress, without deep concern and inexpressible anguish. It will be impossible, after the part that I have taken with regard to two of them — the impending foreign and domestic war — for me to dodge either of the questions. I led the House upon both of them in the last session. I cannot shrink from advising the House concerning them at the next."

To two of these three issues, — those involving the probability of " foreign and domestic war," — it is unnecessary here to refer, for their further consideration by the father did not involve the son. It was otherwise with the third issue, that arising out of the participation of the Senate, through its power of confirmation, in the patronage, aud, by means of the patronage, in the most intimate executive functions of the government. J. Q. Adams had himself been President; and, as President, he had grown to look with deepest apprehension on the tendency of the Senate, one branch of the legislative body, to arrogate authority to itself. His experience and sagacity thus led him early to forecast what has since developed into a great constitutional evil, from that day to this of steady, portentous growth. So, for the moment putting aside the issue with France, and even nullification, as matters of minor consequence, — "The Patronage Bill," he wrote to his son, "is that upon which my feelings and my apprehensions are most intense. I can grind it to impalpable powder before any tribunal but that of Whig federalism, nullification, and ochlocracy; but that is precisely the combination against which I have to contend." Perhaps it would have been as intelligible if, instead of "Ochlocracy," J. Q. Adams had here used the modern substitute for that term, "Democracy;" but he was at the moment writing, not for publication, but familiarly. So, using such words and figures as first suggested themselves, he went instinctively back to the harassing, nerve-destroying trials of his own administration; and, in terms of invective as vehement as they were characteristic, proceeded to give his view of the slow

genesis of this measure, and of its subtile and
dangerous character as interfering with the constitutional allotment of functions. The history
of the now forgotten Patronage Bill of 1835 can
be briefly told.

In view of the wholly unprecedented course
pursued by Jackson in his distribution of offices,
— the introduction in fact of the modern " spoils
system " into our politics, — Mr. Calhoun, during the nullification excitement of 1835, reported
a measure calculated to reduce the political influence exerted by the Executive through its
control of the public patronage. Unfortunately,
however, this result, very desirable in itself, was
reached through what Mr. Adams held to be the
even more pernicious evil of making one branch
of the legislative body a participant in the control of that patronage. If this theory obtained,
he saw clearly enough — he was told by his own
experience — that office-peddling between the
President and the Senate would become a recognized system, to the lasting deterioration of each
as a branch of the government. In the ripeness
of time, as history shows, exactly that result
came about. Driving at once to the heart of
this issue, Mr. Adams saw the thing in all its
remote and latent bearings. Unfortunately, Mr.
Webster, in his dislike and deep distrust of
President Jackson, had in the session of 1835

made a speech in support of the Calhoun "Patronage Bill," in which he indicated a dissent from the construction given to the Constitution in 1789, by which the power of removal from office was exclusively conceded to the President. His position was unquestionably not in the line of Federalist doctrine or authority; and, in assuming it, he incurred the outspoken wrath of Jackson's predecessor. After describing and denouncing, with a vehemence almost ludicrous, the combination — Calhoun, Clay, Webster, and White — which, on February 21, 1835, carried this measure through the Senate, he thus went on in his letter to his son : "The most utterly inexcusable [of this combination] because the most glaringly treacherous to his own professed principles is Webster. He is the only Federalist of the gang. The Constitution was the work and the highest glory of the Federal party. The exposition of it which declares all subordinate executive officers removable by the President was the hard-earned victory of the Federal party in the first Congress. Without it the Constitution itself would long since have been a ruin ; and now Daniel Webster, the Federal Pharisee of the straightest sect, brought up at the feet of Gamaliel, betrays at once to nullification and Bentonism his party and his country, — tells the world that James Madison blundered in not knowing that by the Constitution of the United States the appointing power was vested in the President and Senate, that the executive power is no power at all, that no man can tell what is or is not executive power, and that Congress, if they please, may make a secretary of state or an attorney-general for life.

" ' Semper ego auditor tantum ? numquamne reponam ? ' "

It is open to question whether J. Q. Adams here stated the position of Mr. Webster quite as accurately as he quoted Juvenal's famous line ; but, however this may be, the fierce denunciation produced its effect on his son. The seed this time fell on fertile soil. Once when the younger Oliver Wendell Holmes was discussing some revolutionary views of philosophy with Ralph Waldo Emerson, the transcendentalist advised the neophyte, in bringing out his ideas, to "strike at a king ! " — nothing less than dethroning the Stagyrite himself should satisfy. So, in this case, the younger Adams, then twenty-eight years old, and eager to distinguish himself, was incited by his father to assail on a vital constitutional issue the great "Defender of the Constitution," then fresh from his triumph over Hayne.

J. Q. Adams returned to Quincy early in June, 1835, and, during the months which fol-

lowed, his son went to work, making, with his
assistance and suggestions, a thorough study of
the constitutional questions involved in the "Patronage Bill." The results, read by his father,
were "returned with commendation more than
enough," and appeared during the summer in a
series of communicated articles printed simulta-
neously in the columns of the "Boston Advocate" and the "Centinel." In the autumn,
after careful revision, they were published in
pamphlet form, under the title, boldly appropri-
ated from Burke, of "An Appeal from the New
to the Old Whigs, by a Whig of the Old
School." This effort of his younger days Mr.
Adams always afterwards looked back upon
with peculiar satisfaction; and more than forty
years later, when, under the administration of
General Grant, the same question again presented itself for discussion and copies of his
pamphlet were in some request, after looking it
over he laid it down, remarking on its vigor,
and expressing the belief that he could not then,
in his later and riper life, have done it so well.
When published it was by some attributed to the
father. "Mr. Woodbury" (then secretary of
the treasury), wrote J. Q. Adams from Washington at the end of the following November,
"told me that he had read it, and that it was
unanswerable. He said that he had perhaps

voted [the other way] upon Mr. Benton's proposed bill in 1826, but that the question had not been discussed upon its true principles. He said that no one could read the pamphlet without being convinced of the true intent of the Constitution. I said the pamphlet had been erroneously ascribed to me. I had not written a line of it, but I told him who was the author." This denial was hardly necessary; for the production, though in point and vigor well worthy of the supposed author, bore none of his ear-marks. It was distinctly a better piece of work than he was capable of at that time and upon that topic; for, while in no way lacking in spirit and earnestness, it was more comprehensive, calmer in style, and, from the literary point of view, better ordered. There was in it less of that vehemence of tone, that eagerness for controversy and wealth of invective, which always marred the productions of the father, and which also, curiously enough, instead of being mitigated by years, grew ever upon him.

To return to the son's pamphlet: no reprint of the "Appeal from the New to the Old Whigs" has ever been called for; but at the time and since, whenever the allocation of powers under the federal Constitution has been in discussion, copies have been in request. Even so late as 1897, — sixty-two years after its publication, — a brief note was received by a member of Mr. Adams's family, from one of the justices of the Supreme Court of the United States, saying that the old question was once more before that tribunal, that he had in vain sent to the Congressional Library for a copy of the pamphlet, and asking if one could not be procured for him at Quincy. Though it caused no noticeable sensation, — the Patronage Bill of 1835 having then already become a yesterday's political excitement, — the Appeal when published was remarked upon for its research, its grasp of principle and vigor of statement, bringing the author, among other letters, one of kindly commendation from ex-President Madison.

The "Appeal from the New to the Old Whigs" thus secured for Mr. Adams what he then deeply hungered for, — a degree of personal recognition ; for, in entering upon life, he found himself overweighted by the great reputation of his grandfather and his father, while the latter also overshadowed him by instant prominence. The acts and utterances of the preceding generations were ever on the lips of men, and they had neither knowledge nor expectation of that then rising. So when Mr. Adams thought " to play off his own bat," as Lord Palmerston would have expressed it, people, naturally enough,

attributed the strokes to the veteran in the game.
" They say it is from my pen, but my father's
brain," the younger man wrote of the " Appeal,"
in 1835 ; and, indeed, it was not until he was
over fifty that Mr. Adams fairly succeeded in
asserting his right to be considered as something
more than the son of his father.

The great political issue of his generation,
the issue over African slavery, the agitation of
which, really beginning to make itself felt only
in 1835, was not to culminate for twenty-five
years, had not up to this time (1835) apparently
attracted the notice of Mr. Adams; at least,
he makes no mention of it. The publication
of the " Liberator " was begun in 1831, and
in October, 1835, Garrison was mobbed in
Boston. At that time he represented nothing
but an idea, — the first faint movement of an
awakening public conscience ; but it is curious
to notice the instinctive correctness with which
the great slave-power and its affiliations divined
impending danger. Not guided by reason, their
anger and alarm were out of all proportion to
the apparent menace; but at the first whisper
of attack they, like some fierce wild beast of
prey scenting harm from afar, bristled up sav-
agely and emitted an ominous growl.

On the other hand, the gradual growth of
the anti-slavery sentiment, the arousing of the

Puritanic, New England conscience not less in-
grained in Mr. Adams than in his father, as
from time to time now set down in his record,
is an instructive study, suggestive of what was
then quite generally going on. On August
20th, just two months before the Garrison mob,
he notes : " The town is full of the abolition
projects and the meeting to be held to counteract them. This takes place to-morrow night at
Faneuil Hall ; the application is signed by most
of our respectable citizens. I am glad I have
nothing to do with it." A few days later, September 8th, speaking of one of a series of communications he was then making to a newspaper,
he says : " The last takes up the recent excitement about slavery and abolition, a subject
which it might be wiser not to touch." Of the
Garrison mob, six weeks afterwards, he merely
remarks that, " among other things, we have
had a mob to put down abolitionists, as if the
country was not going to pot fast enough without extraordinary help." Then presently : " The
news from Washington is that the question of
slavery is driving everything else out of view.
My father has opened upon it, rather to my regret though not to my surprise. The excitement
seems to be so intense as to threaten the worst
consequences." A month later comes the de-
spairing groan : " My father at Washington is

in the midst of a painful struggle, which his unfortunate permanency in public life brings upon him. My judgment was not mistaken when I dissuaded him from it. But, as he is in it, I must do my best to help him out." This resolve on the part of the son was certainly commendable; though it is to be feared that, if the father had been able to find no other resource in the difficult position in which he had then placed himself, his danger would have been extreme. Fortunately, on this, as on divers subsequent occasions, he proved quite sufficient in himself; and when, a few weeks later, he emerged in triumph from the conflict, with the floor of the Representatives Hall strewed thick with discomfited opponents, the son could only remark: "It is singular how he continues to sustain himself by the force of his mere ability." From that time forward, however, the " I-told-you-so " refrain was no longer heard.

The anti-slavery educational footprints are next found in entries like the following: "Finished this morning Dr. Channing's pamphlet upon slavery. It is certainly a very powerful production, and worthy of deeper consideration than it has yet been in the way of receiving. Our fashion here is to vote a man down at once without hearing his reasons. This saves much trouble, and dispenses with all necessity

for argument. Dr. Channing may not be wise
to encroach upon a political field, but what he
says may have much weight without considering
the author." The man, so far as he had now
got, showed the influence of environment, — it
was still questionable " propriety " on the part
of a minister of the church of Christ to express
any views on man's property in man ! By the
following July he himself had begun to write
on the subject in the " Boston Advocate." " In
my own opinion it is the best thing I ever wrote ;
but whether it will meet with much approbation
in the world is more than doubtful to me." A
few months later, when his sentiments were
asked for, he said : " While I entirely dissented
from the abolition views respecting the District
of Columbia, I was yet clearly in favor of discussion, and would by no means give to the principle of slavery anything more than the tolera-
tion which the Constitution has granted." This
position certainly could not be regarded as extreme. Events, however, moved rapidly. His
father next had, " as usual, fallen into a great
trouble," rousing " the passions of the Southern
members to the boiling point." This was the
somewhat famous occasion when Mr. Adams,
from his place in the House of Representatives,
inquired of the Speaker as to the disposition
which would, under the rules of that body, be

made of a petition purporting to come from slaves. The result of the contest thus precipitated was again extremely disastrous to the assailants of Mr. Adams, who found themselves badly scalded at his hands by the overflow of their own " boiling passions ; " and two days later the son wrote : " The uproar in Congress has ceased, and my father has carried the day. I hope he will use his victory in moderation." The months then rolled on, and in November, 1837, came the news of the Alton riot with the brutal murder of Lovejoy. It was the legitimate outcome of the Garrison mob of two years earlier, and the distant forerunner of border ruffian outrages twenty years later; it was also fuel to the kindling flame. Even when young Mr. Adams was a cold man outwardly, and not quick to move ; but once fairly in motion he was apt to be impetuous. Accordingly, when now the Boston city fathers undertook to refuse the use of Faneuil Hall on the application of Dr. Channing and others for a public meeting to protest against mob-rule even in Illinois, Mr. Adams wrote : " The craven spirit has got about as far in Boston as it can well go. I had a warm argument in Mr. Brooks's room with two or three of my [wife's] connections there. They are always of the conservative order, and I cannot often be." The following day, after listening to a sermon in which he traced a disposition to deprecate the excitement over " the case of this Lovejoy," he met one of his brothers-in-law, who intimated some degree of sympathy with his views ; and, recording this surprising fact, he insensibly made use of a form of speech subsequently very familiar : " We are not all broken in to the cotton interest then."

The following Friday the Faneuil Hall meeting was held, — the meeting at which Wendell Phillips, then a young man of twenty-six, made his memorable first appearance as a public speaker. Mr. Adams went : — " The hall was very full, and not much time was needed to show that two parties existed in it. Dr. Channing was speaking when I went in. He looked to me somewhat agitated and anxious ; but his manner was slow and drawling, which produces more effect in the pulpit than here. His speech seemed to be a kind of justification of himself in moving the public meeting and in preparing the resolutions, which he said he expected and wished to be known [as his] here and everywhere. He was followed by G. S. Hillard, who, in a brief and well-turned speech, explained the ground of the public meeting. Thus far things were quiet ; but Mr. James T. Austin thought proper to put in a bar to the proceedings. It did not seem clear to me what good object he

could have had, for he produced no substantial
course, and limited himself to insulting the motives and proceedings of the abolitionists. This
was easily enough done in a city corrupted heart
and soul by the principles of slavery, and with
a majority present almost ready to use force to
bear him out, if necessary, right or wrong. His
argument was that the mob of Alton was justified by the case. Lovejoy was acting against the
safety of the people of Missouri, in a place on
the border of the State where the law of that
State could not touch him; that, the laws of
two States thus conflicting, in a case of imminent danger the people rose up in their might
and decided for themselves. They did in this
case no more than our ancestors, who threw
overboard the tea in Boston harbor, — and who
thinks of censuring them for a riot? The fact
of a clergyman's falling only showed that a
clergyman was out of his place when meddling
with the weapons of the flesh, and that he died
as the fool dieth. The course of the abolition
party was like that of a man who should insist
on the liberation of the wild animals of a mena-
gerie. Such was the substance of a speech in
Faneuil Hall in 1837 of the attorney general
of Massachusetts, applauded at every sentence
by a large and powerful party of respectable
men! I confess my nerves did not stand it very

well; and, from that moment, I went with the meeting. A young Mr. Phillips followed with some very spirited and ready remarks, which were too stinging not to arouse the feeling of the opponents, and more than once I thought strong symptoms of a riot to be impending. But he finished quickly, and Mr. Bond got up with a mild view of the whole course of proceeding, full of moderation and good practical sense. The resolutions were then voted, though not without opposition, and adjourned. On the whole, it was the most excited public meeting I was ever present at; and, I confess, nothing could exceed the mixed disgust and indignation which moved me, at the doctrines of the learned expounder of mob law."

As they worked up their new theory for putting, through riot, a stop to discussion, "the friends of law and order" were at that time manufacturing anti-slavery sentiment rapidly. So a fortnight later Mr. Adams noted that his hereditary and college associate and friend, young Edmund Quincy, had "come out a warm abolitionist, his letter being published in the 'Liberator,' and he having made a speech last evening;" and added, with a touch almost of sadness: "I wish I could be an entire abolitionist; but it is impossible. My mind will not come down to the point." So the result showed. In that contest he had his place; but not amid the sharp spattering fire of the skirmish line. His place was just behind that fire, in the front rank of the solid, advancing array of battle. To this conclusion he himself had evidently come when, during the following spring, he passed a month in Washington. The fraudulent "Cherokee Treaty" was then under debate. One day he wrote: "News from Philadelphia of the destruction by a mob of the hall lately erected for free discussion. Such is the nature and extent of American liberty;" and, shortly afterwards, speaking of the House of Representatives: "We heard first General Glascock, and then Mr. Downing, a delegate from Florida, the latter violent and savage. A strong proof of the debased moral principle of the House may be found in the fact that such a speech as this could be listened to with even tolerable patience. It is slavery that is at the bottom of this. I am more satisfied of the fact every day I live; and nothing can save this country from entire perversion, morally and politically, but the predominance of the abolition principle. Whether this will ever take place is very doubtful. I have not much hope." Then on May 29th, being still in Washington, he adds: "Much talk of an insurrection of the blacks, supposed to be about to break out at eleven o'clock this night, instigated by an abolitionist from New York or elsewhere. The alarm of the whites sufficiently shows the horrors of the slavery system, without the need of exaggeration. Their fears magnify their own danger, and this produces all the violence they dread. I imagine the whole story grows out of a very small affair ; but such is the character of the whites that it may not improbably lead to bad consequences. My mother and the family are always apprehensive at such times of the possible direction of the public feeling against my father, for having taken so much part in the matter. I hope she has no cause."

Slavery, however, did not yet occupy the mind of Mr. Adams to the exclusion of all other political topics. That time was coming; it had not yet come. Questions connected with currency and revenue were meanwhile under constant discussion, — for those were the days of the battle over the United States Bank, Jackson's removal of the deposits, the sub-treasury scheme, and the devastating commercial panic of 1837–38. Upon all these topics, now absolutely devoid of interest, Mr. Adams was an active thinker and constant contributor to the newspapers. Series after series of articles from his pen appeared in the " Boston Centinel " and " Advocate ; " and that they attracted so little attention, failing to take the world at once by

storm, was to him, as to most other ambitious
young writers before and since, matter for surprise, and almost, if not quite, of grievance.

As an interlude in these occupations Mr.
Adams, having at last abandoned in despair all
hope of interesting his father in that sacred
duty, was slowly overhauling the family manu-
scripts; and while doing so, he came across the
yellowing files of Revolutionary correspondence.
" A packet I opened," he wrote one day, " contained the love letters of the old gentleman in
1763–66, just before his marriage. They were
mostly written during the three or four weeks
when he went up to Boston to be inoculated for
the smallpox. The subject is, of course, an odd
one for lovers, but they both seem so honest and
simple-hearted in discussing it." And again:
" With what a mixture of feelings do I look
over these old papers. They contain the secret
history of the lives of a single couple. Joy and
sunshine, grief and clouds, sorrow and storms.
The vicissitudes are rapid, the incidents are interesting. Happy are those who pass through
this valley with so much of innocence. Vice
stains no one of these pages." At last the
father, evidently in consequence of the talk of
the son over what his researches had brought
to light, suggested to him the idea of writing
a biography of his grandmother. " I do not

know that this would be beyond my ability," Mr. Adams modestly wrote; and so he set to work upon it.

Early in May, 1840, the copy for the "Letters of Mrs. Adams" was submitted to James Brown, then the leading publisher of Boston, who at a glance took in the value of the proposed book, and "strongly recommended going right on;" so it went to press at once. In August the memoir of Mrs. Adams, which was to accompany it, was completed, and the hesitating author submitted it to his wife; who, with more frankness than literary discernment, pronounced it "wordy and conceited, and recommended its being wholly cut down and written over;" whereat, observed Mr. Adams, "I go on rather under discouragement." The "discouragement" was, under the circumstances, not unnatural, but fortunately proved uncalled for. Published early in October, the success of the "Letters" was immediate and, for a book of the kind in those days, phenomenal. The first edition was exhausted almost at once, and a second of fifteen hundred copies was called for, which was eagerly taken up as fast as it came from the press; for, of the first batch of two hundred copies, nearly all were sent away "to supply orders from the South, and the remainder were sold [over the counter] before twelve o'clock."

Deeply gratified as he was at the success of this his first literary venture, Mr. Adams would have been more gratified yet could he have read the subsequent diary record of his father; for J. Q. Adams was not a demonstrative man, and rarely, except when communing with himself, gave expression to his inmost feelings. So now, on Sunday, September 27, 1840, he wrote that, attending, as was his wont, divine service in the afternoon, whereat a certain Mr. Motte preached upon the evidences of Christianity from the text, John xx. 31, " my attention and thoughts were too much absorbed by the volume of my Mother's Letters which my son has published, and of which he sent me this morning a copy. An admirable Memoir of her life written by him is prefixed to the Letters, and the reading of it affected me till the tears streamed down my face. It disabled me for all other occupation, and the arrears of this diary and the sermon of Barrow were forgotten."

CHAPTER III

THE MASSACHUSETTS LEGISLATURE

THOUGH now in his thirty-fourth year, Mr. Adams had up to this time evinced no desire to enter active public life. A nomination to the Massachusetts legislature was offered him in 1839; but, though equivalent to an election, he had declined it. Governor Everett, Isaac P. Davis, a warm political and personal friend of Mr. Webster, and Robert C. Winthrop, then speaker of the Massachusetts House of Representatives, all spoke of this to J. Q. Adams, expressing their regret; and he earnestly remonstrated with his son. It was too late to reconsider the matter that year; but when, in 1840, a nomination was again offered him, yielding to the very distinctly expressed wish of his father, Mr. Adams accepted. It was the year of the famous 1840 " Log Cabin " and " Hard Cider " presidential campaign — probably the most ridiculous, and, so far as political discussion was concerned, the lowest in tone, the country has ever passed through. As its result, Martin Van Buren was voted out of the presidential chair,

and William Henry Harrison into it, — for the
period of one month. He was then succeeded
by John Tyler. In this campaign Mr. Adams
acted with the Whig party; in 1836 he had
voted for Van Buren, though "horrified" by
that gentleman's support, in the Senate, of "the
bill to suppress incendiary publications." He
had then looked upon the New Yorker "as a
choice of evils;" and it shows the rapid advance
of the anti-slavery sentiment in the mind of Mr.
Adams, that he now, four years later, wrote:
"Mr. Van Buren bids fair to have in the free
States but the seven electoral votes of New
Hampshire. So much for ruling the North by
party machinery. So much for the Northern
man with Southern principles. May this year's
experience be a lesson to all future politicians
who sacrifice the interests that ought to be most
dear to them, for the sake of truckling to slaveholders."

The representatives from Boston to the Massachusetts General Court, some forty in number,
were in those days elected on a general ticket,
the utterly pernicious district system not having
yet been substituted for the original New England town representation; and the complete
groundlessness of the lamentations Mr. Adams
was at this period of his life wont to indulge in
over supposed family and personal unpopularity

must have dawned on his mind when, three days after the election, he wrote: "The 'Daily Advertiser' of this morning tells us that I have received the highest number of votes on the ticket for representatives." A few days later came a letter from his father, written just after reaching Washington. It closed with this paragraph: "You are about to enter on the career which is closing upon me, and I feel much more solicitude for you than for myself. You have so reluctantly consented to engage in public life, that I fear you will feel too much annoyed by its troubles and perplexities. You must make up your account to meet and encounter opposition and defeats and slanders and treacheries, and above all fickleness of popular favor, of which an ever memorable example is passing before our eyes. Let me entreat you, whatever may happen to you of that kind, never to be discouraged nor soured. Your father and grandfather have fought their way through the world against hosts of adversaries, open and close, disguised and masked; with many lukewarm and more than one or two perfidious friends. The world is and will continue to be prolific of such characters. Live in peace with them; never upbraid, never trust them. But — 'don't give up the ship!' Fortify your mind against disappointments — æquam memento rebus in arduis

servare mentem, — keep up your courage, and
go ahead ! ''

Mr. Adams remained five years a member of
the Massachusetts legislature, — three in the
House of Representatives, two in the Senate.
In those days its individuality had not been
wholly reformed out of the constitution of Massachusetts, and the House still represented the
towns, as the Senate did the counties, of the
Commonwealth. Both were elected annually,
and by a majority vote; the House being a
large popular body of some four hundred members, while the Senate numbered only forty.
As the delegations from the large cities and
towns were chosen on a general ticket, more or
less men of prominence, especially from Boston,
were almost sure to be sent to the lower house,
while the Senate was apt to be made up of members having at least a county reputation. The
narrowing influence of the district and rotation
systems was yet to make itself felt.

As Mr. Adams wrote, when first mentioned
in connection with it, the place of a representative in the Great and General Court of Massachusetts is " one of little consequence ; " and
yet it is not too much to say that his election to
that place in 1840, at the age of thirty-three
years, was the turning point in his life. The
educational influence of his subsequent legisla-

tive service was immense, — that of Harvard
College and of the law were, for him, as nothing
to it; for this took him out of himself, brought
him in hard contact with others, widened his
vision, developed his powers, gave him confidence in himself. He ceased to be wholly in-
trospective and morbid; becoming less of a student, he grew to be more of a man. Gradually
and insensibly he came to realize that no prejudice, either personal or because of family, really
existed towards him; but, on the contrary, the
great mass of the community actually felt an
interest in him and a kindliness to him because
of his name and descent, — an interest and a
kindliness which, had he himself possessed only
a little of the sympathetic quality, had he been
only a degree less reserved in nature and repellent in manners, would have found expression,
then and afterwards, in ways which could not
have been otherwise than grateful to him.

As the self-assigned limit to this form of public service was in 1845 drawing to a close, Mr.
Adams wrote: " After all, the legislation of one
of our States is a fatiguing business, — there is
a very large amount of small topics of detail.
As a school of practice it may answer very well
for a time, but perseverance in it has a tendency
to narrow the mind at last by habituating it to
measure small things. I have endeavored as

far as possible to avoid this effect by keeping
myself on topics of general concern." This was
strictly true ; and not without ground did he,
for his own satisfaction, record a belief that his
legislative action had influenced the course of
political events, and given him a certain degree
of reputation, not only in Massachusetts but in
the country at large. " My position, and I may
say it here [in my diary] without incurring the
charge of vain-glory, has been earned by hard
and incessant labor, in opposition to popular
opinion and to the overshadowing influence of
my father. The records of the State show that
during the five years I have not been wholly
idle. The report on the [northeastern] boundary, the passage of the districting bill, the
repeal of the remnant of the slave code, the
protest against the salary bill, the report and
law on the Latimer case, the policy concerning
Texas, and this South Carolina matter will remain to testify for me when I am gone. In all
of them my belief is that the same general principles will be visible." Finally, on the 26th of
March, 1845, the day upon which the last legislature in which he ever sat was prorogued, referring to the close of its business, he exultingly
wrote : " My resolutions placing the Whig party
and the State on the basis of resistance to slavery in the general government, passed the House

by a vote of five to one, and constitute, as it seems to me, a fair termination of all my labors. No proposition of mine has failed since I have been there ; nor have I on the whole committed any error deserving to degrade me in my own estimation or that of the public.   My defects of temper and excessive impetuosity have now and then brought me into error, which I have repented.   I parted company with the other senators with feelings of regret and good-will."

The record was indeed creditable, and, for a State legislature, in some ways remarkable ; for five of the seven subjects which had chiefly occupied his attention, and in respect to which the final statute-book record had taken its shape from him, involved national issues which have left their mark on history.   These were (1) the question of the northeastern boundary, settled by the Ashburton treaty of 1842 ; (2) the law authorizing the marriage of persons of different color ; (3) the Latimer fugitive slave case ; (4) the controversy arising out of the expulsion of Mr. Hoar from South Carolina by the mob of Charleston ; and (5) the resistance to the annexation of Texas.   All of these questions are now past history, — all save only mere preliminaries, remote educational stages, to the great conflict of twenty years later : but, at the time, they had their importance ; and each of them has left its literature, now rarely disturbed, — and, when disturbed, exciting only a languid interest. One day in the early summer of 1833, Mr. Adams busied himself in sorting over and arranging the accumulation of pamphlets in the mansion at Quincy. "A large collection," he wrote; "many good ones, and many very flat, stale and unprofitable. Perhaps it is one of the most singular subjects we have to speculate on, the feeling with which one examines the effusions, personal, political, and miscellaneous of past times. All dead and buried in the tomb of the Capulets. All the evidences of the restlessness of the human mind." To these have since been added Mr. Adams's own discussions of the several issues, then very burning, which have just been enumerated. They here call for no further mention.

CHAPTER IV

THE "BOSTON WHIG"

"WEDNESDAY, 20 May, 1846 : — Went up by agreement to see Mr. Palfrey, and consult with him about the matter of the newspaper. We finally decided on calling a meeting of those who may be considered as likely to favor the measure, for Saturday morning at 10 o'clock."

"Saturday, 23d May, 1846 : — Called at the State House on Mr. Palfrey,[1] and went with him up to Lobby No. 13, where were assembled the persons I had suggested as fit to be consulted at the present crisis. Stephen C. Phillips, John G. Palfrey, Charles Sumner, Henry Wilson and myself. I laid before them the state of my negotiation with the printers, and the terms which had been drawn and accepted. Much discussion ensued. Mr. Phillips seemed more doubtful of the expediency of the project than any of us. He apprehended ugly discussions, growing out of the complicated condition

---

[1] John G. Palfrey at this time held the position of secretary of the Commonwealth ; and the office of that functionary was then in the west wing of the State House.

of our foreign affairs. Mr. Palfrey seemed earnest to go on. Mr. Wilson, the same. Mr. Sumner also. The two last, however, could not aid in money. It then fell between us three. Mr. Palfrey agreed to assume one fifth; I took two fifths; and Mr. Phillips, not without some hesitation, the balance. The general result was to go on; so here I am about to assume a very great risk."

Such is the record, made at the time by Mr. Adams, of a somewhat memorable meeting. The little group of men thus brought together in "State House Lobby No. 13" had very faint if, indeed, any conception of the fact, but the business they had in hand was nothing less than planting the seed from which, in due order of events, was to spring the Republican party of Massachusetts, — indeed it might almost be said, the Republican party of the United States. In other respects, also, the group was noticeable; for three out of the five persons who made it up had before them eminent public careers in connection with events of great historical moment; while, of the remaining two, one was to achieve a lasting reputation as the historian of New England. They were all still comparatively young men; Palfrey, the eldest, being just fifty, while Wilson was but thirty-four. Sumner, born in 1811, was a year older than Wilson;

Mr. Adams was not yet thirty-nine. The last three were destined, during the memorable war which was to result from the success of the political party into which they were that day breathing life, to represent Massachusetts in the national Senate, and the United States at the court of St. James. Stephen C. Phillips, a man then of forty-five, of great public spirit, most active and useful in the early days of the new party, shortly after withdrew from political work, and in 1857 lost his life in a steamboat disaster on the river St. Lawrence. He had then long ceased to be an active factor in the Massachusetts political situation.

The years between 1860 and 1868 were so altogether cataclysmic, and the changes then worked so great, — during them the situation was, in a word, so wholly altered, — that the immediately preceding, and preparatory, period has already assumed an antediluvian aspect. Hence, it is not altogether easy even to understand the posture of political affairs prior to 1850, or the motives under which men acted, either in Massachusetts or the country at large. Moreover, while a great deal of what then took place has been quite forgotten, the residuum, still remembered, is remembered vaguely, and in the deflecting light of subsequent events. Thus what Mr. Adams and his four friends wanted on that 23d of May, 1846, is now not immediately apparent; neither is it altogether clear whom they were opposing, or why they felt so pressingly the need of a newspaper. The fact was, their time had come. They were simply responding to a need in the process of political evolution. In spite of lamentations then, as always, freely indulged in over the apathy of the public mind and the hopelessly lethargic condition of the popular conscience, the United States in 1846 was neither a moribund, nor yet even a decadent, country. It was, however, threatened with disease, and that of a very portentous character. A cancer was steadily eating into its vitals. Though few people, if indeed any, then realized it, the knife was in point of fact already necessary; a surgical operation, and that a severe one, would alone meet the exigencies of the case. The only real questions were : — first, whether the patient could be brought to submit to the necessary operation; and, second, whether he would survive the operation if he did submit to it. Most fortunately, however, these unpleasant alternatives were not apparent either in 1846 or, indeed, during the dozen or more years that ensued. The five men gathered on May 23, 1846, in Lobby 13 of the Massachusetts State House certainly did not appreciate the gravity of the affair, or measure the distant, far-reaching results they were challenging. They took in the present situation only. That the case was bad, they knew. They saw clearly enough the progress which slavery, as an institution, had already made, and the rapidity with which it was advancing; but they did not fully appreciate the extent to which it had struck its roots into the national existence, much less realize the nature of the conflict they were invoking. That, if they had realized it, they would, after a long pause and grave deliberation, have gone straight on in the path upon which they were entering, can hardly admit of question; but it does admit of very great question whether they could have induced the North to follow them in that path. The historical truth is, that in the great anti-slavery discussion which began in 1844 and culminated in 1860, the North never really believed that an appeal to force was necessary and inevitable, until, in April, 1861, it found the country face to face with it. It certainly cannot be said that what then occurred had not been predicted. It had been predicted by numerous voices, on many occasions, in the clearest possible manner, and with all necessary emphasis; but, on the other hand, it is equally clear that those who predicted failed to see that, short of death by disease, there was no other way.

What Mr. Adams and his associates did then

clearly see and all they clearly saw, was the immediate work cut out for them to do. It was for them to rouse the country to a consciousness of the danger of the situation, and the consequences inevitably involved if events went on unchecked. They were mere agencies. To revert to the figure already used, their movement was, in the economy of nature, merely an instinctive effort of the body politic to contend against disease and throw it off. It was long an open question whether the effort would succeed. That depended on the general health and vitality of the organization; for, in a politico-pathological sense, the health of a community, — its power to resist and overcome disease, may be said to be in almost direct proportion to its moral receptivity, — its tendency to altruism. Loyalty, patriotism, and even religious devotion, very admirable and potent in their way, are qualities of a much lower order. Indeed, these are found quite as fully developed in the savage, as in civilized, man: for barbarous Patagonian tribes, semi-developed Scotch clans, and states far sunk in Spanish decadence are conspicuous for them. When, however, in any given community, many individuals, regardless of ridicule, epithets, and denunciation, — shouts of " firebrand," " fanatic," and " traitor," — revolt at wrong, or quickly respond to a cry of injustice,

whether raised on behalf of a person or a class,
— Jew, African, or Malay, — the presence of
such individuals affords evidence incontroverti-
ble of vitality in the community to which they
belong ; and the quickness and volume of the
response to their appeal measure not inaccu-
rately the moral and political soundness of that
community. During the period between 1830
and 1850 the tendency to what are known as
" isms " in the free States of the Union, and
especially in Massachusetts and those of New
England progeny at the West, was notorious.
The land seemed given over to philanthropists
and reformers of the kind generically classified
as " cranks," — long-haired men and short-haired
women. Dickens, who was then here, depicted
them, and made fun of them ; they shocked anti-
slavery men like Richard H. Dana.[1] None the
less, they were the unmistakable symptom of a
redundant moral activity. They indicated a
body politic full of quickening force. Had these
not appeared, or had they been silent, had the
United States as a whole then been in at all a
decadent state, — in the condition, for instance,
of the later Roman Empire, or of Turkey and
Spain since the commencement of the seven-
teenth century, — the attempt would unquestionably have failed. The appeal on behalf of the

[1] *Biography of R. H. Dana,* i. 68.

African, — the despised "nigger," — wasted in the air, would have elicited no response.

In 1845 the abolition movement had spent its force. Begun by Garrison in 1831 it had, in awakening the public conscience, done a great work, — a work wherein its success was in largest degree due to the almost insane anger which its utterances and actions aroused among the slaveholders. In other words, under the irritation of those highly drastic applications, the diseased portion of the body politic became acutely inflamed. The whole system throbbed angrily, — almost suppurated. Thus the "Liberty" movement, as it was called, was effectively advertised; and, without that advertisement, Garrison's most strenuous and sustained efforts, and Wendell Phillips's most eloquent and incisive utterances would never have reached beyond a narrow and in no way influential circle. After the presidential canvass of 1844, the situation rapidly changed, and the extra-constitutional abolition movement, as it had then declared itself, did not thereafter increase either in force or in influence. On the contrary, it distinctly dwindled; for, so far as concerned nationality, — the growing and intensifying spirit of Union, — the Garrisonians thenceforth preached non-resistance and self-destruction; the two especial doctrines against which all the instincts of the

country rose in revolt. Thus, contending with
the spirit of the age, the abolitionists met with
the fate usual for those who engage in that contest. Accordingly, from 1844 onward, one great
effort of those who afterwards brought the conflict to a practical, though to them wholly unan-
ticipated, issue, was to distinguish their policy
from that advocated by Mr. Garrison, and to
work the problem out within the Union and in
subordination to the Constitution. It is, therefore, historically a mistake to treat either Mr.
Garrison or Wendell Phillips, after 1844, as
leaders in the later and really effective anti-
slavery movement, or, indeed, as political factors
of consequence. By nature, as well as from long
habit, irregulars, at home nowhere except on the
skirmish line, very necessary in the earlier operations, they, having brought on the conflict, had
done their work ; and when the solid lines of
battle crashed together, their partisan operations
ceased to count. Had they in 1845 wholly disappeared from the field, the result would have
been in no way other than it was ; for, by the
country at large — those who had to be reasoned with, educated, and gradually brought into
line — Mr. Garrison was from 1844 to 1861
looked upon as an impracticable, cracked-brained
fanatic, and Mr. Phillips as a bitter, shrill-
voiced, political scold. Not influencing results,

they, like guerillas in warfare, were in the later stages of the contest quite as much a hindrance to those with whom, as they were an annoyance to those against whom, they acted.

On the other hand, in the free States, as well as at the South, the old conventional anti-slavery feeling, — that handed down from the War of Independence and the Fathers of the Republic, and based in greatest part on sentiment and tradition, — was fast fading out. That African slavery, as an industrial institution, was not going to die a natural death had become apparent. On the contrary, most vigorous and decidedly aggressive, it was visibly developing. There were in this or in any other country no more really useful, public-spirited citizens than the shrewd, energetic, clear-headed men, generally belonging to the Whig party, who now in Massachusetts, arraying themselves instinctively in behalf of the Union and the Constitution, earnestly deprecated all agitation of slavery, as a political issue. They were right, also, from their point of view. With them the Union was supreme. They rather disliked slavery, and still declaimed against it, averring their abstract abhorrence of it in certain phrases rapidly degenerating into cant; but it may fairly be said that there was no limit to the concessions they would ultimately have been willing to make as

the alternative to a disruption of the Union.
Rufus Choate, for instance, argued earnestly
that the return to slavery of a few fugitives
from time to time was an insignificant sacrifice
on that altar, as compared with the hecatombs
inevitably to be sacrificed through civil convul-
sion.   Leaving honor and self-respect out of the
question, he was unquestionably right; but with
nations as with individuals, honor and self-respect are worth something.   Accordingly, when
at Cambridge, in June, 1851, Choate took occasion to enunciate this latter-day dispensation,
the everlasting verities underwent no change.
That

> " rightly to be great
> Is not to stir without great argument,
> But greatly to find quarrel in a straw
> When honor 's at the stake,"

remained just as true then as it was when
Shakespeare wrote the words two hundred and
fifty years before ; or as, ten Junes later, it
proved to many of those who listened to the
eloquent advocate of honor's effacement.   In
common with the great mass of the most respectable and comfortably circumstanced individuals of the community to which he and they
belonged, Mr. Choate failed to realize that the
self-respect of a people could not but be more
or less blunted, if they saw the land of boasted

liberty in which they dwelt converted into a
" nigger hunting-ground ; " while they themselves were from time to time called upon in
ordered ranks to bear a hand in the work. At
best it was repulsive, even though Union-saving. Still, historically speaking, it is not unsafe
to say that, between 1845 and 1852, there was
no concession, so far as the " peculiar institution " was concerned, at which the representative leaders of the Whig party, North as well
as South, would have stopped, provided disunion appeared to be the alternative. If need
be they would have submitted, under protest of
course, to the complete nationalization of slavery. They would have held it the lesser of two
evils.

The fact here stated was recognized at the
South by the exponents of the new gospel of
slavery. Calhoun counted on it as the prime
factor of success in the policy he now laid
down. He was never a Disunionist ; but he
called on the South to bring the North face to
face with a dissolution of the Union as the alternative to unconditional submission. In presenting this alternative he did not believe that it
would lead to disruption, being firmly convinced
that, with disruption certain to result from persistency, the North would consider no price too
great to pay for a united, even though bickering,

household. For, as he scornfully expressed it, "measureless avarice was its ruling passion." [1]

In this belief the South Carolinian was, as South Carolina afterwards found, dreadfully mistaken ; but, for the time being, it did not so seem. Then and afterwards, Massachusetts was the storm centre ; and in Massachusetts the antislavery movement, after 1844, assumed a wholly new phase. It organized ; and, while it became constitutional, became also distinctly opportunist and practical. It drew its inspiration from the Declaration of Independence, and sought, so far as African servitude was concerned, to convert the national government from a propagandist to a repressive agency.

An organ — a newspaper — thus became necessary; for the new doctrine — after all a species of homœopathic faith-cure — must be voiced, and voiced constantly by those who believed in it. The situation, also, was becoming more and more grave. The admission of Texas had been finally consummated on December 22, 1845 ; and, on the 11th of May following, President Polk sent to Congress his message, at once famous and infamous, declaring that " War exists, and notwithstanding all our efforts to avoid it, exists by the act of Mexico itself." A war of spoliation had thus been entered upon, — a war the pur-

[1] Von Holst, iii. 315–318.

pose of which, whether avowed or not, was well known to be the propagation of slavery. The disease was in an obviously acute stage; the cancer was manifestly spreading.

The President's war message bore date May 11th; the unnoticed, and apparently scarce noteworthy, meeting in State House Lobby No. 13 took place just twelve days later, on the 23d, — a mere incident, it was, none the less, in a way the response to the great event; for, though it caused no loud or echoing reverberation, it was, as the event showed, the answering gun which signified an acceptance of the challenge. Meanwhile, so far as Massachusetts, and more particularly Boston, was concerned, the situation had been further complicated. On May 11th, Mr. Robert C. Winthrop, representing the Boston district in Washington, had gone upon the record as voting in favor of the war measures at once reported to the House of Representatives in consequence of Polk's message. In Massachusetts that vote of his was an event of far-reaching consequence. It made complete and permanent the division between the " Conscience " and the " Cotton " Whigs; and Mr. Adams was now to become the recognized mouthpiece of the former.

So far as the establishment of a newspaper was concerned, the feasibility of so doing had

for some time been under consideration. Dr.
Palfrey advocated it earnestly; and the more
Mr. Adams thought of it, the more the idea
took possession of him. In dead earnest now
on the slavery issue, he had a strong inclination
generally towards newspaper utterance. For
years he had liked to set forth his views on current political topics in communicated articles,
usually, as was the custom in those days, running into series, signed "Publicola," "Junius,"
"Sagitta," or the like. The trouble was that,
with some little experience, not very encoura-
ging, as an editorial writer, he had no knowledge
whatever, or even conception, of editorial functions in the modern sense of the term.

On the other hand, journalism in 1846 was in
the plastic stage. In almost no aspect did it
resemble what it has since become. In 1846, the
electric telegraph was only two years old; the
suburban railroad service was new and imperfect;
the street railway did not exist. People had not
yet accustomed themselves to any of these neces-
sities of modern existence, much less grown to
depend upon them. A newspaper, accordingly,
did not then imply its present organization and
expense. It was a comparatively simple affair,
usually the property and mouthpiece of one man,
— its editor and proprietor. In fact, it is now
difficult to realize what a thing of yesterday the

newspaper of 1846, though the progenitor of the modern newspaper, then itself was. The " Advertiser," the first daily paper which had been able to sustain itself in Boston, dated only from the year 1813. The " Courier " followed in 1824; and then came the " Transcript " (1830), the " Post " (1831), the " Atlas " (1832), the " Journal " (1833), and finally the " Evening Traveller " (1845). The cheap one-cent paper, sold on the street or at the news-stand, was looked upon as an undignified publication, carrying no weight. Among the high-priced, old-fashioned subscription " blanket sheets," the " Daily Advertiser " — " the respectable Daily " — meant Mr. Nathan Hale; the " Courier," Mr. Joseph T. Buckingham; and the " Post," Mr. Charles G. Greene. They were all organs, too; for independent journalism was only then assuming shape in New York, and the older and more established newspapers depended for their existence on the subscriptions, advertisements, and patronage of some mercantile interest or political organization. The " Advertiser," for instance, was inspired by Mr. Webster; the " Post " was the recognized organ of the Jackson Democracy; the " Liberator " — a weekly paper — was the mouthpiece of Mr. Garrison and the extreme abolitionists. The circulation of that day would also now be considered almost ridicu-

lously small. It is very questionable whether
the subscription list of any of the sheets which
have been named contained over four thousand
names; while an annual net income of $20,000
was thought enormous. A circulation of two
thousand was looked upon as very respectable.
The New York "Evening Post," for instance, in
1842, printed two thousand five hundred copies;
the noted and influential "Courier and Enquirer"
only seven thousand; while the "Herald," the
great sensational journalistic innovator, could
boast of but fifteen thousand. The influence of
a paper was not, however, by any means measured by its circulation; far less so, indeed,
then than now: and hence in great degree,
in the mind of Dr. Palfrey, the necessity as
well as the feasibility of an organ. Between
1840 and 1850 the local — what would in Europe be called the provincial — press was vigorous and potent. Rapid transportation had
not yet laid down the journal of the great city
on the doorsteps of every country town as
promptly as the news carrier laid it down at
those of the houses adjoining the press-room.
So every considerable centre in Massachusetts
had its paper, — its "Argus," its "Spy," its
"Republican," its "Mercury," its "Courier,"
— which again looked to the recognized Boston
organ for its news and its inspiration. As Gar-

rison had already demonstrated in the case of
the "Liberator," a limited circulation by no
means implied a correspondingly restricted influence.

Notwithstanding all this, the showing made to
Mr. Adams by the publishers of the "Whig" was
the reverse of inspiring. "It " [the paper], he
wrote, "is far from flourishing. It has but two
hundred and twelve paying subscribers, and its
debts run on all fours with its income." It is true
that only eleven years before this time the New
York "Herald" had been launched on its won-
derful career with cash resources of only $500
behind it; and, more remarkable still, the
"Tribune" had started out so recently as 1841
with a borrowed cash capital of but $1000 : but
both these journals were backed by the enterprise, energy, and experience of two of the most
remarkable born journalists of the century, and
they had been merely the prizes in a fascinating
lottery which had turned up almost innumera-
ble blanks. It is needless to say, also, that Mr.
Adams had very few attributes in common with
either James Gordon Bennett or Horace Greeley. He was rather modeled on the old-fashioned pattern of William W. Seaton and Nathan
Hale, — types fast vanishing. He had absolutely no conception of the journal of the future,
as it then loomed vaguely up; while for the

work such a journal implied he was in every respect lacking. Nevertheless the editorship of
the "Boston Whig," while it carried with it
some danger of ignominious failure, did not
involve any excessive pecuniary risk. It was
only necessary to secure the few hundred dollars
immediately needed to keep the concern afloat.

This sum was forthcoming from the sources,
and in the proportions, already indicated. So,
on going to town from Quincy on June 1, 1846,
Mr. Adams found himself "saluted with a
great bundle of newspapers, the sign of a new
vocation," and, at the same time, read his own
opening editorial. The "Whig" was a blanket sheet, as it was called, of the pattern then in
vogue. Twenty-two inches by sixteen in size,
one of its six-column pages was devoted to editorial matter and news, while the three others
were filled with advertisements, with the exception of a single column, the first of the first
page, which contained the instalment of a serial
story, or some other mild literary nutriment of
that character. This was the form the "Whig"
had when Mr. Adams assumed editorial charge
of it; and this form it retained until his connection with it ceased. A two-cent paper, with
a subscription price of $5.00 per annum, Mr.
Adams's name nowhere appeared upon it as its
editor; nor was he ever its proprietor. He re-

ceived no compensation for his services ; in fact
the paper, while under his editorial control, was
never prosperous enough to pay any compensation.

The position assumed by the " Whig " was,
from the outset, simple.   Remembering the disastrous results which followed the Birney movement in 1844, it was, in 1846, no believer in third
parties as political factors; though, only two
years later, in 1848, its action led to the formation of a third party.   But parties were merely
the means to the attainment of political ends ;
and the end which the " Whig " had in view
was explicit.   " Either," it declared, " the present tide, which is carrying all of our institutions,
excepting the forms, into a vortex of which
slavery is the moving power, must be stayed by
the people of the free States, or, if left to its
course, it will bring on, in no very long time, a
sudden and total dissolution of the bond of our
Union. . . . We feel tolerably confident it may
be avoided ; but it can only be by one way.
That way is the total abolition of slavery, —
the complete eradication of the fatal influence it
is exercising over the policy of the general government."

Such was the attitude of the organ of the
" Conscience " Whigs of Massachusetts.   The
limits assigned to this sketch permit hardly more

than a reference to the bitter controversies, personal and political, which in Massachusetts
between the years 1846 and 1856 marked the
breaking up of the Whig party and the formation of the Republican.   The story is not lacking in interest ; but it has already in main been
told both by Henry Wilson, himself an actor in
it, and by Edward L. Pierce, not only an actor
in it, but subsequently an untiring investigator
of it.   Upon it Mr. Adams's contemporaneous
record throws much additional light.   The
period was, too, not only important, but, as revealed in his papers, extremely interesting.   It
has its distinctly humorous, as well as tragic,
side.   There was in it a vast play of character,
and of strong character, as J. Q. Adams, and
Webster, and R. C. Winthrop pass off the stage
and new men force their way upon it.   They all
tell their story, and often in their own words as
well as by their acts ; and while the earnest,
angry, acrimonious debate goes on, the dark,
ugly, ominous war-cloud rises and spreads in
the distant background.   It is absorbing, as
well as impressive ; but the narrative attains
almost the dimensions of a history, and will not
be compressed into a sketch.   Its salient features only can here be referred to.

   In 1846, when the war with Mexico was engineered by the slave power, through the agency

of President James K. Polk in firm possession of the national government, there were two Massachusetts public men of the first rank whose attitude, while of especial significance, was altogether uncertain, — Daniel Webster and Robert C. Winthrop. The course of the former, as subsequently developed during the next six years, is matter of familiar history. But it was with the course of the latter that Mr. Adams was more immediately concerned : for the vote of Mr. Winthrop in favor of the Mexican war bill during the previous May was already, in June, 1846, a burning issue ; and, as the months rolled on, it became steadily more so. In regard to that vote Mr. Adams took occasion presently to express himself in the columns of the " Whig," though not until two months were gone since it was cast. " We know not, or care not, what the feelings of others may be upon the subject, or whether Mr. Winthrop may not become ten times more popular than ever for this act ; but, according to the best estimate we can form of political morality, if he could expunge the record of it even by the sacrifice of the memory of all his preceding brilliant career, he would make a bargain. . . . Either the preamble to the war bill tells the truth, or it tells what is not true. If it does tell the truth, then indeed are we all of us wrong, and no one is

more wrong than Mr. Winthrop, in having heretofore described the administration policy as
inevitably bringing on a state of war on the
part of Mexico. If, on the other hand, it does
not tell the truth, how could Mr. Winthrop justify it to his own conscience to set his name in
perpetual attestation to a falsehood ? "

America has never been looked upon as a
field conspicuous for a delicate journalistic regard for the amenities of political discussion ;
but between 1840 and 1855 certain of the editorial writers — it was the " We " period — set
much store, in Boston at least, on what may
perhaps best be defined as " tone." It is needless now to say that there was in this " tone " a
good deal of that which approximates closely to
cant. A spade, after all, is a spade ; and, when
referring to it, little is gained by describing it
as an agricultural implement used in turning
the soil. Mr. Adams, as respects slavery and
the Mexican war, was thoroughly in earnest;
and a man thoroughly in earnest is apt to be
outspoken. Neither, until he fairly takes to
vituperation, as, unfortunately, is altogether too
frequently the case, is the editorial writer open
to any just criticism because he makes use of
language which does not allow his meaning to
escape the reader. As to Mr. Winthrop's vote
of May 11, 1846, as a matter of policy on his

part, much may be said in extenuation. None
the less, the measure for which he that day voted
had been unnecessarily and wantonly amended
so as to declare that the war, for which it made
provision, existed "by the act of the Republic
of Mexico." This was a falsehood. That it
was a falsehood, and a flagrant, palpable, un-
blushing falsehood, no man now denies ; and
history has not failed so to brand it.[1] Nor at
the time was this disputed, except for hypocrisy's sake. Henry Clay, for instance, was an
unquestioned authority in Whig circles, whether
in Massachusetts or elsewhere ; but Henry Clay
did not hesitate to describe that measure as "a
bill with a palpable falsehood stamped on its
face," and almost passionately exclaimed that
he "never, never could have voted" for it. In
like manner the "National Intelligencer," the
official Whig organ, declared that the two
Houses of Congress, in passing the bill with
that declaration in it, gave "the seal and sanction of their authority to a false principle and a
false fact." Yet when Mr. Adams, writing editorially, asked the question how the Boston representative in Congress could justify to his
conscience thus setting "his name in perpetual
attestation to a falsehood," the regular Whig
papers of the city found their sense of propriety

[1] Von Holst, iii. 250–255.

greatly shocked by language, which they referred to as " rude and indecorous," and, moreover, " unfounded in truth."

The vigor and direct personal character of the
assault were, it must be admitted, of a nature
calculated to excite surprise in the breasts of
the very respectable and altogether well-mean-
ing and public-spirited gentlemen who now
found themselves the object of almost daily attack ; but, on the other hand, subsequent events
showed unmistakably that the measures resorted
to, and the language used, were no more drastic
and severe than the exigency called for. At a
grave crisis in political affairs the public mind
was lethargic, and it had to be aroused. No
two citizens of Boston then stood higher in public estimation than Abbott Lawrence and Nathan
Appleton. They stood, too, deservedly high ;
for they were men of great business sagacity,
high character, and of a public spirit which
had been often in evidence. In fact there have
not been before or since better examples of the
strong, virile, adaptive, and resourceful stock
which made and sustains Massachusetts. Solid
and intelligent, they were representative men.
As respects slavery, however, their views were
of the sentimental and submissive order. It was
a bad thing, they were wont to say, — very bad ;
but one dangerous to agitate, especially from the

business point of view; and, after all, no affair
of theirs. Like honest Dogberry, having, as in
the case of Texas, bid the "vagrom" man stand,
if he would not stand, they would then "take no
note of him, but let him go;" and presently
thank God they were "rid of a knave." Mr.
Garrison boldly preached a dissolution of the
Union as a remedy, and the only remedy, for
the existing state of affairs. Mr. Appleton
frankly believed that the so-called "Conscience" Whigs were, as he expressed it,
"playing into the hands of the disunionists;"
and he intimated the strong desire he really felt
to save "one of them," meaning Mr. Sumner, —
then looked upon in Beacon Street as a young
man of uncommon promise, — from the courses
and contamination into which he was then headlong rushing. Seeing things as he did, Mr. Appleton frankly admitted that he held "all the
evils of bad legislation and bad administration,"
— including slavery, Texas, and the Mexican
war, — "light, compared to those which must
inevitably flow from a disruption of the States."
That, of course, settled the matter. The "vagrom" man, when bid to stand, had but to
refuse to do so, and they would forthwith "take
no note of him, but let him go." And moreover, like Dogberry, Messrs. Lawrence and
Appleton, and those who thought as they

thought, would on this score make no noise in
the streets; "for to babble and to talk" about
slavery and other matters, which in no way concerned Massachusetts, was "most tolerable and
not to be endured."

This way of looking at the situation did not
commend itself to Mr. Adams. It had received
practical illustration the preceding spring in
the point blank refusal of Messrs. Lawrence and
Appleton to put their names to the final remonstrance against the admission of Texas to the
Union. This proceeding Mr. Adams had not
forgotten; and the "Whig" at once proceeded to
hold Messrs. Lawrence and Appleton personally
to account. The latter had in his letter to the
anti-Texas Committee used the expression that,
to his mind, the Texas question had, as a result
of the election of 1844, been "for all practical
purposes settled." Dr. Palfrey now, in the columns of the "Whig," rang the changes on that
expression. "The question was settled! What
if it had been? Did Massachusetts owe nothing
then to her principles, her pledges, her character? Did she owe no record of honorable action
to future history? Have Mr. Appleton and his
friends always reasoned thus? . . . The demonstration of Mr. Appleton and his friends, coming, as it did, as unexpectedly as a thunderclap
in a clear sky," did much to embarrass and

check " the vigorous movement of the people,"
then daily gathering momentum. Mr. Adams
also a few days later added his opinion that,
" when a gentleman of such standing in the cotton manufacturing interest as Mr. Appleton
insults the founders of the Constitution so far
as to maintain that ' it is questionable whether
the abolition movement is reconcilable with duty
under it,' we are driven to the conviction that
he is not a safe guide in the construction of his
neighbor's duties either to his country or his
God." At the same time Mr. Adams took Mr.
Lawrence in hand in a series of letters signed
" Sagitta," addressed directly to him, after the
manner of Junius. These also contained some
vigorous specimens of style, — the following for
example. As a manufacturer Mr. Lawrence had
evinced a deep interest in the tariff on wool.
The remonstrance against the admission of
Texas to the Union, Mr. Adams now wrote,
" simply asked the representatives of the Union
not to sanction a form of government in Texas
designed to make slavery perpetual there. And
this petition you refused to sign on the ground
that the question was already settled, at the very
moment when you were ready to move heaven
and earth to resist a change in the Tariff of
1842. . . . You, who would not give a dollar
to defend the rights of man, are announced as

having paid the expenses of circulating twenty
thousand copies of Mr. Stewart's defense of
sheep. . . . To sacrifice mankind, to fasten forever the galling chain around the neck of the
black man, the other end of which, though you
did not know it, was to press upon your own,
you were not unwilling to agree beforehand. It
was only for the sheep that you preferred to go
to the death."

Before Mr. Adams had been five months in
charge of the " Boston Whig " the issue between
" Conscience " and " Cotton " was defined. Mr.
Winthrop's vote of May 11th presented it; it
was emphasized and embittered by a sharp correspondence, as yet unpublished, between him
and Mr. Sumner, all the details of which were
long subsequently recounted by Mr. Pierce [1] and
by Mr. Winthrop's son.[2] The Whig house was
clearly divided against itself ; which faction
was the larger remained to be seen. The
strength of the " Conscience " element lay in
the country ; in Boston and the larger manufacturing towns, the " Cotton " influence was
more than dominant, it was supreme. The
question of mastery was to be decided in the
state Whig convention to be held in Faneuil
Hall on September 23d. That convention was

[1] *Life of Sumner*, iii. 114–119.
[2] *Memoir of R. C. Winthrop*, 51–56.

memorable, marking, as it did, an epoch in the
anti-slavery movement. In it Winthrop and
Sumner struggled for the ascendency; and an
issue was forced. Under the throes of upheaval
from the young party of the future within it,
the Whig house trembled to its foundations. As
the day wore on, the traditional party magnates,
alarmed by the strength the new movement developed, and the courage and persistency of its
leaders, appealed, as a last resort, to the personal authority of Mr. Webster. E. L. Pierce,
in his life of Sumner, has given a detailed
and striking account of what now took place,
and still another account, too long for insertion
here, is to be found in the diary of Mr. Adams.
Suffice it to say that no more striking scene was
ever witnessed in Faneuil Hall. The entrance
of Webster upon the stage was a veritable *coup
de théâtre*, admirably arranged and skillfully
timed by the hard-pressed respectabilities of the
organization. It worked also like magic. The
tide was running strongly for " Conscience,"
and against " Cotton," when, late in the September day, and after hasty conference among
the gray-haired conservatives, Mr. Webster's
son, Fletcher, hurriedly left the hall. Presently
he came back, and, whispering to Abbott Lawrence, who was seated on the platform, that
gentleman rose and went out. When he came

back, Daniel Webster was on his arm. The two walked slowly through the excited chamber. The debate had ceased in the presence thus evoked, and all parties rose and joined in a loud demonstration of applause. Without uttering a word the great Whig chieftain took his seat on the platform, — grand, gloomy, impressive. Not a word was necessary; his presence, thus heralded, sealed the fate of the amendments moved by the " Conscience " faction, and then in debate. It was in the brief speech that followed the decisive vote — the " few generalities intended as a soother," as Mr. Adams described them in his account of what occurred — that the great orator made use of a striking simile, since famous, which may well have been suggested to him by a figure of speech used only a few days before by Mr. Adams in an open letter to Mr. Lawrence: " Others rely on other foundations and other hopes for the welfare of the country ; but, for my part, in the dark and troubled night that is upon us, I see no star above the horizon promising light to guide us but the intelligent, patriotic, united Whig party of the United States." And this, delivered through the lips of Daniel Webster, was the answer of Abbott Lawrence to the challenge of " Sagitta."

CHAPTER V

THE FREE-SOIL PARTY

THE Massachusetts canvass of 1846 resulted, as might naturally have been expected, in the total discomfiture of the " Conscience " Whigs. With them it was as yet only the seeding time. The election that year took place on November 10th ; and, as the outcome of the fierce and sustained assaults made upon him, Mr. Winthrop was triumphantly sent back to Congress from Boston. Dr. Palfrey, on the other hand, the " Conscience " Whig candidate for Congress in the adjoining Middlesex district, failed to secure a majority, though chosen some weeks later by a narrow margin of votes at a special election. " This is all of it very bad," wrote Mr. Adams, " and it depressed me much for the rest of the day." But the depression of his friends he found even greater than his own, " inasmuch as they attach more consequence to the immediate result. Yet it is unpleasant to meet with a large majority of persons who disagree with you, and who are disposed to rejoice at your defeat. I am prepared for this with a good share of philosophy, and submit to it."

Immediately after the election Mr. Adams accompanied his mother and his father's family to Washington, leaving his father himself in Boston.   When on his way from New York to Philadelphia he saw in the newspaper the announcement that J. Q. Adams had suffered a paralytic shock on the previous Thursday ; and it is noticeable as evidence of how very slowly information traveled in those days, only half a century ago, that information of an event of such public, and, to him, domestic interest, occurring Thursday morning in Boston, reached him only while leaving New York on Saturday, and then through the newspapers.   Indulging in no delusive hopes of recovery, he realized the full extent of the loss.   "However light that blow may be," he wrote on the day he heard of it, " there it is ; and, at eighty, not to be remedied."   It so proved.

A period of political gloom, as of domestic anxiety, now ensued.   In spite of a languishing subscription list, the " Whig," with a firm front, persisted in its course ; and when, the following autumn, the next annual convention of the Whig party was held, this time at Springfield, the struggle between the two factions was renewed. The as yet unwritten history of this gathering can here be no more than alluded to, though it still has an interest, and, at the moment, was of great historical significance. Mr. Webster was present in person, pleading' for a nomination to the presidency. Winthrop and Sumner both were there, renewing their wrestle of the year before. George Ashmun, George T. Curtis, Charles Allen, Stephen C. Phillips, and Dr. Palfrey all figured prominently; while Mr. Adams outlined the policy and directed the operations of the "Conscience" element. Practically it resulted in a drawn battle.

Though Mr. Webster on this occasion favored the convention with an address two hours in delivery, his biographer has made no mention of the fact, notwithstanding he was himself a delegate and listener. The reason is obvious. Mr. Webster at that time was engaged in the difficult politico-acrobatic feat of endeavoring to ride two horses at once, they going in opposite directions. On the one side was the Southern wing of "the intelligent, patriotic, united Whig party of the United States," fast drifting into the pro-slavery Democracy; on the other were the "Conscience" Whigs of Massachusetts driving headlong towards the Republican organization of the future. Mr. Webster's wish was to hold the two together in support of himself. That day he had to plead his cause before the "Conscience" tribunal; and, in doing so, he touched what proved for him the high-water mark of anti-slavery sentiment. He

even claimed the famous " Wilmot proviso " as
his " thunder." In return, he secured an indorsement, such as it was, for the presidential nomination of the following year. In view of the
course he subsequently pursued and his later
utterances, the fact that Mr. Curtis ignored the
incident in his biography affords no more occasion for surprise than that Mr. Webster's remarks are omitted from the authorized edition
of his Speeches.

Mr. Pierce refers briefly to the convention, in
his biography of Sumner; [1] but that day Mr.
Webster's successor in the Senate did not score
more of a success than Mr. Webster himself.
Mr. Sumner's speech had the merit of brevity,
for him ; but no other : and, as it appears in his
" Works," [2] it is characteristic of his worst style,
— the overloaded, rhetorico-classical. Mr. Adams wrote that, in delivery, it " sounded out of
place and pointless." The honors of the occasion belonged distinctly to Mr. Winthrop, who
not only spoke several times, but carried his
point, greatly to his own satisfaction ; [3] and for
satisfaction, he had good cause. That day he
made a long stride towards Whig leadership.
" Sumner," Mr. Adams wrote, was " the only
one of our friends much depressed ; " though his

[1] Vol. iii. pp. 144–146.   [2] Vol. ii. pp. 76–88.
[3] *Memoir*, p. 65.

own speech in the convention, he added, was
" much resented by [Mr. Webster's] friends."

That day, there were two real points at issue ;
one, the indorsement of Mr. Webster as the
next presidential candidate of the Whig party ;
the other, a resolution offered by Dr. Palfrey,
and designed to preclude the support of General Taylor. The former was carried in a per-
functory, half-hearted way ; the latter was voted
down, though by a narrow majority only. But
it was in regard to the latter that Mr. Winthrop
exerted himself, and influenced the result. To
every one but Mr. Webster, it was apparent
that the Webster candidacy was a form only.
General Taylor was the coming man ; and Mr.
Winthrop was now the Whig leader of the future. Thus the " depressed " condition of Mr.
Sumner's mind was easily accounted for. Meanwhile the Palfrey resolution had outlined the
action of the " Conscience " Whigs in a contingency which every day rendered more probable.
An immediate split was impending in " the
intelligent, patriotic, [but no longer] united,
Whig party."

A month afterwards, in the early days of November, 1847, J. Q. Adams, going with his
family to Washington, left Quincy for the last
time. Four months later he was brought back
for burial. It lacked, on the day he left, just

two weeks of seventy full years since, a boy of
ten, he had for the first time gone forth from
his native town, then Braintree, embarking in
the midst of the Revolutionary trials on the
frigate Boston, then lying in the bay, sent to
carry his father to France. The intervening
period covered the whole national existence,
from the war for independence with Great
Britain to that for slavery with Mexico. On
his part they had been threescore years and ten
of almost uninterrupted public life, now approaching an end not less fitting than dramatic.
" I dined with them," wrote the son, " and felt
a great deal of the dullness which overspread us
all. I do not wonder ; it is difficult to see what
six months will bring forth at such an age. It
will not do to look forward."

After a short contest, Mr. Winthrop was
elected speaker of the House, in the Congress
that now met; J. Q. Adams, to the great chagrin
of his son, voting for him. This Dr. Palfrey
found himself unable to do. The latter was
accordingly, at the very outset of congressional
life, thus put in a most trying position, in which
he found support at home from the " Whig "
alone. Into the now wellnigh forgotten controversy, which arose out of this speakership
election, there is not room here to enter. It was
long, bitter, and, in some features — as seen

through the vista of fifty years — amusingly instructive. The parties to it were very much in earnest and, as a consequence, exceedingly unjust to themselves, as well as to each other. The death of J. Q. Adams suddenly broke in upon it, and, during the painful observances which ensued, the extremely considerate demeanor of Speaker Winthrop to Mrs. Adams and the members of her husband's family extricated her son, though at the time he failed to realize it, from a position which was fast becoming false. The controversy was obviously degenerating into one of a personal character, — an organized, if not very promising, effort to break down Mr. Winthrop. The "Whig" also was far from flourishing, and Mr. Adams, with reason, was getting extremely weary of it. So far as editorial work was concerned, it was becoming more and more plain to him that he had no vocation that way. Indeed, how the paper sustained itself at all under his management, it is difficult now to understand. Voicing an unpopular cause, it was without capital, patronage, or enterprise. The consciousness of forever tugging at a dead weight is not inspiriting, and the zeal with which Mr. Adams took hold of his new work in June, 1846, was, in February, 1848, fast degenerating into a sense of hopeless drudgery. He was, however, at least cured of his taste for newspaper writ-

ing. He had of it enjoyed a surfeit. Of Mr.
Winthrop, Mr. Adams now in private exclaimed:
"He is wrong, and grievously wrong; and what
is worse, he is leading Massachusetts wrong.
And now I am in a manner handcuffed in my
opposition." This at the moment he looked
upon as one of "the heaviest of [his] trials:"
but, as the weeks went on, he grew to see it in
another light; and when, a few months later,
the course of events compelled his complete
severance from the paper, he accepted the situation with a sigh of profound relief. The experience was one he never cared to repeat. One
of the most thoroughly creditable episodes in
Mr. Adams's life, it carried with it ever after a
memory of thankless labor, necessary, but in
character most repellent. The seed had to be
sown; but the husbandman's work was hard,
the hours long, and his harvest to the last degree meagre.

The National Convention of the Whig party
met at Philadelphia on June 7th, and the next
day nominated General Taylor as its candidate
for the presidency, resolutely and significantly refusing to put forth any declaration of principles.
A candidate whose political views, if he had any,
were quite unknown was the party's unwritten
platform. In the convention, four ballots were
had. One hundred and forty votes were necessary

to a nomination; Mr. Clay, beginning with ninety-seven, ended with thirty-two; Mr. Webster had twenty-two votes on the first ballot, and thirteen on the last. So far as the " Conscience " Whigs of Massachusetts were concerned, the issue was now made up under " the Palfrey resolve." A Southern man and an owner of slaves, General Taylor could not have their support. They had so declared in advance; and their two special representatives in the convention, Charles Allen and Henry Wilson, after voting loyally on every ballot for Mr. Webster, formally withdrew when General Taylor was declared the nominee. In doing so Mr. Allen publicly and boldly announced that, in his belief, "the Whig party is here and this day dissolved;" while Mr. Wilson exclaimed, amid the wild uproar of a tumultuous demonstration: " Sir, I will go home; and, so help me God, I will do all I can to defeat the election of that candidate." The more immediate friends of Mr. Webster acquiesced. Like Mr. Webster himself, they did so silently, sullenly, slowly; but, by degrees, they acquiesced.

Meanwhile on June 3d, when already the result at Philadelphia was anticipated, a consultation had been held at the office of Mr. Adams, in Boston, and the steps preliminary to an organized "bolt" discussed. It followed, close and sharp, on the announcement of the nomination of Taylor and Fillmore ; and, in a few days, the call went forth for a convention to be held in August at Buffalo. To this convention Mr. Adams was appointed as one of the delegates from his father's old congressional district; and, on August 5th, he started on his way thither, going first to New York, where he met Mr. Giddings, and had with him an exchange of views. "He is averse to taking up Mr. Van Buren, and so am I," he wrote. On the 8th he reached Buffalo, and at once found himself involved in the whirl of the political storm centre. Thirty years later, referring to the Buffalo Convention of 1848, Mr. Adams recorded his mature conviction of it. "There have," he said, " been many such assemblages since, far larger in numbers, and perhaps more skillful in their modes of operation ; but for plain, downright honesty of purpose, to effect high ends without a whisper of bargain and sale, I doubt whether any similar one has been its superior, either before or since."

The convention of the Democratic party, which met at Baltimore on the 22d of May, had, after a sharp contest, nominated Lewis Cass, of Michigan, as its candidate ; a Northern man with Southern principles, General Cass stood on a distinctly pro-slavery platform. The real question, therefore, which the Buffalo Conven-

tion had to decide was, whether General Taylor
or General Cass should be President of the
United States for the term then approaching.
The " Conscience" Whigs wanted to defeat
Taylor; but they did not want to elect Cass.
The "Barnburners," the bolting New York contingent at Buffalo, bitterly resented the treatment of their chief, ex-President Van Buren, in
the last two Democratic presidential conventions.
In that of 1844, he had been defeated through
the instrumentality of Cass; and in that just
held Cass had received the nomination. No
matter who was elected, the " Barnburners "
were now eager for revenge. In the end they
had their way; and they secured it through a
very simple pact, or compromise. The " Barnburners " said to the "Conscience " Whigs:
" Give us the naming of the candidate, and you
may frame the platform of principles on which
the candidate shall stand." So far as political
tenets were concerned, the opponents of Mr.
Van Buren were thus given absolute *carte
blanche;* and with this they had to be content.
Mr. Adams was made chairman of the convention; and finally, at the very earnest request
of the Ohio delegation, among whom his father's
name was a thing to conjure with, he was associated on the ticket with Mr. Van Buren, as
the third party's candidate for Vice-President.

CHAPTER VI

THE EBB OF THE TIDE

HAVING completed its labors, the Buffalo Convention of 1848 adjourned on August 10th; the presidential election took place on November 9th following. While polling close upon 300,000 votes in the country at large, the new party failed to carry a single electoral college; but, none the less, as between the two dominant divisions, it decided which should carry the day.

So far as Mr. Adams personally was concerned, the vote was unmistakably gratifying. To him had been assigned the second place on the ticket, representing the element in the new organization to be drawn from the Whigs; and he had to go before the anti-slavery people of Massachusetts weighted down by the name and the record of Martin Van Buren. Nevertheless, the proportion which the Free-Soil vote bore to the total vote cast in Massachusetts (twenty-eight per cent.) was larger than in any other State, except Vermont (twenty-nine per cent.), and materially exceeded that reached in New York (twenty-six per cent.). In other words,

Mr. Adams contributed his full share to the strength of the ticket on which he ran. The lessons of his father, supplemented by his own years of almost daily teaching from the editorial office of the "Whig," bore their fruits. Both the old parties were shaken to their centres by the new demonstration.

Mr. Adams, also, came out of this canvass with a national reputation of his own, which thenceforth he retained and increased. This meant a great deal for him ; for probably in the whole experience of the country there has not been another case where a man was so persistently estimated at less than his real value because of the eminence of his immediate ancestors. To a certain extent this was a natural presumption ; but it was intensified in the case of Mr. Adams by peculiarities of manner, and a shyness of temper which caused merely casual observers to mistake an innate indisposition to push himself for lack of capacity. Growing up under the overshadowing fame of John Quincy Adams, it was not until 1848 that he was generally recognized as something more than the bearer of a distinguished cognomen. This, too, was a point on which he was sensitive, — and unduly so. Never claiming anything, or even seeking recognition, because of his father and his grandfather, constant reference to them

in connection with himself annoyed, and at times
irritated him. He could not habituate himself
to it, nor learn to take it lightly and as matter
of course, — at one time the commonplace utterance of some not unkindly man, devoid of good
taste, and at another the obvious retort of a
coarse and commonplace opponent, quick to
avail himself of a telling personal allusion. For
all such, it was so very easy to refer to a noticeable family deterioration, — " sharp decline "
was the approved form of speech, — and the
reference was sure to elicit a sneering laugh, and
round of blockhead applause from the benches
of the groundlings. Nor was it only the clumsy
who had recourse to this unfailing method of
bringing down the house. In the course of the
campaign of 1848 even Rufus Choate, the kind-
est, the most genial and charming of men and
acquaintances, both by nature and training
courteous and considerate of opponents, — even
Rufus Choate, in the Whig state convention,
held that year at Worcester, was not above this
wretched, worn-out claptrap; and, with rhe-
torical pause, referring to J. Q. Adams, then
scarcely six months dead, as " the last of the
Adamses," he elicited from his audience a noisy
and delighted response. It was a hit, — a very
palpable hit; but none the less somewhat un-
worthy of Rufus Choate. It was all in the

rough give-and-take of the hustings ; but there is no doubt it annoyed Mr. Adams more than he cared to admit or, indeed, than it should have done. To have one's ancestors unceasingly flung in one's face is unpleasant, and listening to the changes incessantly rung upon them becomes indubitably monotonous. This, however, all through life, was to an unusual degree the fate of Mr. Adams, and never so much so as in the campaign of 1848. None the less the rallying cry of the new party, formulated by Stephen C. Phillips at Buffalo, — " Van Buren and Free Soil ; Adams and Liberty," — echoed all through the North, and through it Mr. Adams's individual name became known far beyond the limits of Massachusetts.

In other respects the outcome of that campaign was not so gratifying. The fact was, and it could not be sophisticated away, that Martin Van Buren, the political heir of Andrew Jackson and the "little magician" of New York politics, was a strange candidate for earnest anti-slavery men to select. The association was undeniably incongruous. Of course, Mr. Adams's own record and utterances in regard to his new political running-mate were industriously hunted up, and he was confronted with them. They were, to say the least, the reverse of respectful. Only four years before he had in print alluded to Mr. Van Buren as one who, making " a trade of public affairs," was fixed to nothing " but his own interest;" and whose " cold and temporizing policy " at that time was " symptomatic of treachery hereafter." Referring to such expressions, he now wrote : " These opinions I then held, but [Mr. Van Buren] has done much to make me change them ; and it singularly happens that, in the particular in which I then predicted he would fail, he falsified my anticipation : — he did oppose the annexation of Texas. Mr. Van Buren is a mixed character. In early life, right ; in middle life, swayed to the wrong by his ambition and his associations, — he seems towards the close of his career to be again falling into the right channel. But, as a candidate, his main defect is that he wants warmth to give an impulse to his friends."

In presenting their case in 1848, the Free-Soil speakers always met the objection of Mr. Van Buren's candidacy by saying that it was a case of " principles, not men." As Von Holst has since pointed out,[1] this phrase in connection with a presidential canvass has a somewhat empty sound. If it was meant that the candidates of the party stood no chance of an election, and consequently that the voter, in casting

[1] Vol. iii. p. 398.

his ballot for them, merely recorded himself as in favor of a principle, the proposition might be accepted ; though scarcely one calculated to attract recruits. On the other hand, when ardently supporting principles, it is at least questionable wisdom to choose to office men who, in office, cannot be relied on to make those principles effective. Furthermore, Mr. Adams's position was now not logical. He had objected to Mr. Webster as the exponent of the anti-slavery sentiment because he was deficient in moral stamina. He had insisted that, if Mr. Webster was elevated into leadership, he would, sooner or later, by leading the movement over to the enemy, betray it to its destruction. Not grounded in the faith, Daniel Webster was consumed by a craving for the presidential office. This was probably true ; but, in these respects, how was it with Martin Van Buren ? Was he, as studied in a record at once long, varied, and sinuous, conspicuous for moral stamina ? How had he stood, and what had he said on the great question at issue ? If again elevated to the presidential chair, could he be depended upon to carry out the principles enunciated at Buffalo ? In point of fact, it needed but the development of a single year to show the eager and honest participants in the Buffalo convention that the leaders among their New York associates were simply playing a game. Headed by Mr. Van Buren's son, the popular " Barnburner" idol in the campaign of 1848, they in 1849 marched in a body back into the regular Democratic fold. Their late allies in other States looked on at the spectacle in blank amazement; but the fact could not be gainsaid. It is not easy to see what more, or worse, under similar circumstances, Mr. Webster could have done.

In the way those concerned then approached it, the difficulty, however, was insoluble. The nascent party did not feel able to stand alone; and, that being so, it would have made no difference at the stage of evolution it had then reached, whether it put forward as its exponent Van Buren or Webster, Corwin or M'Lean. As Mr. Adams one day somewhat ruefully wrote, " We must do with what we have;" and whichever of the candidates they might select from the men prominent in either of the old organizations, the Free-Soilers of Buffalo would have been sure to regret not selecting another. In J. Q. Adams the anti-slavery sentiment had a leader, and from him it drew an early inspiration. When, in 1845, years and failing strength incapacitated him from service, no successor of national reputation presented himself. Those then foremost on the stage had, so far as the free States were concerned, been educated on national lines. On the slavery issue they were, one and all, wholly unreliable when subjected to any severe test. They would roll off platitudes by the yard, and accept endless formulas ; but they could not lift themselves to a level with the subject, or be convinced that it was beyond a charlatan treatment. The party of the future, therefore, had to educate its own leaders, — slowly evolve its exponents. Precipitated into existence by the events of 1848, it had no confidence in itself. That must be its excuse; and, as an excuse, it is fairly satisfactory. Nevertheless, for the young party of high standards and noble aspirations to select Martin Van Buren as its standard-bearer was absurd; and, thereafter, the genuine earnestness which pervaded the movement alone saved it from collapse under ridicule. Even so, in making its first nomination the Free-Soil party, to use the words of the translator of Von Holst, "destroyed its own viability." Had it been thoroughly consistent and true to itself, it would have nominated John P. Hale, Salmon P. Chase, or William H. Seward, treating the canvass of 1848 as a subordinate and temporary issue, which, so far as any ultimate result was concerned, might safely be left to decide itself.

Practically, in the end, it did decide itself. Millard Fillmore became president; a compromise was patched up; the slave - power ruled

supreme. Meanwhile, in spite of the prominence given him during the canvass of 1848, the
political leadership in the Massachusetts anti-
slavery movement within the lines of the Constitution was passing from Mr. Adams. Charles
Sumner, on the one hand, and Henry Wilson,
on the other, were rapidly coming into greater
prominence and more pronounced activity. Sumner's larger and more imposing presence, combined with magnetism, eloquence, and zeal, were
then gaining for him that personal ascendency
which, firmly cemented by the brutal assault of
May, 1856, was to continue unbroken to his
death. Henry Wilson, on the other hand, failing in business, had now devoted himself to
politics as a calling from which incidentally the
means of livelihood might be extracted. With
untiring activity he was organizing the new
party throughout the State; and he was not organizing it with an eye to the political advance-
ment of Mr. Adams. He meanwhile was writing in his diary: "I look upon this period as
simply an episode to what ought to be the true
purpose of my next few years."

In this entry he referred to the work before
him in connection with the family papers, now
his, the John Adams accumulation having now
been augmented by the yet larger accumulation
of his son. Twenty-two years had then already

elapsed since the death of the second president,
and his grandson felt no disposition longer to
defer a task which, moreover, was one altogether
congenial. So already, while the presidential canvass of 1848 was still in progress, arrangements
for the publication of the "Life and Works
of John Adams" had been effected, and a pro-
spectus issued. Wholly freed at last from journalistic work, Mr. Adams, now turning from politics, devoted himself wholly to literature and
the study of "stale political excitements."

The massive ten volume publication of the
John Adams papers, begun in 1848, was not
completed until 1856; nor was it until 1860
that Mr. Adams again exercised an appreciable
influence in the direction of public affairs. The
intervening years, passed in his library, or at
most touching on politics quite remotely and in
a way not productive of any considerable result,
only here and there offer anything of historical
value. Not in a position to be consulted, or to
enjoy special means of information, his diary
became a mere record of private reflections and
local or family incidents. In it, also, the absence of his father makes itself greatly felt, the
inspiration of his large activity and restless,
eager temper being distinctly gone. Though he
himself did not know it, the single element of
the picturesque and broadening had in Febru-

ary, 1848, been taken out of Mr. Adams's existence, and he now fell easily and naturally back into the narrow circle of New England life.

So far, also, as the anti-slavery cause was concerned, there now followed a succession of dull, dragging years, — years of reaction, discouragement, and hope deferred. In national politics, the death of Taylor, at the moment when to anti-slavery men his administration promised results as happy as they were unexpected, was followed by the accession of Fillmore, the recreancy of Webster, and the passage of the compromise measures of 1850. Then came the canvass of 1852, and the election of Franklin Pierce; the Free-Soil party of four years before being now reduced to little more than a contemptible political fragment. The Whig organization did not, however, survive its defeat of that year, and perceptibly melted away in the agitation which followed the repeal of the Missouri Compromise. Finally the Republican party emerged from the chaos, and in 1856 almost secured the presidency. Fortunately for itself and the country, it failed to elect Fremont; but in 1858 it carried a majority in the House of Representatives, preliminary to its election of Lincoln two years later. Mr. Adams's time, long deferred, then came.

CHAPTER VII

THE ANTE-BELLUM CONGRESS

In 1858 it was for Mr. Adams either to find his way into active public life, or make up his mind to permanent exclusion from it. Fifty-one years of age, he had been prominent; and he no longer was so. He was in the familiar and dangerous position of a man well known to nourish political aspirations, who has been much and long discussed in various connections, but who, for one reason or another, has never received preferment. Of such, in the end, people weary. The man everlastingly named, who never "gets there," becomes, so to speak, shopworn, — lacking novelty, he is a bit out of fashion; and, moreover, he is in the way of the younger and more energetic aspirants. Already, when his father died in February, 1848, Mr. Adams had been more or less talked of as his congressional successor; but Horace Mann had then been preferred to him. In 1850, the compromise year, Mr. Mann became involved in a bitter controversy with Mr. Webster, growing out of the compromise measures, and Mr. Adams was one of the most zealous advocates of his reëlection. Two years later, in 1852, Mr. Mann voluntarily withdrew; but Mr. Adams was then a Free-Soiler, and those were the dark days. He was nominated by his party for the district; but, on the second trial, — for a majority of all the votes cast for the office was then necessary to a choice at the first or regular election, — his Whig opponent, a highly respectable Boston business gentleman of the Webster following, was chosen over him by a narrow plurality. The Democrats, as ever, were disinclined to Mr. Adams. The old Jackson antipathy would not away, and the instinctive Irish dislike to the essentially Anglo-Saxon made itself felt. In 1854 the Whig and Free-Soil parties both disappeared in Massachusetts under the native American, or " Know-Nothing " cataclysm, and Mr. Adams found himself a leader absolutely without a following. In the Norfolk district, William S. Damrell, a man whose name had never been heard of in politics before, of whom the dictionary of Congress says that, " by trade a printer, [he] never had the privilege of even a common-school education," was evolved as a candidate from the sessions of a secret order, and elected by a majority larger than any by which the district had ever honored either of his two immediate, and better remembered, prede-

cessors, Horace Mann and John Quincy Adams.
Though incapacitated by paralysis from any
active performance of his duties, Mr. Damrell
served through a second term ; but as that drew
to its close in 1858, the Know-Nothing deluge
had in great degree subsided, having in Massachusetts brought to the political surface absolutely nothing but driftwood and scum. A way
was at last thus opened for Mr. Adams. But
in the district the native American element was
still strong, and almost as set in its hostility to
Mr. Adams as were the Irish ; so his nomination
was effected not without trouble. Indeed, he
owed it largely to the unseen, personal intervention of Mr. Sumner, and to the generous
withdrawal in his favor of George R. Russell,
the natural candidate of those of Whig antecedents, in that district a large element. When,
however, the day of the convention came, Mr.
Adams was nominated on the first ballot by a
decisive preponderance ; and, in common with
the rest of the Republican ticket, he was returned at the November election by a clear
majority of nearly 1200 over two opposing candidates. He was thus at last fairly launched
into national public life.

The Thirty - sixth Congress, the only one
in which Mr. Adams ever sat, assembled on
Monday, December 5, 1859. The Republican

party at that time was at a great disadvantage
socially in Washington. It had no foothold in
the executive departments, and few officers of
the army and navy were in sympathy with it.
The ordinary run of office-holders regarded it with
traditional aversion, and an apprehension ever
increasing. The whole social atmosphere of the
capital was in fact surcharged with pro-slavery
sentiment. Among the prominent Republicans
in Congress, Governor Seward almost alone
dwelt in a house of his own, or made any
pretense of hospitality. Mr. Sumner lived in a
bachelor apartment of modest proportions and
severe simplicity, taking his dinner at a restau-
rant, when not the guest of some member of the
diplomatic corps. Most of the Republican members of Congress lived at the wretched hotels,
or still less inviting boarding-houses, then characteristic of Washington; and they and their
wives, when the latter were there, haunted cor-
ridors and public parlors. Sensible of the obligation which in this respect was upon him,
Mr. Adams had engaged a large house, as houses
in Washington then went, and prepared to
make of it a Republican social centre, so far as
such a centre was possible under existing conditions.

The session of 1859–60, as usual with sessions
next preceding a national election, was almost

wholly given up to president-making. The
Buchanan administration was already moribund.
All the high hopes and sanguine expectations
with which that " old public functionary," as he
described himself, had entered upon his high office
had, one by one, been disappointed, and utter
failure now stared him in the face; though, in
that respect, no imaginings could for him have
equaled the realities which the immediate future
had in store. The Democratic party was rent
in twain over the slavery issue; while, for Mr.
Douglas, his great panacea of popular sover-
eignty had proved in the result a veritable boom-
erang. In spite of his victory over Abraham
Lincoln in the election which followed the memorable Illinois senatorial debate of 1858, Stephen
A. Douglas was now hardly less out of favor
with the Southern leaders than were the more
moderate Republicans. None the less, he was
still the favorite presidential possibility of the
Democracy of the North; while the South looked
about anxiously, but in vain, for somebody on
whom they could unite as " available," in opposition to him. Every possible combination was
considered. On the Republican side, John C.
Fremont had long dropped out of consideration. It was instinctively recognized, and tacitly
conceded, that he did not possess the stamina
required; and men already began to feel a degree

of mortification and a certain sense of shame-
facedness as they called to mind the way in
which they had been stampeded into his nomination four years before. The recollection was
the reverse of inspiring. Had Governor Seward
then been nominated in Fremont's place, — as
he always after felt he should have been, — his
position as the recognized leader of the Republican party would have been thereby established,
and a renomination in 1860 would have followed
as a matter of course. As it was, he had since,
by force of ability and incisive utterance, risen to
be the most prominent member of the party in
Congress and before the country; but in the
former he did not attain the position which
Henry Clay had held so long among the Whigs.
He lacked certain of the personal elements essential to American political leadership. Still, so
far as the impending nomination was concerned,
he was distinctly in the lead, with Salmon P.
Chase as a not very formidable second. Abraham Lincoln was as yet hardly considered seriously. The Whigs were a mere rump; the
Know-Nothing party had disappeared.

The House of Representatives of the Thirty-
sixth Congress was a wholly impotent body, in
that it was hopelessly divided. Of its 237 members, 109 were classed as Republicans, 88 as
Administration Democrats, 13 as Free State

Democrats, and 27 as "Native Americans," all but four of the last named being from former Whig districts of the South. A contest, and a long and bitter contest, over the choice of a speaker was inevitable from the outset; and the situation, mixed and bad at best, was further complicated by the extreme agitation into which the whole South had been thrown by the John Brown raid at Harper's Ferry in the previous October. Never had a Congress assembled containing so many elements of such dangerous discord. As subsequent events showed, it was rather an unmanageable mob insensibly premonitory of conflict, than a parliamentary body. Above all, the arrogance and anger of the Southern contingent scarcely brooking constraint, the manners of the plantation overseer were constantly in evidence, as also an eagerness for the fray. Among the more prominent members on the Republican side were Thaddeus Stevens, of Pennsylvania, who, having already served two terms in the House between 1848 and 1853, now again returned to it to remain in continuous service until his death in 1868; John Sherman, of Ohio, then commencing his third term, and shortly to be transferred to the Senate; Roscoe Conkling, of New York, a man of only thirty and just entering on his brilliant congressional career; the three famous brothers Washburn, Israel, from Maine, Elihu B., from Illinois, and Cadwallader C., from Wisconsin; and to these might be added Owen Lovejoy, a brother of the "martyr of Alton," Galusha A. Grow, of Illinois, and Lot M. Morrill, of Vermont.   Besides L. Q. C. Lamar, of Alabama, Roger A. Pryor, of Virginia, and Laurence M. Keitt, of South Carolina, infamous as the coadjutor of Brooks, the list of those serving on the other side of that House bristles with names of men who subsequently died in the Confederate service. Vallandigham, of Ohio, afterwards notorious as a "copperhead," was also a member.

The contest over the speakership began on December 5th, the opening day of the session, and came to a close on February 1st; when, on the forty-fourth ballot, William Pennington of New Jersey, then serving his first and only term in Congress, was chosen. John Sherman was the candidate of the Republicans from the second ballot to the thirty-ninth, when he withdrew his name to save his party from clearly impending defeat.   The contest was within three days as long as the similar struggle of four years previous, which had resulted in the election of Banks; but here the resemblance stopped. There was in it, as compared with the other, a significant increase of bitterness;

on both sides an exasperation as of men who could with difficulty be restrained from laying violent hands on each other. Thus, while good-humor and courtesy had marked the contest of 1856, that of 1860 was noticeable for its acrimony and spirit of fierce defiance.

The House was thus organized. When, however, it came to the assignment of committee positions, Mr. Adams, so far as influence in the House was concerned, was, as he at the time well understood and, later on, more and more appreciated, courteously, and in a dignified, considerate sort of way, shelved. Failing to bear in mind an injunction earnestly imposed upon him by Mr. Giddings at a meeting in Boston in December, 1858, "not to permit any delicacy or scruples to stand in the way," it never occurred to Mr. Adams to bring to bear on the new and inexperienced occupant of the speaker's chair any pressure to secure recognition for himself. Indeed, he would not have known how to set about such a business. Accordingly, acting under almost unendurable pressure from every other quarter, Mr. Pennington lent a ready ear to the ingenious suggestion conveyed to him by a not disinterested Massachusetts colleague, that Mr. Adams should be appointed to the same committee positions which had been assigned to his father when, nearly

thirty years before, the latter first entered the
House of Representatives as an ex-President.
The scheme was effective, and Mr. Adams was
thus promoted out of his colleague's way. The
committee on manufactures, of which his name
appeared as chairman was, under the rules for
the disposition of business then and since in
vogue, a mere name. It had not even a room
assigned to it; nor had it been called together
within the memory of any member of that Congress. To be announced as its head was equivalent to what is commonly known as "honorable mention." Nevertheless, for a new member
of Mr. Adams's peculiar temperament and very
retiring disposition, this practical shelving had
its advantages in affording him time in which
to become familiar with his new surroundings.
His subsequent prominence came naturally and
in due order of events, and under a positive
call; he was not prematurely thrust into notice.

In this, his maiden session, except in answer
to the call of the clerk, Mr. Adams's voice was
heard but once in the House. He would much
have preferred to maintain an unbroken silence;
but a presidential election was impending, and
set speeches were in order. These speeches, of
the abstract, educational kind, while addressed
to the House, were meant for the constituencies.
Some of Mr. Adams's friends at home insisted

that he must make himself heard; and, in response to their urgency, he spoke. His speech
was thoroughly characteristic. In no way sensational or vituperative, — its calm, firm tone,
excellent temper, and well-ordered reasoning
naturally commended it to an audience satiated
by months of turgid rhetoric and personal abuse.
This his Southern colleagues appreciated; for,
conscious what sinners they were in those respects, they the more keenly felt in others moderation of language and restraint in bearing.
A few days later one of the most extreme among
them, Mr. Cobb, of Alabama, went out of his
way to refer to Mr. Adams as "the only member never out of order;" and the person thus
curiously singled out noted, "there is something
singular in the civility formally paid me on the
other side of the house. I have never courted
one of them; but I have insulted no one." It
was to these men — the members from the
South, and more especially to those from Virginia — that Mr. Adams now addressed himself,
setting forth the cause of being — the *raison
d'être* — of the Republican party in a natural
resistance to the requirements and claims of a
property interest, which, alone of all interests,
was directly represented on the floor of the
House by a solid phalanx of its members. Then
passing on to an appeal from the modern inter-

pretation of the Declaration and Constitution to
the understanding of the framers, he closed with
a distinct statement of the constitutional limitations as respects slavery recognized and accepted
by the Republican party, and his own belief in
the utter futility and foreordained failure of
any attempt on the Union.

The Republican National Convention met at
Chicago, on May 16th. Mr. Adams was an
earnest, though quiet, advocate of the nomination of Governor Seward. Seward was the
leader of the Republican party ; more, far more,
than any other one man, he had formulated its
principles and voiced its feelings. He was entitled now to be its standard-bearer. Suddenly,
at the moment when that result of the convention's action was most confidently anticipated, a
rumor spread through the House of Representatives, then engaged on a contested election
case, that the prize had fallen to Mr. Lincoln.
Mr. Adams the next morning thus commented
on this momentous selection : " [The report] was
received with general incredulity, until by repeated announcements from different quarters
it appeared that he had carried the day by a
union of all the anti-Seward elements. The
effect upon me was to depress ; for, though no
partisan of Governor Seward, I did feel as if he
was the man to whom the party owed the nomi-

nation.   But I could not fail to perceive in the
faces of many of our friends the signs of a very
opposite conviction.   In truth, the western section and the middle States are exceedingly
timid, and desire as far as possible to escape so
direct an issue on the slave question as the nomination of Mr. Seward would have made.   Mr.
Lincoln is by no means of so decided a type;
and yet he is in many respects a fair representative.   I believe him honest and tolerably capable; but he has no experience and no business
habits."

Mr. Adams was no stump speaker or campaign orator.   It was not in him to "move the
masses;" but, in the long and exciting canvass which now ensued, he took a somewhat
active part, accompanying Governor Seward in
his memorable electioneering journey through
the States of the Northwest, going as far as
St. Paul.   Renominated to Congress without
opposition, he was elected by a majority of
some 3000 votes.   This was on November 6th;
upon which day ended the canvass most pregnant of consequences of all the country has ever
witnessed, before or since.   On November 10th
Mr. Adams closed the old mansion at Quincy,
and moved with his family to his house in Boston, there to remain for the few weeks yet to
intervene before his departure for Washington.

The effort of fourteen years had been crowned with success. The anti-slavery movement, at last proving irresistible, was about to take possession of the government. The final evening he was destined to pass in Quincy for more than seven years was marked by a celebration of the great political victory just won, and was marred by no premonition of the trials to come. The curtain fell amid rejoicings, illuminations, the blazing of rockets and the shoutings of victory; shortly it was to rise again to the sound of alarm-bells struck in the night. For the moment, however, satisfaction over the past was as unalloyed as the anticipation of the future was confident.

CHAPTER VIII

THE AWAKENING

RETROSPECT is the one infallible test of political, as of private conduct, in times of emergency. To its cold and altogether unsympathetic scrutiny, the statesman's policy and the methods of the tradesman are in the close equally subjected. Having, too, the last word, from its verdict there is no escape. Accordingly, it is apt to go hard before posterity with a public character when his biographer feels himself under the necessity of defense or explanation. Fortunately nothing of the sort is necessary for Mr. Adams in connection with the course of events subsequent to the election of 1860, and leading up to the catastrophe of April 13, 1861.

Not that Mr. Adams ever subsequently persuaded himself, as did so many others, both in and out of public life, that, during the winter which preceded the outbreak of the civil war, he had foreseen the whole terrible outcome, anticipating just what occurred. On the contrary, claiming no prescience in that regard, when

the struggle came he frankly confessed himself
astonished and horrified. His forecast had for
years been all wrong. He had assured the
country that the South was not in earnest, that
its threats were mere braggadocio, that its interests and its safety combined to keep it in the
Union. Now he had slowly to wake up to his
error, and address himself to a new and unan-
ticipated situation. He did so, step by step
feeling his way; but, afterwards, had his foresight during the winter of 1860–61 been as perfect as his retrospect became, he would in no
essential respect have done otherwise than he
did.

So far as the loyal people of the United
States were concerned, the course of political
events from the election of Lincoln to the bom-
bardment of Fort Sumter — from November 6,
1860, to April 13, 1861 — afforded a curious
exemplification of what can only be described
as national good luck ; for, absolutely without
intelligent human guidance, those events developed themselves in a way which, under the
peculiar conditions then existing, hardly admitted of improvement. This, of course, was
not apparent at the time. On the contrary, as
the ship of state slowly and irresistibly drifted
into the breakers, the cry for guidance — for a
hand at the helm — was only less loud than the

wail of despair over its manifest absence; this, however, did not alter the fact that, the catastrophe being inevitable, it came about, though in a way purely fortuitous, at the right time, in the best place that could have been selected, and, so far as the elements of the country loyal to nationality were concerned, in the most desirable form.

The facts, not open to dispute, need to be briefly recalled. On November 6, 1860, when a large plurality of those voting chose Lincoln as President, they, like Mr. Adams, never believed that secession would ensue. When they were speedily undeceived on this head, the situation in which the country found itself could hardly have been worse. Four months were to elapse before the change of administration was to take place. The interim was full of danger. It was a veritable interregnum, during which the government might well be wrecked. The administration was indeed in the hands of the wreckers; while the President, wholly out of sympathy with the man chosen to be his successor, and in no way in communication with him, was almost, if not altogether, pitiable in his timorous vacillation. A better opportunity to complete their work, conspirators could not have desired. It so chanced, however, that, South as well as North, public sentiment was

divided.   The cotton States, so-called, — South
Carolina and those contiguous to the Gulf of
Mexico, — unanimous within themselves, were
for all practical purposes also united in a common line of action ; but in all the more Northern, or, as they were now called, border slave
States, there was a strong Union sentiment — a
reluctance to being swept headlong into the
uncertainties which secession would unquestionably entail.   Virginia and Maryland, during
the interregnum, held the key of the situation.
This fact is fundamental to any correct understanding of the situation.   Had those two
border slave States then promptly followed
the lead given by the cotton States, their action would unquestionably, with Buchanan at
the head of the national government, have been
decisive of the result.   The conspirators, seizing
the national capital before the change of administration was effected, would have overturned
the government.   Fortunately, the traditions of
Virginia and the material interests of Maryland
were not readily overcome ; and, actuated by
the spirit of conservatism, a strong party in
favor of delay at least, if not of the Union, developed itself in each of those pivotal States.   It
was manifestly of vital importance to the loyal
North to keep alive and encourage this visibly
languishing Union sentiment, if only as an ob-

stacle which the Southern extremists would have to overcome, thus making of it a factor of delay, consuming an interval of time fraught with danger. Not until March 4th would the machinery of state — the War Department and the Navy Department — be transferred; and, for the North, it was a matter, as is now apparent, of simply vital importance that the catastrophe — if a catastrophe was inevitable — should be deferred until after that date. Throughout that trying winter, therefore, the eyes of all thinking, cool and clear-headed men were steadily fixed upon the ides of March.

On the other hand, it was plainly the interest of the conspirators to precipitate a conflict. By so doing they might not impossibly secure the national capital, thus becoming, when the change of administration necessarily took place, the *de facto* government. So far as foreign nations were concerned, this would have been conclusive. The hesitating attitude of the border slave States, especially of Virginia, was the obstacle in the way. Those States were, however, in that unstable psychological condition which made it very necessary to deal carefully with them. To bring on a conflict was easy; but by unduly precipitating such a conflict, the border States might not impossibly be shocked and repelled rather than attracted. The Southern extremists, therefore, instinctively recognized the fact that it would not be safe yet to put themselves manifestly in the wrong through any act of aggression, at once overt and wanton. For that, conditions were not ripe. Premature action on their part, while consolidating the North, might divide the South. Accordingly, unless the entire Southern heart should by good luck be fired by some premature attempt of the national government at the "coercion of a State," the conspirators had perforce to wait.

Meanwhile, the free States were in a condition of moral chaos. The old union-saving, compromising sentiment was there both strong and outspoken. It had to be cautiously dealt with. The Republican party was thus under heavy bonds to keep in the right. It must show itself reasonable, conciliatory, and law-abiding; it must hold out the olive-branch conspicuously; avoiding anything like provocation, it must await attack. Only by so doing could it, when the moment came, rally public sentiment to its support. So far as the North was concerned, the day for diatribes and denunciation, for philippics and incrimination, was, therefore, over. Though there were those, and not a few, who seemed unable to realize this fact then, it is obvious now.

Under these difficult conditions, the loyal element labored under great disadvantage in the important matter of leadership. The Southern conspirators, knowing exactly what they were driving at, had, immediately after the election, gone effectively to work to secure it. They enjoyed perfect means of information; for they were actually represented in Congress, as well as in the executive departments. They were united as one man. Every point in the game was thus in their favor; they apparently stood to win. Not so the incoming party of loyalty and freedom. Divided by jealousies, distracted in council, those of the North knew absolutely nothing of that man whom the voice of a political convention, little above a mob, had selected to be their leader; and he, an untried executive, far away from the centre of action in "his secluded abode in the heart of Illinois," made no sign. All eyes were turned thither, all ears were intent; but during all the fateful days from early November to late February, nothing was there seen and little thence heard. Yet, as in the end it turned out, even this absence of lead in the time of crisis — so deplored at the time, and which on any received doctrine of chances should have been fatal — proved opportune. The country drifted more fortunately for itself than it would probably have been directed even by the most sagacious of politicians. For the

moral conditions time in which to mature was
absolutely essential. A community fairly agon-
ized with fear was being slowly educated to the
fighting pitch. The process was one, not of
days, nor yet of weeks, but of months.

A succession of events then occurred, — all
fortuitous, and yet all as they should have been.
On December 26th, acting within his orders but
on his own responsibility, Major Robert Anderson, in command of the United States forces in
Charleston harbor, transferred his skeleton garrison from Fort Moultrie to Fort Sumter. A
catastrophe, then imminent, but for the North
altogether premature, was thus deferred; and
the eyes of the whole country were thereafter
fixed, and its thoughts concentrated, on a single
point of danger. An attack on the flag flying
on an island in Charleston harbor became from
that moment an assault on the Union. Chance
thus selected the point of collision, and selected
it most advantageously for the North; for while
South Carolina, laboring under a record of nearly
forty years, was in the South looked upon with
apprehension, in the North, deemed a firebrand,
she had no friend. Memories of nullification,
of assaults in the senate chamber and of counsels always extreme, there arose uncalled at the
mere mention of her name. Human foresight
thus could not have better designated the point
of danger.

A few days later, on January 9th, the attempt to reinforce Anderson with men and supplies by the steamer Star of the West failed, the relieving steamer being fired into and driven back to New York by the guns of South Carolina; while, most fortunately, and almost as matter of chance, those of Sumter did not reply. The act of aggression was thus on the part of the conspirators ; and yet no catastrophe was precipitated. It would then have been premature — to the Union probably fatal ; for March 4th was still nearly two months in the future.

Again, in the early days of February, when the tension was fast becoming too severe to last, Virginia held an election for delegates to a convention to decide on the course to be pursued ; and a decisive majority of those chosen were found to be opposed to immediate secession. Most fortunately Henry A. Wise was no longer governor of that State. Had his tenure of the office continued, it is impossible to say what might or might not have been attempted. John Letcher, a Virginian of the states-rights school but not a secessionist, had succeeded Wise in 1859, and, though a few months later on he acted with decision in favor of the Confederacy when the Virginia convention at last passed its ordinance of secession, he now for the time being maintained a conservative attitude. The Vir-

ginia election, resulting as it did at just this juncture, was, therefore, a piece of supreme good
fortune. It checked the rapid course of events.
As Mr. Seward, with a deep sigh of relief, wrote
on hearing of it: " The danger of conflict before
March 4th has been averted. Time has been
gained." Time at that juncture was precious.

Then came the futile Washington Peace Conference, called at the request of Virginia. More
discussion and new suggestions of accommoda-
tion followed; and, though nothing came of
them in the end, they were most useful, for they
consumed the few days still remaining before
the fateful ides. And all this time the ship of
state, under influences quite irresistible, steadily
drifted on a rocky lee shore. There was no
hand at the helm; but nothing untoward occurred, no reef was struck.

On March 4th, the transfer of the government was effected quietly and safely. A hand
was now at the helm, and something positive in
the way of direction was looked for. Luckily
for the country, Mr. Lincoln's lack of familiarity with the situation, the very habit of his
mind and the fact that he was more intent on
the distribution of offices than on the gravity of
the crisis, then also stood the country in good
stead. The immediate question related to the
course to be pursued in respect to Fort Sumter.

Something had to be decided. Should the garrison be withdrawn? — or should the government, in the attempt to relieve it, provoke a collision? And here, whichever course was decided on, serious doubts suggested themselves, grave danger was incurred. If the garrison had been, as Secretary Seward then advocated, quietly withdrawn, the country would have been humiliated and a great opportunity lost. Its self-respect gone, it would have sacrificed its prestige in the eyes of foreign powers. The result might well have proved disastrous; for, itself practically recognizing the Confederacy, it would have invited its recognition by others. On the other hand, if South Carolina were attacked, and the garrison at Sumter relieved by a successful naval operation, it would have been an overt act of aggression precipitating the South into a war of defense. Upon that issue the slave States would have been a unit, while the free States might have been divided. Had the Confederate leaders been wise and far-seeing, they would in this way have provoked the now inevitable conflict, compelling the national government either to humiliate itself or to strike the first blow, they then replying strictly in self-defense. Again luck, for it was nothing else, served the United States better than the counsels of its statesmen. Taking the bit in their teeth,

the hot-heads of South Carolina precipitated the
issue.   Blunderers — aggressors in civil strife,
the disciples of Calhoun caused the Confederate
batteries to open fire on the flag of the Union.
The rest followed.   From that moment the loyal
North was a unit.   All the conditions were ripe,
the educational process was complete, and the
psychological crisis followed.

Such was the course of events.   That Mr.
Adams did not at the time fully appreciate the
gravity of the situation, or the irresistible force
of the influences at work, or the earnestness and
strength of his opponents, has already been said.
He never did appreciate them.   Referring to the
secession movement of 1861, he twelve years
later expressed the astonishing belief that " one
single hour of the will displayed by General
Jackson " in 1833 " would have stifled the fire
in its cradle."   A similar opinion was expressed
by Charles Sumner in 1863,[1] and by the biographers of Lincoln seventeen years later.[2]   That
a decided lead and vigorous action on the part
of the federal executive would, in December,
1860, or January, 1861, have united the North
earlier, and have in this way greatly influenced
subsequent results, is hardly questionable ; but,
in view of the temper and self-confidence then
there prevailing, that the attempt to " coerce a

[1] *Works*, vii. 518.   [2] Nicolay and Hay, iii. 123.

State " in January, 1861, would have cowed the
South into submission, and so prevented the four
years of desperate conflict which ensued, is altogether improbable; nor would it have been
desirable. The thing had been brooding too
long and gone too far to escape a copious blood-
letting. At some time, a little sooner or later,
nationality had once for all to be established.
Nevertheless, mistaken as he was as to the conditions under which he was called upon to act,
and their inevitable outcome, — still holding the
irremediable to be not beyond remedy, — Mr.
Adams, in December, 1860, considered carefully his course. Though dictated by instincts
of high statesmanship, that course was at the
time distinctly opportunist, — a course in which,
amid changing circumstances, but always in
presence of a great danger, he felt his way from
day to day. None the less, whether viewed from
the standpoint of the moralist and Christian, or
that of the statesman, or that of the astute
player in the game of politics, the line of action
Mr. Adams then followed was completely justified by results.

In the first place, he recognized the fact that
in their hour of victory a change of tone and
bearing on the part of the victors was wise as
well as becoming. Invective and threat were
now to be replaced by firmness, moderation,

conciliation ; fears were to be allayed ; confidence established. Assurance was to be given that the ascendency gained would not be abused. This was something which a large portion of those associated with him, of whom Mr. Sumner was a type, could not understand. That a man should in the hour of triumph demean himself towards his opponents otherwise than as he had demeaned himself in the heat of conflict seemed to pass their comprehension. To their eyes moderation always savored of weakness. In the next place, whichever way he looked at the actual situation, the course to be pursued seemed to Mr. Adams plain. If he looked at it from the standpoint of high moral responsibility, — as a Christian, — it was incumbent on him to do all in his power to do, short of the concession of some vital point at issue, to avert civil strife. He would yield nothing really essential ; but so far as non-essentials and points of pride were concerned, he would make smooth the way. The soundness of this view cannot well be controverted. Taking next the lower plane of the statesman, his eye was riveted on the transfer of the government from the hands of those who then held it to its friends ; as he twelve years later said, it was manifest that something had to be done " to keep control of the capital, and bridge over the interval before

the 4th of March in peace and quiet." To this
end it was not sufficient to guard carefully
against any premature catastrophe, the result of
some governmental action, not the less ill advised because well meant; but such a catastrophe, if cunningly contrived by the enemies of the
government, must, if possible, be averted. Mr.
Adams, therefore, advocated the appointment of
committees and the summoning of conferences,
— the presentation and discussion of schemes, —
anything, in fact, which would consume time and
preserve the peace, until the interregnum should
end. Finally, as an astute politician, he labored
to divide his enemies and concentrate the friends
of the government by the plausibility and fair-
ness of his proposals. He hoped to the last to
hold the border States, fully believing that, if
an armed conflict could by judicious caution be
averted, the Gulf States would, when the time
for sober second thought came, find their position untenable, and so be forced ignominiously
back into the Union. In this belief he was over
sanguine, failing to recognize the deadly inten-
sity of the situation. Nevertheless, in the stage
of that tremendous game then developing, it was
a point worth playing for. Its loss would not
jeopardize the stakes.

This, however, was remote. The 4th of March,
— the possession of the seat of government when

the change of administration should take place,
— this was the first point in the game, the securing which was essential to the result.   All
through that long, anxious winter, it was never
absent from the mind of Mr. Adams.   He now
also rose, at once and as if by common consent,
into great congressional prominence.   Almost
the first legislative act of the session was to provide for a large Special Committee of Thirty-
three, one from each State in the Union, to
frame, if anyhow possible so to do, some measure, or measures, to extricate the country from
the danger into which it was manifestly drifting.   Mr. Corwin, of Ohio, was chairman of this
committee, and upon it Mr. Adams represented
Massachusetts.   The fate of the measures of
conciliation and adjustment, which Mr. Adams
drew up and submitted in this committee, subsequently constituting the basis of its report, well
illustrated how, to the very last moment, he was
intent on the change to be effected on Inauguration Day.   These measures were before the
House of Representatives, causing discussion
and consuming time to the close of the session;
they were then at last disposed of in some parliamentary way which made them no longer
effective.   Walking home that day from the
Capitol with a member of his family after the
adjournment of the House, his companion ex-

pressed to Mr. Adams regret at the disposition
thus made of his measures. The reply, conveyed with unmistakable cheerfulness of tone,
was, on the contrary, expressive of profound
satisfaction that they were thus well out of the
way, having done the work for which they were
designed. Matters for discussion, they had occupied time which might otherwise have been dan-
gerously employed. But the expediency of using
every device to bridge over the interregnum did
not admit of public expression, and in the North
the purpose of Mr. Adams was only in part understood. The support he received was emphatic and general; but underneath there was a
current of dissatisfaction and distrust.

This, however, anticipates the narrative.
Throughout December Mr. Adams had, in the
Committee of Thirty-three, been constantly
manœuvring for position, and to gain time.[1] It
was yet many weeks before Lincoln would be
inaugurated. On December 8th, Howell Cobb,

[1] Reuben Davis, of Mississippi, a member of the Committee
of Thirty-three and an influential " fire-eater," at the time
pronounced that committee " a tub thrown out to the whale,
to amuse only, until the 4th of March next, and thus arrest
the present noble and manly movements of the Southern
States to provide by that day for their security and safety out
of the Union. With these views I take my place on the committee, for the purpose of preventing it being made a means of
deception by which the public mind is to be misled and mis-
guided." *Globe*, December 11, 1860, p. 59.

of Georgia, had resigned the portfolio of the Treasury to throw in his lot with the seceders; and on the 15th, in anger, disgust, and despair, his secretary of state, General Cass, had abandoned President Buchanan. On the evening of the 26th Major Anderson had transferred his command from Fort Moultrie to Fort Sumter. Up to this time, coolly watching his opponents in the Committee of Thirty-three, the effort of Mr. Adams had been directed towards making them show their whole hand. With extremists at both ends, — Sumner and Chandler on the one side, and Davis and Chestnut on the other, — the North and the South were equally divided, the advocates of compromise in the free States vainly struggling against the influence of the "Black Republicans," as they were designated, and the Unionists in the slave States against that of the "fire-eaters." Mr. Adams instinctively sought to show to the North that compromise was out of the question by forcing the representatives of the South from one position to another, until their final demands were shown to be impossible of concession; and, while by so doing he united the North, the conciliatory tone adopted would tend temporarily to paralyze the South, if not permanently to divide it. The border States were in dispute.

His diary, and still more his letters written at

the time, show the skill, temper, and clearness of
head with which Mr. Adams played the hand
assigned to him in this delicate game. The real
object of the secession movement, the end to
which his opponents were working, was not so
plain in the winter of 1860–61 as it has since become; for what the leaders of the Confederacy
then secretly had in view, they in public carefully disavowed. It is now well understood that
what they planned was the ultimate establishment of a great semi-tropical republic, founded
on African servitude, which, including all, or
nearly all, the slave-holding States of the old
Union, should find ample field for almost unlim-
ited expansion in Mexico, Central America, and
the West Indies. The reopening of the slave
trade, as an inexhaustible source for the supply
of cheap labor, was a recognized feature of the
scheme, for obvious reasons sedulously disavowed
until a more opportune occasion.[1]

As a whole, and in the more or less remote
future, the project was large and essentially aggressive; at the commencement it professed to

[1] This subject has been well discussed by both Rhodes and
von Holst (Rhodes, ii. 34, 241, 367–373; iii. 119–124, 294,
322; von Holst, v. 13–16, 30, 477–490; vi. 336; vii. 263, 264);
and of the main features of the project, as it rested, more or
less clearly defined, in the minds of the leaders of the Confederacy, there can be no question. See, also, Nicolay and Hay,
iii. 177.

be modest and strictly defensive. Those maturing it even assumed an attitude of injured
innocence, and seem at times almost to have
persuaded themselves, as well as tried to persuade the world, of the wrongs which they
loudly averred. These were principally three
in number. First, and that most harped upon,
was the exclusion of slaves, as property, from
the territories, the common possession of the
Union, not yet organized into States. Next,
the alleged fear of the anti-slavery sentiment as
an aggressive force, in time disregarding constitutional barriers and interfering with a strong
hand in the domestic institutions of the South.
And, finally, the Personal Liberty Acts passed
by legislatures of many of the free States,
practically nullifying in those States the constitutional provision looking to the rendition of
fugitives from labor. Such were the capital
grievances of the South specifically alleged;
but, in reality, a mere cover to the greater, unavowed, and as yet carefully disavowed, scheme
of southern empire and the slave trade. The
effort of Mr. Adams was to remove the mask,
and disclose to the free States, and yet more to
the hesitating border States, the reality beneath. To this end, he framed the propositions advanced by him in the Committee of
Thirty-three: (1.) So far as the common ter-

ritory was concerned, rather than quarrel, let
us, he said, dispose of the matter finally by admitting the region in dispute into the Union as
a State, with or without slavery as its constitution when framed shall provide. (2.) As to
the Personal Liberty bills, the Fugitive Slave
Law can be modified in its repulsive and uncon-
stitutional features, and those laws shall then be
repealed. (3.) Finally, the Republican party
had always carefully disavowed in every declaration of principles all right, or any intent, to in-
terfere with slavery as a state institution ; and
so far as that cause of apprehension was concerned, as a pledge of its good faith in making
its declarations, the Republican party would
agree to any reasonable additional constitutional
guarantee that might be asked for.

Confronted with these proposals, advanced in
perfect temper and apparent good faith, the
representatives of the slave States were in a
dilemma. If they accepted them, all cause of
complaint was removed, and secession became
mere wanton revolution. If they rejected them,
it must be because other and unavowed ends
were aimed at. If so, what were those ends?
The Southern extremists of the Gulf States,
the men of the Reuben Davis type, knew well
enough, and seceded without further discussion.
The representatives of the border States were

less precipitate, and, in presence of their constituents, more embarrassed.   They, in their
turn, were well aware that, in presence of the
aroused anti-slavery sentiment of the free States,
the Fugitive Slave Law was a dead letter.   The
modification of the Personal Liberty Acts to
conform to constitutional requirements was, they
felt, an empty concession; but they could not
refuse to accept it.   One article of grievance
was thus removed.   The alleged fear of interference with slavery as a state institution was
next disposed of.   They could ask no more than
the additional guarantees freely offered.   The
second article of grievance was thus removed.
There remained only the territorial question.
That, from conditions of soil and climate, slavery as a system could not find a profitable field
for development in New Mexico, the only territory open to it then belonging to the United
States, had already been proved by experience.
The concession thus offered, as the representatives of the slave States well knew, was absolutely empty; none the less its acceptance removed the last alleged cause of grievance.

Feeling themselves thus steadily pressed back
in discussion, the attitude of such members of
the committee from the slave States as still remained upon it now underwent a change.   The
mask had to fall.   The complaint over exclusion

from territory already owned ceased to be heard,
and, in place thereof, it was claimed that the
existence of slavery and rights of slaveholders
should be recognized, and in advance affirmed,
in all southward territory thereafter to be acquired. No longer modest and on the defensive,
the aggressive spirit and imperial ambition of
the slaveocracy were avowed. It had been driven
from cover. The only other question, that of
a reopened slave-trade, was not then at issue,
and the wish for it would have been promptly
and emphatically denied. Meanwhile the object
Mr. Adams had in view was attained. Accordingly, the moment his opponents acknowledged
their alleged grievances as mere pretenses, and
disclosed their real purpose, he ceased to urge
on them his measures of adjustment. Before
the free States and before the border States the
issue was made, and was clear. The demand
simply could not be complied with.

Such were the views of the situation at Washington entertained by Mr. Adams during that
momentous winter, as described in his diary
and letters, as yet unpublished, with that vivid-
ness only possible in records contemporaneous
with events, when hopes and fears fluctuate
daily. As he himself summed it all up in a
letter relating to other matters addressed to
Mr. Sumner's brother George, dated April 24,

1861: "Our only course in the defenseless condition in which we found ourselves was to gain time, and bridge over the chasm made by Mr. Buchanan's weakness." That this was the one practical course for a statesman to pursue, under the circumstances, seems now self-evident; that it was the course which would instinctively suggest itself to a natural diplomat is apparent. This Mr. Adams was. Looking upon him as such, his line of action throughout that crisis becomes explicable, and was right. He played his hand for time and the occasion; they came, and he won.

The single set speech Mr. Adams made in the course of this session was on January 31st, and it completely justified with the general public the course he had taken. So far as the House of Representatives was concerned, it was unquestionably the speech of the session. Keenly expected, listened to intently, published and republished in the leading papers of the country, the response it elicited was immediate, emphatic, and favorable. Mr. Adams had now come to occupy a position of great prominence; only a few days earlier Sherrard Clemens of Virginia, one of the few border-state representatives really sincere in their loyalty, had earnestly exhorted him to declare himself; and now what he said was listened to with an almost feverish in-

terest. In that speech, far the best and most
finished production of his life, Mr. Adams rose
to the occasion; and few occasions anywhere or
at any time have been greater. Though long
since lost sight of in the mass of utterances of
that time, — a mass so great as not to admit of
measurement except by the cubic foot or pound,
— this speech, when read by the historical investigator, speaks for itself. While delivering it
Mr. Adams stood near the centre of the great
Hall of Representatives, the galleries of which
were densely packed and breathlessly silent.
When he took the floor there was a general
movement of Southern members from their side
of the chamber towards him, and some of the
most extreme, in their anxiety to hear every
word he uttered, were imperceptibly attracted
until they found themselves occupying the desks
of their Republican opponents. Mr. Everett,
Robert C. Winthrop, and Governor Clifford, of
Massachusetts, all then in Washington, occupied
members' seats close to the speaker; and, when
he finished, extended to him thanks and con-
gratulations. Indeed, it was a droll and highly
significant reversal of conditions when Robert
C. Winthrop was present and outspoken in commendation, while Charles Sumner was noticeable
for his absence. The next day the correspondents pronounced it " the ablest, most polished,

and clearly argued speech delivered in House or Senate the present session;" and the "Louisville Journal," when reprinting it in full a week later, commended it to readers in the border States, "as the most finished and masterly, as well as the most significant, expression of the spirit of conciliation that has yet been made on the Republican side." That it contributed to the unification of sentiment at the North was nowhere more clearly shown than in a declaration of George S. Hillard, at the Union meeting held a few days later in Boston. Mr. Hillard, a devoted personal adherent of Mr. Webster, then voiced more nearly than any other the sentiments of the " Webster Whigs ; " and Mr. Hillard now declared that, in his speech, Mr. Adams had yielded all " that an honorable opponent ought to ask." On the other hand, the division effected in the Southern ranks was shown by the declaration of Mr. Nelson, an influential member from Tennessee, that "at a most critical moment" he had been led to take " an entirely different course of action by a timely suggestion made " by Mr. Adams. His line of conduct and utterance had thus tended to unify and educate the supporters of the government, while, dividing its opponents, it held the border States in suspense.

When it came to forming the Cabinet of the

new administration, the name of Mr. Adams
was much discussed. Governor Seward urged
him upon the President elect, through the potent agency of Thurlow Weed; and the Massachusetts delegation united in a formal recom-
mendation of him for the Treasury Department.
Mr. Lincoln, however, had his own ideas as to
who his advisers should be. One portfolio he
had assigned to New England; and, out of consideration to Mr. Hamlin, of Maine, his associate
on the presidential ticket, he left it to that
gentleman to designate the person to whom
the portfolio in question should be confided.
At the same time he advised Mr. Hamlin that
those to whom most consideration had been
given were Mr. Adams, Governor Banks, of
Massachusetts, and Gideon Welles, of Connec-
ticut. For reasons which he stated to Mr.
Lincoln, Mr. Hamlin, though himself of Democratic antecedents, objected strongly to Governor Banks, of the two preferring Mr. Adams.
Finally, with a view to the more even division
of the Cabinet, both Mr. Lincoln and Mr. Hamlin agreed that it was advisable that the member of it from New England should have come
from the Democratic camp. Fortunately, as it
turned out, for him, this eliminated Mr. Adams,
as Governor Banks had been eliminated before;
and the choice settled down on Mr. Welles.

Mr. Lincoln certainly was not predisposed in favor of Mr. Adams for any position; though the evidence is clear that he entertained no particular objection to him.   When it came, however, to the assignment of the other more prominent posts under his administration, the President elect, acting on his own volition, had pitched upon William L. Dayton, of New Jersey, for the English mission, and John C. Fremont for that to France; thus providing for the candidates made familiar to the country as the nominees of the Republican party in the election of 1856.   This arrangement, made without consultation with Mr. Seward, was, of course, scarcely courteous to the secretary of state; and moreover, in the case of one of the two selected, was obnoxious.   William H. Seward was no admirer of John C. Fremont.   The President, however, did not yield the point readily; and it was only as the result of persistent effort that the secretary brought about the transfer of Mr. Dayton to Paris, and Mr. Adams's appointment to St. James.   Even then Mr. Lincoln is alleged to have excused himself for yielding by the characteristic remark that the secretary of state had begged very hard for it, and " really, Seward had asked for so little ! "

Mr. Adams made at the time his own diary record of the single official interview he was ever

destined to have with President Lincoln. His
half-amused, half-mortified, altogether shocked
description of it, given contemporaneously to
members of his family was far more graphic.
He had been summoned to Washington by the
secretary of state to receive his verbal instructions. The country was in the midst of the most
dangerous crisis in its history ; a crisis in which
the action of foreign governments, especially of
England, might well be decisive of results. The
policy to be pursued was under consideration.
It was a grave topic, worthy of thoughtful consideration. Deeply impressed with the responsibility devolved upon him, Mr. Adams went
with the new secretary to the State Department, whence, at the suggestion of the latter,
they presently walked over to the White House,
and were ushered into the room which more than
thirty years before Mr. Adams associated most
closely with his father, and his father's trained
bearing and methodical habits. Presently a
door opened, and a tall, large-featured, shabbily
dressed man, of uncouth appearance, slouched
into the room. His much-kneed, ill-fitting trou-
sers, coarse stockings, and worn slippers at once
caught the eye. He seemed generally ill at
ease, — in manner, constrained and shy. The
secretary introduced the minister to the President, and the appointee of the last proceeded

to make the usual conventional remarks, expressive of obligation, and his hope that the confidence implied in the appointment he had received might not prove to have been misplaced. They had all by this time taken chairs; and the tall man listened in silent abstraction. When Mr. Adams had finished, — and he did not take long, — the tall man remarked in an indifferent, careless way that the appointment in question had not been his, but was due to the secretary of state, and that it was to " Governor Seward " rather than to himself that Mr. Adams should express any sense of obligation he might feel; then, stretching out his legs before him, he said, with an air of great relief as he swung his long arms to his head : — " Well, governor, I 've this morning decided that Chicago post-office appointment." Mr. Adams and the nation's foreign policy were dismissed together ! Not another reference was made to them. Mr. Lincoln seemed to think that the occasion called for nothing further; as to Mr. Adams, it was a good while before he recovered from his dismay ; — he never recovered from his astonishment, nor did the impression then made ever wholly fade from his mind. Indeed, it was distinctly apparent in the eulogy on Seward delivered by him at Albany twelve years afterwards.

CHAPTER IX

THE PROCLAMATION OF BELLIGERENCY

Leaving Boston on May 1st, Mr. Adams got to London late on the evening of the 13th. Hardly had he reached his hotel, when Joshua Bates was announced. Though the head of the great English banking firm of Baring Brothers, — reputed the first commercial house in the world, — Mr. Bates was Massachusetts born, having come from Weymouth, likewise the birthplace of Mr. Adams's grandmother, Mrs. John Adams. Long settled in London, and rising by pure force of business capacity to the first place in the Royal Exchange, to Mr. Bates then and afterwards belonged the honorable distinction of being, in those dark and trying times, the most outspoken and loyal American domiciled on British soil. As such he now came first of all "to express his satisfaction in seeing" the newly arrived American minister, "and his uneasiness respecting the proceedings of the government." "I confess," added Mr. Adams, after mentioning the visit of Mr. Bates, "the speech of Lord John Russell has excited in me no small surprise." The speech referred to was that in which Lord John Russell, then secretary for foreign affairs, had announced the purpose of the government to recognize the Confederacy as a belligerent, though not as an established and independent power; and the royal proclamation to that effect met Mr. Adams's eyes in the columns of the "Gazette" of the following day. Since his nomination, exactly eight weeks before, events had moved hardly less rapidly in Europe than at home; though at home they had witnessed the fall of Sumter and the consequent uprising of the North.

So far as the United States was concerned, — meaning by the term United States that portion of the Union which remained loyal, — the European conditions at that time, bad, very bad, in appearance, in their reality were still worse. Well calculated to excite alarm at the moment, looking back on them now, as they have since been disclosed, the wonder is over the subsequent escape. Indeed, it is not going too far to assert that, between May and November, 1861, the chances in Europe were as ten to one in favor of the Confederacy and against the Union. But, to appreciate the critical nature of the situation in which Mr. Adams now found himself, its leading features must be briefly reviewed.

In London, Paris, Madrid, and St. Petersburg,

and more especially in London and Paris, those
entrusted with the management of the foreign
relations of the several countries were, during
the spring of 1861, following the course of
American events with curious eyes, — eyes of
wonderment. That course was in fact mislead-
ing, if not bewildering, to a degree not easy now
to realize. The uprising of the North took place
in response to the proclamation of President
Lincoln and to his first call for troops, issued
on April 15th, the day following the fall of
Sumter. It was immediate and unmistakable;
but before that response, the outcome of the
secession movement had been to all outward
appearance as uncertain in America as, a month
later, it seemed still to be in Europe. Up to
the very day of the firing on Sumter the attitude
of the Northern States, even in case of hostilities,
was open to grave question; while, on the other
hand, that of the border slave States did not
admit of doubt. General disintegration seemed
imminent; nor was it clear that it would encounter any very formidable cohesive resistance.
Not only were influential voices in the North
earnestly arguing that the "erring sisters"
should be permitted to "depart in peace," but,
even so late as April 1st, the correspondents of
the European press reported men as prominent,
and shortly afterwards as decided, as Charles

Sumner and Salmon P. Chase — the one a senator from Massachusetts, the other the secretary of the treasury — intimating more than a willingness to allow the " Southern States to go out with their slavery, if they so desired it." At the same time the mayor of the city of New York, in an official message to the municipal legislative department, calmly discussed and distinctly advocated the expediency of that municipality also withdrawing itself from both Union and State, and proclaiming itself a free port of the Hanse type. Not without ground, therefore, did the London " Times " now declare that, to those " who look at things from a distance, it appears as if not only States were to be separated from States, but even as if States themselves were to be broken up, the counties assuming to themselves the same rights of sovereign power as have been arrogated by the larger divisions of the country." All this time the Southern sympathizers throughout the loyal States were earnest, outspoken, and defiant; while Mr. Seward, the member of the President's Cabinet in charge of foreign affairs, both in his official papers and his private talk, repudiated not only the right but the wish even " to use armed force in subjugating the Southern States against the will of a majority of the people; " and declared that the President " willingly "

accepted as true the " cardinal dogma " of the
seceding States, that " the federal government
could not reduce them to obedience by conquest,"
— the very thing subsequently done.   All philosophical disquisitions of this character were a
few days later effectually silenced in a passionate outburst of aroused patriotism ; but, none
the less, for the time being they were in vogue,
and, while in vogue, they puzzled and deceived.
European public men could not understand such
utterances ; and, not understanding them, put
on them a false construction.

The continental nations in those days got the
little knowledge they had of American affairs at
second-hand, — from English sources ; and England looked largely to the " Times." The legend
of " the Thunderer," as portrayed by Kinglake
in his history of the Crimean War, still held
sway, and " the Thunderer " had sent out to
America Dr. William H. Russell, the famous
special war correspondent with the army before Sebastopol, to enlighten Europe as to the
true inwardness of affairs.   Dr. Russell landed
in New York in the middle of March, 1861, —
just one month before the great uprising ; and
the feature in the situation which seemed to impress him most was the *dilettante, insouciant*
tone with which in all circles the outcome of the
political situation was discussed.   In his own

words, describing the atmosphere he found in the foremost social, monetary, and political circles of New York, " there was not the slightest evidence of uneasiness on account of circumstances which, to the eye of a stranger, betokened an awful crisis, if not the impending dissolution of society itself." This was written on March 19th, the day the appointment of Mr. Adams was announced from Washington ; and a fortnight later, having then got to that city, Dr. Russell wrote : " Practically, so far as I have gone, I have failed to meet many people who really exhibited any passionate attachment to the Union, or who pretended to be actuated by any strong feeling of regard or admiration for the government of the United States in itself." Such were the views and conclusions of an unprejudiced observer, communicated through the medium of the most influential journal in the world to Europe in general, and, more especially, to those then comprising Her Majesty's government.

In May, 1861, the so-called Palmerston-Russell ministry had been in power a little less than two years, having displaced the preceding conservative government, of which Lord Derby was the head, in June, 1859. So far as the individual talents of those composing it were concerned, this ministry was looked upon as the strongest ever formed. Lord Palmerston was Premier, and led the Commons; Lord John Russell, as he still was, had charge of foreign affairs; Mr. Gladstone was chancellor of the exchequer; and Sir George Cornewall Lewis was secretary for war. The long list of subordinate positions was filled with other names of mark and weight. When the returns of the parliamentary election were first complete, the Liberal party was supposed to be almost hopelessly broken up. Afterwards, through an understanding reached between the two chieftains, Palmerston and Russell, it had become singularly compact; and, under a strong government, confronted, with a small but reliable majority, a vigorous opposition skillfully led by Mr. Disraeli. In 1861 Lord Palmerston was in his seventy-seventh year, and Lord John Russell was eight years his junior; both were among the oldest and most experienced, and were ranked among the ablest, of European statesmen. So far as the complications in America were concerned, the current supposition was that the sympathies of Lord John would naturally incline towards the loyalists as representing the anti-slavery sentiment, while Lord Palmerston would almost certainly array himself more or less openly on the side of the slaveholding secessionists. The position of France was not understood. In America,

a vague impression prevailed, based on old Revolutionary memories, of a friendly feeling between the two countries as against Great Britain.
Traditionally they were allies.   Accordingly Dr.
Russell noted, so soon as he began to mix in
New York social life and listen to the conversation at its dinner-tables, that "it was taken for
granted that Great Britain would only act on
sordid motives, but that the well-known affection of France for the United States is to check
the selfishness of her rival, and prevent a speedy
recognition."   This was the loose, uninstructed
talk of the club and street; but in better informed circles it was whispered that the French
minister at Washington was advising his government of the early and inevitable disintegration of the Union, and suggesting that formal
recognition of the new Confederacy for which a
little later Louis Napoleon intimated readiness.
The Emperor, in fact, was already maturing his
Mexican schemes, and, in connection with them,
covertly making overtures looking to the early
and complete disruption of the United States.

So far as public opinion was concerned, Great
Britain, and more especially England, was in a
curious condition.   Sentiment had not crystal-
lized.   The governing and aristocratic classes,
especially in London, were at heart in sympathy
with the slaveholding movement, and, regard-

ing the trans-Atlantic experiment as the pioneer
of a popular movement at home, now hoped and
believed that " the great Republican bubble in
America had burst." Of this they made no con-
cealment ; but, constrained to an extent by their
old record and utterances as respects slavery and
its wrongs, — their lionizing of Mrs. Stowe, and
their reflections on the depth of that barbarism
which made possible such brutalities as the assault on Sumner, — reflecting on all this, they
now had recourse to one of those pharisaic, better-
than-thou moods at times characteristic of the
race. People, who in their own belief, as well as
in common acceptance, were the best England
had, vied with each other in expressions of astonishment that such a condition of affairs as that
now day by day disclosed in America could exist,
and, with wearisome, just-what-I-expected itera-
tion, pretended bewilderment over what their kin
across the sea were generally about. Quietly forgetful of Ireland, English men and women wondered why Americans should object to national
suicide, or, as they euphemistically phrased it,
friendly separation. Language quite failed them
in which adequately to express their sense of the
violence, coarseness, and lack of Christian and
brotherly feeling which marked the controversy.
Aristocratic England was in fact in one of its
least pleasing mental and moral phases, — a phase

in which the unctuous benignity of Chadband
combined with the hypocritical cant of Peck-
sniff. Such was the prevailing social tone.
When, it was declared, "calmer reflection shall
have succeeded to that storm of passion now
sweeping over the North," the citizens of the
United States would consider as their "sincerest
friends" those who now sought to secure the recognition of the Confederacy ; for such were
moved so to do "not from any hostility towards
them, nor from any advocacy of slavery, but
from love of peace and unrestricted commerce,
from horror of civil war and unrestrained
hatred ; " and so on *ad nauseam* in that familiar, conventicle strain so dear to the British
Philistine, in which the angry bulldog growl
grates harshly beneath the preacher's lachry-
mose whine. On the other hand, the large non-
conforming, dissenting, middle-class element, —
that best represented by Cobden, Bright, and
Forster, — the friends of free labor and advocates of a democratic republic, naturally well
disposed to the loyal side in the American contest, — the men of this class were taken by
surprise and quite demoralized in action by the
rapidity with which events moved. They were
bewildered by the apparent and quite inexplicable indifference which seemed to prevail in the
free States, while the procession of slave States

was noisily flaunting out of the Union. Time
was necessary in which to enable these men —
the real rulers of England — to inform themselves as to the true situation, and to concentrate their scattered forces. Unless swept off
their feet by some blind popular impulse, such
as those only a few years before engineered by
the wily Palmerston in the " opium war " and
the Crimean war, Bright and Cobden and
Forster could be relied on, working upon the
old lines, gradually to arouse the moral sense
of their countrymen.

Meanwhile the foreign ministers appointed
under the Buchanan administration were still at
their posts, though expecting soon to be relieved,
— among them, Mr. Dallas, of Philadelphia, at
London, Mr. Faulkner, of Virginia, at Paris,
and Mr. Preston, of Kentucky, at Madrid.
Pending the appointment and arrival of their
successors these gentlemen had been notified by
a circular from Secretary Seward, issued as
soon as he entered upon the duties of his office,
to " use all proper and necessary measures to
prevent the success of efforts which may be
made by persons claiming to represent [the seceding States] to procure recognition." In com-
pliance with these instructions, Mr. Dallas, on
April 8th, had an interview with Lord John
Russell, in the course of which he received assur-

ances, which he transmitted to Washington, that
"the coming of Mr. Adams would doubtless be
regarded as the appropriate occasion for finally
discussing and determining the question " of
the attitude to be taken by Great Britain in
view of the American troubles. The dispatch
from Mr. Dallas containing this assurance was
received at the State Department shortly after
the middle of April, and to the confidence caused
by it that nothing would be done until the arrival of Mr. Adams, was due the fact that Mr.
Adams was not earlier hurried to his post. As
it was, his instructions, bearing date the 10th,
did not reach Mr. Adams until Saturday the
27th of April, and he sailed four days later, on
Wednesday, the 1st of May. Meanwhile the
startling news of the fall of Fort Sumter had
preceded him, reaching London on April 26th,
seventeen days before he landed at Liverpool ;
and during those days the agents of the Confederate government then in Europe, Messrs.
W. L. Yancey, of Alabama, and P. A. Rost, of
Louisiana, had not been idle. First on the
ground, they had, though in an "unofficial"
way, also obtained access to the British secretary for foreign affairs.

James L. Orr, of South Carolina, for a time
chairman of the House Committee on Foreign
Affairs of the Confederate Congress, is author-

ity for the statement that the Confederacy
"never had a foreign policy, nor did its government ever consent to attempt a high diplomacy with European powers." Historically
speaking, this assertion does not seem to have
been inconsistent with the facts; and the absence of a sagacious, far-reaching, diplomatic
policy on the part of the Confederacy was apparently due to a double error into which its
executive head, Jefferson Davis, early fell. He
at once overestimated the natural influences at
work in behalf of the Confederates, and under-
estimated his enemy. Immediately after his inauguration at Montgomery on February 18th,
and before making any civil appointment, Mr.
Davis had sent for Mr. Yancey and offered him
his choice of positions within the executive gift.
Upon his intimating the usual modest preference
for service in a private capacity, Davis insisted
on the acceptance by him of one of two places,
— a cabinet portfolio, or the head of the commission to Europe for which the Confederate
Congress had already provided. At the same
time, the new President intimated a wish that
the latter might be preferred. The selection was
not in all respects judicious; for while Jefferson
Davis in his dealings with European nations naturally desired to keep slavery, as a factor in secession, in the background, and above all to deny

any desire, much more an intention, on the part
of the Confederacy to reopen the African slave
trade, Mr. Yancey was, both by act and utterance, more identified in the public mind than
any other Southern man with both those
causes. That gentleman, however, now submitted to his brother, B. C. Yancey, who had
some diplomatic experience, the Davis proposition. Should he accept the first place in the
proposed European commission? B. C. Yancey advised strongly against his so doing, and
the points he urged showed a very considerable
insight into the real facts of the situation as
they subsequently developed. The year before,
while returning from a diplomatic mission to
one of the South American states, B. C. Yancey had passed some time in England, and,
while there, had sought to inform himself as to
the currents of public opinion, and their probable action in case a slave confederacy should
be formed and should seek recognition. Though
the British suffrage had not then been so enlarged as to include the laboring classes, he
became satisfied that the government was on
that account hardly the less respectful of their
wishes. Cobden and Bright were the leaders of
the working classes; and Cobden and Bright
would oppose any recognition of a government based on a system of African slave labor.

Unless, therefore, the Confederacy was prepared to authorize through its commission commercial advantages so liberal as to outweigh all other considerations, no British government, however well disposed, would in the end venture to run counter to the anti-slavery feeling of the country by a recognition of the Confederacy. Unless armed in advance with authority to commit the Confederacy to this length, B. C. Yancey advised his brother to have nothing to do with the proffered mission.

Under the provisions of the Confederate Constitution it was for the President to determine the scope of any diplomatic function. At this point, therefore, Jefferson Davis became the leading factor in the situation. His idiosyncrasies had to be taken into account; and they were so taken. Though an able man and of strong will, Mr. Davis had little personal knowledge of countries other than his own, or, indeed, of more than a section of his own country; but, most unfortunately for himself and for the cause of which he became the exponent, he was dominated — for no other word expresses the case — by an undue and, indeed, an overweening faith in the practical world-mastery enjoyed by that section through its exclusive production and consequent control of cotton, its great agricultural staple. That Cotton was indeed King, and would in the end so be found, was his unswerving conviction. As Mrs. Davis subsequently expressed it in her biography of her husband: "The President and his advisers looked to the stringency of the English cotton market, and the suspension of the manufactories, to send up a ground swell from the English operatives, that would compel recognition;" or, as Dr. Russell, writing to the same effect from Montgomery, put it at this very time: "They firmly believe that the war will not last a year. . . . They believe in the irresistible power of cotton, in the natural alliance between manufacturing England and France and the cotton-producing slave States, and in the force of their simple tariff." So much for the leading trump card President Davis held in the great game he was about to play. Meanwhile, on the other hand, he entertained a somewhat unduly low opinion, approaching even contempt, for the physical courage, military capacity, and patriotic devotion of his adversaries. He did not permit himself for an instant to doubt the ability of the Confederacy to hold the United States firmly in check during any amount of time needed to enable the cotton famine to do its work thoroughly. Neither, it must now be admitted, did he err on this point. His error lay in his estimate of the potency of a cotton famine, as a factor in foreign politics.

From Mr. Davis's point of view, consequently, the diplomatic problem before the Confederacy was one easy of solution. If no cotton was allowed to go forward, Great Britain would in less than six months be starved into subjection; she must raise the blockade to preserve her internal peace, if not to prevent revolution. Under these circumstances, it was obviously unnecessary to concede through diplomacy much, if anything, to secure that which the Confederacy had the power, and fully purposed, to compel. This was a perfectly logical view of the situation from the Confederate standpoint, and the early events of the struggle went far to justify it. In a few weeks after hostilities began, cotton doubled in price. The Confederate Congress next put a discriminating tax on its production, while in the seceding States it was common talk that all the cotton on hand ought to be destroyed by the government, and formal notice should be served on Great Britain that no crop would be planted until after the full recognition of the Confederacy. On the other hand, the physical power of the South as a resisting force was demonstrated at Bull Run; and, as Mrs. Davis says, the necessary time in which to make the cotton famine felt being absolutely assured after that engagement, " foreign recognition was looked forward to as an assured fact." Such was the diplomacy of President Davis. It at least possessed the virtue of simplicity.

On the other hand there were weak points, — points, indeed, of almost incredible weakness, in the diplomacy of the United States. Fortunately they were only suspected. Even so, they gave an infinity of trouble; had they been known, they could hardly have failed to be the cause of irreparable disaster. At an early stage of the war it became quite apparent both at Washington and at Richmond that by some understanding already reached, partly express and partly tacit, the nations of Europe had decided to leave the initiative in all action touching the American contest to Great Britain and France, as being the two powers most intimately concerned; and France again looked to Great Britain for a lead. Thus from the very outset, so far as Europe was concerned, Great Britain became for America the storm centre; and, in that centre, the danger focused in London. In London the new American foreign secretary was regarded with grave suspicion. Not only was Mr. Seward believed in official circles to be unreliable and to the last degree tricky, but he was assumed to be actuated by a thoroughly unscrupulous disregard not only of treaty obligations but, so far as foreign nations and especially Great Britain were concerned, of international morals.

This impression, vague and accordingly difficult to combat, dated far back, even to the McLeod case when, twenty years previous, Mr. Seward had been governor of New York, and as such had sustained the state courts in some rather questionable legal positions, which occasioned Mr. Webster, then secretary of state, more or less trouble. More recently he had fallen into some indiscretion of social speech, concerning which various accounts were at times current, and these still further complicated a situation at best difficult. The incident is supposed to have occurred during the visit of the Prince of Wales to the United States, in 1860, and at a dinner given to him in Albany. The story is that Mr. Seward, " fond of badinage," as Dr. Russell expressed it, then in a jocose way intimated to the Duke of Newcastle, who was at the head of the Prince's suite, that he [Seward] expected " soon to hold a very high office here in my own country ; it will then," he was alleged to have added, " become my duty to insult England, and I mean to do so." Subsequently Mr. Weed wrote to Mr. Seward about the matter. Mr. Seward, in reply, professed himself greatly surprised, but said the story was so absurd that to notice it by a denial would on his part be almost a sacrifice of personal dignity. None the less, there can be no doubt that such a story did ema-

nate from the Duke of Newcastle ; and, during
the years that followed, it is equally undeniable
that the story in question made its appearance
with great regularity, though in form variously
modified, whenever the relations between the
United States and Great Britain were, in appearance or reality, in any way " strained."
The fact seems to have been that, on the occasion referred to, Mr. Seward indulged in what
he intended for some playful " chaff " of the
Duke, in no degree seriously meant, or to be
taken seriously. It was a form of social intercourse to which Mr. Seward was a good deal
addicted, especially at dinner-table, and when
conversation was stimulated by champagne. Not
that the idle, ill-natured talk, so current at one
time concerning him on this head, was true ; for
it was not. Partly society gossip, and partly personal and political malevolence, it has since been
forgotten. But Governor Seward was social ;
and, at table, in no way abstemious. He enjoyed
his food, his wine, and his cigar ; and, having
in him this element of good fellowship, his
tongue sometimes yielded to its influence. Under
these circumstances and in this mood, not knowing his Grace of Newcastle well, or weighing the
construction that might be put on his words, it
is supposed that the senator, as he then was, in
clumsy, humorous vein, on the occasion in ques-

tion, let the American eagle scream, to the
grave and lasting perplexity of his table neighbor. By that neighbor his talk was afterwards
repeated, and then again by others repeated,
until it assumed the *veritas in vino* form of an
indiscreet dinner-table disclosure.

Fortunately this mere social indiscretion admitted of explanation and denial ; but that, at
a later day, some such idea respecting Great
Britain as that commonly imputed to him, was
really lurking in Secretary Seward's mind, is
shown by the memorandum entitled "Some
Thoughts for the President's Consideration,"
which bore date April 1, 1861, and was first
made public from among his papers by Lincoln's biographers, Messrs. Nicolay and Hay,
nearly thirty years later. This paper, the very
existence of which had probably passed out of
Mr. Seward's recollection, Mr. Adams never
saw ; indeed it was not published until after
his death. He never had an opportunity, therefore, to offer his explanation of the enigma.
Meanwhile he had dined with Secretary Seward
in Washington on the evening of March 30th,
two days before the paper in question was dated
and handed to Mr. Lincoln. It must then have
been in its writer's mind ; but, if so, it was not
reflected in the slightest degree either in his intimate conversation, or in the instructions to

various ministers then lying on his desk, and
submitted to Mr. Adams for perusal. None the
less, it is now undeniable that, so late as April
1, 1861, Mr. Seward was gravely proposing to
the President, as a national distraction from impending troubles, a general foreign war, to be
provoked by that very attitude towards Great
Britain which had been foreshadowed in the
alleged apocryphal dinner - table talk of six
months earlier. That talk caused Mr. Adams,
first and last, almost endless annoyance and
trouble; and it was certainly fortunate for the
outgoing minister to Great Britain that the
secretary had in no degree taken him into his
inmost confidence during that gentleman's visit
to Washington before starting to assume the
duties of his position. Had he done so, the
minister could scarcely have denied as persistently as the exigencies of the case called for
the stories of Mr. Seward's animus towards
Great Britain. As will shortly be seen, also,
the memorandum of April 1st only a few weeks
later exercised an influence not recognized at the
time, nor indeed until long years after, on other
instructions sent to Mr. Adams which only just
failed suddenly to end his mission.

The details of the fall of Sumter and the subsequent proclamation of Lincoln appeared in the
London papers of April 27th, and on May 1st

Lord John Russell sent for Mr. Dallas, in consequence of the reports which immediately began to circulate as to the intentions of President Lincoln regarding a blockade of the Southern coast and the discontinuance of its harbors as ports of entry. At this interview Lord John informed Mr. Dallas of the arrival in London of Messrs. Yancey and Rost, and intimated that an interview had been sought, and that he was not unwilling to see them "unofficially." He at the same time gave notice of an understanding reached between the governments of France and England that the two countries should act together, and take the same course as to recognition. Mr. Dallas in his turn informed Lord John that Mr. Adams was to sail from Boston that very day, and would be in London in two weeks, and it was accordingly again agreed to pay no attention to "mere rumors," but to await the arrival of the new minister, who would have full knowledge of the intentions of his government. The next day (May 2d) in response to questions in the House of Commons, Lord John announced it as the policy of the government "to avoid taking any part in the lamentable contest now raging in the American States." "We have not," he declared, "been involved in any way in that contest by any act or giving any advice in the matter, and, for God's sake, let us if possible keep out of it."

The following day the two Confederate commissioners were received by Lord John "unofficially." They owed this favor to the friendly intercession of Mr. W. H. Gregory, an Irish member of Parliament of strong Confederate proclivities, who must have been very active in their behalf, as, leaving New Orleans at the close of March, they did not reach England until Monday, the 29th of April, and on Thursday, May 2d, the day after Mr. Adams left Boston, they were in the foreign secretary's reception-room. Into the details of this interview it is not necessary here to enter. It is sufficient to say that it afforded a fair example of the Confederate diplomacy. On the part of the Southern commissioners it was essentially weak, — in reality apologetic so far as slavery was concerned, and altogether empty as respects inducements for aid. Lord John Russell was an attentive listener merely.

This was on May 2d; and, on the 6th, the questions involved having in the meantime been considered by the government, and the opinions of the crown lawyers obtained, the foreign secretary formally announced in the Commons that belligerent rights would be conceded to the Confederacy. Five days later, on May 11th, President Lincoln's proclamation of blockade was officially communicated to the British

government by Mr. Dallas, together with a copy
of Secretary Seward's circular of April 20th
addressed to the foreign ministers of the United
States in relation to privateers against American
commerce fitted out in accordance with President
Davis's letter-of-marque notification of three
days previous. A copy of this document had,
however, already reached the Foreign Office,
transmitted by Lord Lyons. The Queen's proclamation of neutrality, announced by Sir
George Lewis in the House of Commons as
contemplated, on the 9th, was formally authorized on the 13th, and appeared officially in the
" London Gazette " of the following day ; the arrival of the Niagara, with Mr. Adams on board,
at Queenstown having been telegraphed to London on the 12th.

Such was the sequence of events. Unquestionably the Queen's proclamation followed hard
upon the " unofficial " reception of the commissioners, — so hard, indeed, as to be strongly
suggestive of connection. The natural inference
was that the one event contributed to the other ;
and the commissioners, with apparent grounds,
professed themselves entirely satisfied with the
results of their conference. But, whether the
representations made to the British foreign
secretary by Messrs. Yancey and Rost on May
3d did or did not affect the decision announced

by Her Majesty's government on the 6th, there can be no question that the proclamation of the 13th was issued with unseemly haste, and in disregard of the assurances given to Mr. Dallas only five days previous. The purpose was manifest. It was to have the status of the Confederacy, as a belligerent, an accomplished fact before the arrival of the newly accredited minister. This precipitate action was chiefly significant as indicating an animus; that animus being really based on the agreement for joint action just reached between the governments of Great Britain and France, and the belief, already matured into a conviction, that the full recognition of the Confederacy as an independent power was merely a question of time, and probably of a very short time.

The feeling excited in America, and among Americans in Europe, by this precipitate act, was intense; and the indignation was more outspoken than discreet, being largely minatory and based on the assumed greater friendliness of France. It must also be conceded that loyal America was then in a mental condition closely verging on hysteria. It could see things only from one point of view; and that point of view its own as then occupied. The *insouciance* of the period prior to April 13th was wholly gone, — something of the forgotten past; and the bitter denunciation now poured forth on Great Britain knew no limit: but there rang through it, distinctly perceptible, a well-grounded tone of alarm. The possible imminence of a great disaster was recognized.

Looking back on the incident in the full light of subsequent events, it will now be conceded that, had Great Britain then been actuated by really friendly feelings, the thing would not have been done at just that time, or in that brusque way, highly characteristic though it was of Lord John Russell; on the other hand, that it was done then and in that way proved in the result most fortunate, not only for Mr. Adams personally but for the cause he represented. Great Britain having through its foreign secretary's action put itself in the wrong, Lord John thereafter, under the steady pressure to which he was subjected, found himself on the defensive, and insensibly became correspondingly over-cautious. The weight of opinion, even among Americans, has since tended to the conclusion that the proclamation of May 13th admitted of justification;[1] but, whether it did or no while issued at that precise time and in that way, it certainly could not have been deferred later than immediately after the arrival of the news of the disaster of Bull Run, shortly before the close of the follow-

[1] Rhodes, iii. 420, note.

ing July : and, if then considered and conceded, it might well have carried with it a full recognition of the Confederacy. As it was, the partial and ill-considered concession proved final, and, as matter of fact, precluded the more important ulterior step. None the less, at the moment Mr. Adams regarded it as a most adverse and unfortunate opening of his diplomatic career.

It so chanced that Lord John's eldest brother, the Duke of Bedford, died at just this time ; so the interview at the Foreign Office which had been arranged for Mr. Adams the day after his arrival could not take place. Meanwhile a dispatch from Mr. Dallas had been received in Washington foreshadowing the course afterwards pursued by the British government, and this dispatch had excited much indignation in the mind of Secretary Seward. He forthwith wrote to Mr. Adams, under date of April 27th, directing him at once to demand an explanation. This dispatch (No. 4) was, however, only preliminary to a far more important dispatch (No. 10) of May 21st, and the two can best be considered later on, and together. They involve a discussion, and if possible some explanation which shall at least be plausible, of the incident most difficult to account for in all Secretary Seward's career, — the incident from which, it is not too much to say, his posthumous reputation has suffered, and will probably continue to suffer, great injury.

In the mean time, acting promptly on the instructions contained in the dispatch of April 27th, Mr. Adams requested an interview, and on Saturday, May 18th, drove out to Pembroke Lodge, where Lord John then was, for the first of his many interviews with the foreign secretary. He found him " a man of sixty-five or seventy, of about the same size as myself, with a face marked by care and thought rather than any strong expression. His eye is, I think, blue and cold." The conversation lasted more than an hour. Mr. Adams wrote that while, in carrying it on, he " avoided the awkwardness of a categorical requisition, it was only to transfer the explanation to the other side of the water ; " and, he added, " my conclusion from it is that the permanency of my stay is by no means certain." In the course of this important first interview, Mr. Adams and his future antagonist must instinctively have measured each other. On neither side, probably, was the conclusion unsatisfactory. The two men were, in fact, from a certain similarity of disposition, naturally calculated to deal the one with the other. Of Earl Russell, as he was then soon to become, it has since been said by a writer very capable of forming an opinion, and with excep-

tionally good means of correctly so doing in
that case, that his "standard of private and
public virtue was as high as that which any man
has ever maintained in practice throughout a
long and honored life;"[1] and those who knew
him best would not be indisposed to assert a similar claim on behalf of Mr. Adams.   Men of the
highest character, public and private, both were
marked by a certain simplicity and directness
of manner and bearing, not unaccompanied by
reserve, which must at once have commended
them each to the other.   Lord John was the older
and much the more experienced of the two; but
he could not, nor did he, fail at once to recognize
in Mr. Adams a certain quiet undemonstrative
force which bespoke one, like himself, of the
genuine Anglo-Saxon stock.   They thus, most
fortunately for the great interests they had in
charge, liked and respected each other, and got
on together, from the start.

All now went quietly until June 10th.   On
that day Mr. Adams received Mr. Seward's dispatch No. 10, of May 21st, written when the
Queen's Proclamation of Neutrality was plainly
foreshadowed.   Of it he wrote on a first perusal: "The government seems ready to declare war with all the powers of Europe, and
almost instructs me to withdraw from communi-

[1] Trevelyan, *The American Revolution*, 8, 9.

cation with the ministers here, in a certain contingency. I scarcely know how to understand Mr. Seward. The rest of the government may be demented for all that I know; but he surely is calm and wise."

CHAPTER X

SEWARD'S FOREIGN WAR PANACEA

" My duty here is, so far as I can do it honestly, to prevent the mutual irritation from coming to a downright quarrel. It seems to me like throwing the game into the hands of the enemy. . . . If a conflict with a handful of slaveholding States is to bring us to [our present pass] what are we to do when we throw down the glove to all Europe?" In these further words, in the extract just quoted from his diary, Mr. Adams set forth the whole policy which guided his action at London from the day he arrived to the day he left. During the early and doubtful period of the war it has already been said that Mr. Seward was, in Europe at least, believed to entertain another view of a possible outcome of the situation. That he wished to provoke a foreign war was more than suspected. One great source of Mr. Adams's diplomatic usefulness lay in the confidence he instinctively inspired by his directness and manifest sincerity. In these respects he came at last in Great Britain to be accepted as almost a re-

verse of the secretary. What, as respects the
foreign policy then to be pursued, lay in Secretary Seward's mind in the spring and early
summer — March to July — of 1861? This
difficult problem is now to be considered.

The dispatch just referred to as that numbered ten, bearing date May 21st, and received
by Mr. Adams on June 10th, was certainly a
most extraordinary public paper. Its full secret history, also, did not come to light until
disclosed by Messrs. Nicolay and Hay nearly
thirty years after it was written.[1] It has been
seen how it puzzled and dismayed Mr. Adams
when he first received it. The fiercely aggressive, the well-nigh inconceivable, foreign policy
it foreshadowed must, he thought, have been
forced on the secretary by the other members
of the administration ; but, in fact, though Mr.
Adams never knew it, that dispatch, in the
form in which it was originally drawn up by
the secretary of state and by him submitted to
the President, must have been designed to precipitate a foreign war. Moreover, it would inevitably have brought that result about but for
Lincoln's unseen intervention. The documents
speak for themselves. To be read intelligently,

---

[1] The dispatch, as originally drafted by Secretary Seward,
with Lincoln's interlineations and omissions indicated in it, is
printed in full in Nicolay and Hay, iv. 270–275.

the two dispatches to Mr. Adams of April 27th
and May 21st, Nos. 4 and 10, must be read together, and both in connection with the extraordinary paper entitled, " Some Thoughts for
the President's Consideration," already alluded
to, handed by Seward to Lincoln on April 1st.
In that paper the secretary proposed to the
President to take immediate measures calculated
to " change the question before the [American]
public from one upon slavery, or about slavery,
for a question upon union or disunion ; " and to
that end he recommended that explanations, in
regard to their proceedings in the West India
Islands and in Mexico, be demanded " from
Spain and France, categorically, at once. I
would then," he went on, " seek explanations
from Great Britain and Russia, and send agents
into Canada, Mexico, and Central America, to
rouse a vigorous continental spirit of independence on this continent against European intervention. And if satisfactory explanations are
not received from Spain and France, would convene Congress and declare war against them."
Of course, if the policy here recommended had
been followed, " satisfactory explanations " from
the powers addressed would, under the circumstances, have been neither expected nor desired.
War was intended.

The conception of a foreign policy of this

character, at such a time, or at any time, seems so unstatesmanlike, so immoral, from any rational point of view so impossible, that for a public man occupying a responsible position merely to have entertained it, subsequently discredits him. Yet that Secretary Seward did entertain it, long and seriously, in the spring of 1861, and moreover that he abandoned it slowly, and only in the presence of facts impossible to ignore, cannot be gainsaid. This is matter of record. That Mr. Seward was a statesman, astute, far-seeing and sagacious, with a strong grasp on facts and underlying principles, is hardly less matter of record. The thing cannot, therefore, be dismissed as an incomprehensible historical riddle, — a species of insoluble conundrum. It calls for explanation ; and any explanation offered must be at least plausible.

Into the cabinet situation, as it then existed, it is not necessary here to enter in detail. It was undoubtedly more than trying. Seen in the light of subsequent events, it is assumed that the Lincoln of 1865 was also the Lincoln of 1861. Historically speaking there can be no greater error ; the President, who has since become a species of legend, was in March, 1861, an absolutely unknown, and by no means promising, political quantity. During the years intervening between 1861 and 1865 the man de-

veloped immensely ; he became in fact another
being. History, indeed, hardly presents an anal-
ogous case of education through trial. None the
less the fact remains that when he first entered
upon his high functions, President Lincoln filled
with dismay those brought in contact with him.
Without experience, he evinced no sense of the
gravity of the situation or of the necessity of a
well-considered policy. The division of offices
among eager applicants seemed to engross his
thoughts. The evidence is sufficient and conclusive that, in this respect, he impressed others
as he impressed Mr. Adams in their one characteristic interview. Thus an utter absence of
lead in presence of a danger at once great and
imminent, expressed the situation.

There is every reason to believe that in those
early days of their association, Seward, as the
result of close personal contact and observation,
shared in the common estimate of his official
chief. Certainly, close as were his personal relations with Mr. Adams, preserving a discreet
silence as respects his official chief, the secretary
let no intimation escape him that, in the case
of the President, appearances were deceptive.
There can, also, be no question that Secretary
Seward, when he entered upon his duties in
the Department of State, did so with the idea
that he would prove to be the virtual head of

the government, — its directing mind. The early course of events in the cabinet was not what he anticipated. A highly incongruous body, hastily brought together, no member of it saw his way clearly, and differences immediately developed. Without a head, it seemed to have no prospect of having a head. In the direction of its councils, the secretary of state became day by day conscious of the fact that he was losing ground, and it was more and more manifest to him that a line of policy almost sure to precipitate a civil war was likely soon to be adopted. The tension was too great to last; unless a new direction was given to the rapid course of events there must be a break. Plainly, something had to be done.

Governor Seward, moreover, had all along asserted with the utmost confidence that no serious trouble would ensue from the change of administration; that the South was not in earnest. A civil war was no part of his programme. Yet now he found the country confronted with it; and he himself was no longer held in high, if indeed in any, esteem as a political prophet.

When, immediately before the inauguration, Mr. Seward tendered his resignation of the first place in the cabinet, the incoming President, after brief consideration, declined to accept it, characteristically observing that he " could not afford to let Seward take the first trick." Following out this not over-dignified figure of speech, it may be said that now, a month after the change of administration had taken place, Mr. Seward, in the course of the game, found himself "put to his trumps." Under these circumstances he seems to have rapidly matured a policy which he had long been meditating,—a policy reserved as a last resort. Falling back on what was with him a cardinal point of political faith, an almost inordinate belief in the sentimental side of the American character,—its patriotism and its spirit of nationality, its self-confidence when aroused,—falling back on this, he thought to work from it as a basis of action. It was no new or sudden conception. On the contrary, months before, at the dinner of the New England Society in New York, during the previous December, referring to the secession of South Carolina which had then just been announced, he declared that if New York should be attacked by any foreign power, "all the hills of South Carolina would pour forth their population to the rescue." And two years and a half later, during the foreign crisis of the war, in precisely the same spirit he wrote to Sumner: "Rouse the nationality of the American people. It is an instinct upon which you can always rely, even when the conscience that ought never

to slumber is drugged to death." Accordingly
in March, 1861, he only repeated what he had
written in his dispatches to Mr. Adams when
he said to Dr. Russell, of the "Times," that
if a majority of the people in the seceded
States really desired secession, he would let
them have it; but he could not believe in
anything so monstrous. Convinced, therefore,
that the South was possessed by a passing mania,
he was himself a victim of the delusion that, by
a bold and unmistakable appeal to a sentiment
of a yet deeper and more permanent character,
the evil spirit then in temporary possession
might be exorcised; or, as he a few months before had in the Senate expressed it, citing Jefferson as his authority, the "States must be kept
within their constitutional sphere by impulsion,
if they could not be held there by attraction."
This idea others shared with him, and it found
frequent expression : but in his case, during
April, May, and June, 1861, it amounted to
what was almost a dangerous hallucination; for
he was secretary of state.

In itself a morbid conception, the thought was
further strengthened by another belief entertained by him as to the existence of a latent,
but widespread, Union sentiment at the South,
requiring only a sufficient stimulus to assert itself and set everything right. This last article

of faith was immediately due to the great number of appealing letters which, after the election and before the inauguration of Lincoln, had
poured in upon him in steady volume from the
South in general, but more particularly from the
border slave States.   While he probably construed their contents liberally, to these he at
the time made continual reference ; and now he
thought to use the sentiment revealed in them
as the basis of a great educational movement.
It was the material on which he proposed to
work.

The real condition of public opinion at the
South, and the amount of Union sentiment there
latent, was, of course, in the spring of 1861, a
question of fact in regard to which men's judgment varied according to their means of information and warmth of temperament.   In reality,
as Dr. Russell soon afterwards found out and
advised Europe through the " Times," and as
Seward himself later had to realize, those dwelling
in the great region afterwards known as the
Confederate States were of one mind.   In that
region, even as early as May, 1861, there was no
Union sentiment ; or, as Russell, while visiting
the Confederacy in April, wrote to the " Times " :
" Assuredly Mr. Seward cannot know anything
of the South, or he would not be so confident
that all would blow over."   In point of fact, at

the very time Mr. Seward was conjuring up this widespread, latent Union sentiment in the South, the life of any man in the South even suspected of Union sentiments would not have been safe. But in the spring of 1861 a mistaken belief on the subject was not confined to Mr. Seward. Cassius M. Clay, for instance, came from Kentucky, a slave State. Having all his life lived there, his means of information would be supposed to have been good, and his judgment presumably correct. Yet so late as May 29, 1861, six weeks after the fall of Sumter, Cassius M. Clay, then on his way to represent the United States at St. Petersburg, asserted in a communication printed in the London "Times" of May 25th, that "the population of the slave States is divided perhaps equally for and against the Union." More extraordinary yet, weeks later, in his message to Congress when it met on July 4, 1861, President Lincoln put himself on record to the same effect. "It may well be questioned," he then said, "whether there is to-day the majority of the legally qualified voters of any State, except, perhaps, South Carolina, in favor of disunion. There is much reason to believe that the Union men are the majority in many, if not in every other one, of the so-called seceded States." Mr. Seward was not alone in his hallucination.

In like manner, on the other point, — the effect of a foreign war as a diversion, — the American correspondent of the "Times," — not Dr. Russell, — wrote as follows on May 21st, the very date of Seward's dispatch No. 10 which so dismayed Mr. Adams : — " There are those here, high in influence too, who are actively aiming to create a cold feeling between England and the United States, under the belief that that will more effectually reconcile North and South than anything else. They argue that the presence of a foreign foe alone can reconcile the disintegrated States, and they would court a foreign war rather than a civil one. Strange as it may sound, impracticable as it may appear, I assure you that such ideas are entertained and acted upon in New York." The prevalence of this idea was also well known in England, and, on the 15th of June, William E. Forster, the stanchest friend America had, defended to Mr. Adams the action of the British government in sending out troops to Canada " by attributing to our government a desire to pick a quarrel with this country in the hopes of effecting by means of it a reunion."

The letter containing the extract just quoted from the " Times " was written from New York, and the feeling in it referred to may not impossibly have been inspired by the secretary of state. A politician's newspaper feeler, thus reflecting the dispatch of May 21st. In any event the presence of such an idea in Seward's mind at that juncture was plainly a grave additional source of national peril, and it would be interesting to trace the manifestations of it. These, however, though numerous and unequivocal, are scattered through the press and in official and other publications, and would be inappropriate here. The essence of them, moreover, was condensed in a single remark to Dr. Russell, made by the secretary in course of conversation on April 4th : " Any attempt against us " by a foreign power, Mr. Seward then said, " would revolt the good men of the South, and arm all men in the North to defend their government."

The policy thus assuming shape in the secretary's mind was large, vague, visionary. To avert the impending issue, he would, as distinctly shadowed forth in his dispatch of May 21st, challenge a yet greater issue. Confidently appealing to the spirit of Americanism and of the age, to liberty, democracy, and the aspirations of the century, he was prepared to precipitate a general war, not unlike that of the Napoleonic period, fully confident that the United States would emerge from it victorious, purified, and more than ever consolidated. A great conception, it was also a trifle Corsican ; and, though an

able man, Mr. Seward was essentially a New
Yorker, and not a Napoleon Bonaparte. Under
the circumstances, therefore, it must be conceded that the scheme had in it elements not
consistent with what is commonly known as
sanity of judgment.

Recurring to the course of events at Washington and in London, a considerable interval
elapsed between the two days, close together, on
which Seward handed to Lincoln his memorandum of "Thoughts" and had the conversation
just referred to with Dr. Russell, and that other
day on which he wrote the bellicose dispatch
No. 10 to Mr. Adams. The dates were seven
weeks apart. In the interval the situation had
altogether changed. Fort Sumter had fallen ;
the President's Proclamation had been issued ;
Virginia and Tennessee had seceded. Another
dispatch also had reached the secretary from
Mr. Dallas announcing the arrival in Europe of
the Confederate Commissioners, and that Earl
Russell was disposed to accord them an " unofficial " interview. This very contingency had
been anticipated by Mr. Seward in a dinner-
table talk, at which Dr. Russell was present, before April 1st. He had then declared that " the
Southern Commissioners could not be received
by the government of any foreign power, officially or otherwise, even to hand in a document

or to make a representation, without incurring the risk of breaking off relations with the government of the United States."

When he made this remark Mr. Seward must have been meditating his memorandum of "Thoughts for the President's Consideration." Four days later he handed it to Mr. Lincoln. The latter's considerate method of dealing with that document, proposing, as it did, his abdication of the functions of his office, and "two or more" foreign wars as a possible substitute for one domestic, is matter of history. He quietly put it aside. None the less, Secretary Seward evidently did not at once abandon the scheme therein outlined. He apparently still believed in it as a practical recourse, so to speak, — the last and largest trump card in the hand; and, a few weeks later, he seems to have concluded that the time to play it had come. Accordingly he now prepared the dispatch of May 21st, No. 10. Directing Mr. Adams in certain contingencies then sure to occur to confine himself "simply to a delivery of a copy of this paper to the secretary of state," he in it used language to which no self-respecting government could submit, — language so indecorous and threatening as to be tantamount to a declaration of war. If, he announced, Great Britain shall recognize the bearers of Confederate letters of marque as belligerents, and give them shelter from our pursuit and punishment, " the laws of nations afford an adequate and proper remedy, and we shall avail ourselves of it. . . . When this act of intervention is distinctly performed, we from that hour shall cease to be friends and become once more, as we have twice before been forced to be, enemies of Great Britain. . . . We are not insensible of the grave importance of this occasion. We see how, upon the result of the debate in which we are engaged, a war may ensue between the United States, and one, two, or even more European nations. . . . A war not unlike it between the same parties occurred at the close of the last century. Europe atoned by forty years of suffering for the error that Great Britain committed in provoking that contest. If that nation shall now repeat the same great error the social convulsions which will follow may not be so long but they will be more general. When they shall have ceased it will, we think, be seen, whatever may have been the fortunes of other nations, that it is not the United States that will have come out of them with its precious Constitution altered or its honestly obtained dominion in any degree abridged." [1]

---

[1] The wrap-the-world-in-flames hallucination seems to have degenerated into something very like a formula in Mr. Seward's speech during the earlier Rebellion period. On the 4th

It is not difficult to imagine what would have been the effect of a dispatch couched in these terms delivered in June, 1861, to a British government of which Lord Palmerston was the head, with England then acting in full understanding with France. The Confederacy would have been recognized, and the blockade of its coast, at that time hardly more than nominal, would have been disallowed almost before the American minister had rattled out of Downing Street. Thus, as originally drawn up, this extraordinary paper of May 21st was nothing more nor less than a definite commitment of the United States to the policy outlined by Seward in the "Thoughts" of the first of the previous April, — "I would demand explanations from

---

of July Russell of the *Times* had a talk with him at the State Department. In the course of it, six weeks after writing the dispatch of May 21st, the Secretary said : — "We have less to fear from a foreign war than any country in the world. If any European power provokes a war, we shall not shrink from it. A contest between Great Britain and the United States would wrap the world in fire, and at the end it would not be the United States which would have to lament the result of the conflict." (*My Diary*, 381.) More than six months later, January 22, 1862, he wrote to Thurlow Weed : — "Nevertheless, I do know this, that whatever nation makes war against us, or forces itself into a war, will find out that we can and shall suppress rebellion and defeat invaders besides. The courage and the determination of the American people are aroused for any needful effort — any national sacrifice." (*Life of Weed*, ii. 410.)

Spain and France, categorically, at once. I
would seek explanations from Great Britain and
Russia, . . . and, if satisfactory explanations
are not received, . . . would convene Congress
and declare war against them." Fortunately the
memorandum of "Thoughts," of April 1st, had
forewarned Mr. Lincoln, and the influence of the
earlier paper was immediately apparent in his
treatment of the paper of May 21st, now submitted. "It was Mr. Seward's ordinary habit
personally to read his dispatches to the President
before sending them. Mr. Lincoln, detecting
the defects of the paper, retained it, and after
careful scrutiny made such material corrections
and alterations with his own hand as took from
it all offensive crudeness without in the least
lowering its tone; but, on the contrary, greatly
increasing its dignity. . . . When the President
returned the manuscript to his hands, Mr. Seward somewhat changed the form of the dispatch
by [omitting most of the phrases above quoted
and] prefixing to it two short introductory para-
graphs in which he embodied, in his own
phraseology, the President's direction that the
paper was to be merely a confidential instruc-
tion, not to be read or shown to any one." [1]
And in this happily modified form it came into
the hands of Mr. Adams. A collision between

[1] Nicolay and Hay, iv. 269, 270.

the two countries was thus narrowly, and for the moment avoided! Fortunately, as will presently be seen, Mr. Seward's views about this time underwent a change. As a result of the battle of Bull Run two months later, he recovered his mental poise, and, quite dismissing the illusion of a latent Union sentiment to be invoked in the South, ceased to look upon a more or less general foreign war as a means of escape, both natural and legitimate, from dissension at home.

Too much space has, perhaps, been devoted to this bit of secret history. If so, its interest as well as its importance must be a justification. For the United States, it was a piece of supreme good fortune then to have in Great Britain so discreet a representative, unimpulsive and bent on a maintenance of the peace. It would have been very easy at just that juncture to have provoked a crisis, which must have been decisive, though, as the result showed, wholly unnecessary. So far as Mr. Adams himself was concerned, no minister of the United States probably ever had so narrow an escape as his then was from a position which could not have been otherwise than humiliating to the last degree. It was, too, at the threshold of a diplomatic life. As to Mr. Seward, it would be useless to philosophize. His management as a whole of the country's foreign relations during the Rebellion speaks for itself.

It was a magnificent success. Alone of all the departments of the government, the State Department proved from the beginning, and to the end, in every respect equal to the occasion. Carrying things always with a high hand, preserving in each emergency a steady and unbroken front, never betraying sign of weakness, or lowering the national dignity, Mr. Seward extricated the country from whatever difficulty it had to encounter; nor were those difficulties few or slight. His success in so doing was so great and so uniform that it seems since to have been almost assumed as of course. Scant justice has accordingly been rendered him to whom it was due ; for, by averting intervention, he saved the day. The single inexplicable, ineradicable blemish upon the record is contained in that inconceivable memorandum of "Notes" handed by Secretary Seward to President Lincoln on April 1, 1861, and the dispatches numbered four and ten subsequently prepared for Mr. Adams in obvious pursuance of the mad and indefensible policy therein outlined.

The day following the receipt of this modified dispatch Mr. Adams sought an interview with Lord John. In it he "tried to act up to [his] instructions at the same time that [he] softened as well as [he] could the sharp edges." Fortunately for him, in a previous interview with

Lord John, of which he had already sent a report to Washington, he had pressed the foreign secretary quite as far and as hard as circumstances justified.   "In truth," he had written, "if I were persuaded that Her Majesty's government were really animated by a desire to favor the rebellion, I should demand a categorical answer; but thus far I see rather division of opinion, consequent upon the pressure of the commercial classes."   So he contented himself with the highly significant remark to Lord John, that, if Great Britain entertained any design, more or less marked, to extend the struggle then going on in America, "I was bound to acknowledge in all frankness that, in that contingency, I had nothing further left to do in Great Britain. I said this with regret, as my own feelings had been and were of the most friendly character." Secretary Seward seems to have been greatly mollified when advised of this intimation; but now Mr. Adams had again to approach a delicate subject.   Accordingly he proceeded to intimate "in all frankness" that any further protraction of relations, "unofficial" though they might be, with the "pseudo-commissioners" from the Confederate States "could scarcely fail to be viewed by us as hostile in spirit, and to require some corresponding action accordingly." To this diplomatically expressed demand, Lord

John, after reviewing the course pursued by
Great Britain in similar cases, concluded by saying that " he had seen the gentlemen once some
time ago, and once more some time since; he
had no expectation of seeing them any more."
Directness in dealing was not thrown away on
Lord John Russell. Mr. Adams now scored
his first success; Messrs. Yancey, Rost, and
Mann were not again received at the foreign
office. On their side, the commissioners reported
to their government that " the relations between
Mr. Adams and the British cabinet are not entirely amicable and satisfactory to either, and,
both in his diplomatic and social relations, Mr.
Adams is held a blunderer." Mrs. Jefferson
Davis took later a different and more practical
view of the matter, remarking in her life of
her husband : " The astute and watchful ambassador from the United States had thus far fore-
stalled every effort, and our commissioners were
refused interviews with Her Majesty's minister."
Mr. Yancey, thinking the concession of Lord
John to Mr. Adams's demand was in violation of
the rule of neutrality, to which the British government had pledged itself, urged his brother
commissioners to respond to Lord John's notice
of suspension of interviews by a firm though
moderate protest. But Messrs. Rost and Mann
objecting to this course, the matter was referred

to the Richmond government; nor was it again heard of. The commissioners were presently (September 23d) superseded in their functions, so far as Great Britain was concerned, by the appointment of James M. Mason as the Confederate representative in that country.

CHAPTER XI

THE TREATY OF PARIS

THE so-called Declaration of Paris was an outcome of the Crimean war. Up to the time of that struggle the semi-barbarous rules of international law which, during the Napoleonic period, had been ruthlessly enforced by all belligerents, were still recognized, though in abeyance. As an historical fact, it was undeniable that, on the high seas, piracy was the natural condition of man; and, when the artificial state of peace ceased, into that condition nations relapsed. To ameliorate this, Great Britain and France, on the outbreak of the war with Russia, agreed to respect neutral commerce, whether under their own flags or that of Russia; and, at the close of the war, the Congress of Paris adopted, in April, 1856, a Declaration, embracing four heads : —

1. Privateering is and remains abolished.

2. The neutral flag covers enemy's goods, with the exception of contraband of war.

3. Neutral goods, with the exception of contraband of war, are not liable to capture under enemy's flag.

4. Blockades in order to be binding must be effective; that is to say, maintained by forces sufficient really to prevent access to the coast of the enemy.

Great Britain, France, Prussia, Russia, Austria, and Turkey adopted this mutual agreement, and pledged themselves to make it known to states not represented in the congress, and invite their accession to it, on two conditions: — (1) That the Declaration should be accepted as a whole, or not at all; and (2) That the states acceding should enter into no subsequent arrangement on maritime law in time of war without stipulating for a strict observance of the four points. On these conditions every maritime power was to be invited to accede, and had the right to become a party to the agreement. Accordingly nearly all the states of Europe and South America in course of time notified their accession, and became, equally with the original members, entitled to all the benefits and subject to the obligations of the compact.

The government of the United States was also invited to accede, and like the other powers had the right so to do by simple notification. Secretary Marcy informed the French government, July 28, 1856, that the President could not abandon the right to use privateers, unless he could secure the exemption of all private property, not contraband, from capture at sea; but with that amendment the United States would accede to the Declaration.

In other words, in addition to the points agreed on at Paris, the United States contended for the establishment of the same principle on the sea that obtained on land, to wit : — the exemption from capture of all private property, not contraband of war, including ships. The last great vestige of the earlier times of normal piracy was, by general consent, to be relegated to the past. With the exception of Great Britain, the more considerable European maritime powers made no objection to the Marcy amendment. Great Britain was understood to oppose it, for obvious reasons connected with her past history and present naval preponderance.

President Buchanan's was essentially an "Ostend manifesto," or filibuster, administration. When Lincoln succeeded Buchanan the aspect of affairs from the United States point of view had undergone a dramatic change. Threatened with Confederate letters of marque, the government also found itself engaged in, and responsible for, a blockade of the first magnitude. Under such circumstances, it was plainly impossible to forecast all the contingencies which might arise, and it was altogether dubious what policy might prove to be the more expedient;

but, on the whole, it seemed to the administration wisest to endeavor to conciliate Europe.
A circular dispatch from the Department of
State was sent out accordingly, bearing date
April 24th. By it the ministers of the United
States were formally instructed to ascertain the
disposition of the various governments to which
they were accredited; and, if they found such
governments favorably disposed, to enter into
a convention, under the terms of which the
United States became a party to the Paris
compact. This dispatch, it will be observed,
was prepared and sent out after the fall of Sumter, and the consequent proclamation of Lincoln
and letter-of-marque notification of Jefferson
Davis. In view of the widely spread suspicions
entertained respecting the methods of the American secretary of state, the move was one calculated to excite a not altogether unnatural distrust in the minds of diplomats and European
statesmen; a distrust which would not have
been allayed had they been acquainted with the
tenor of the memorandum of " Notes for the
President's Consideration " submitted to Mr.
Lincoln by that secretary some three weeks previous.

Mr. Adams next found himself engaged in a
long, and what he at the time accurately described as a " singular," negotiation on this sub-

ject, into the details of which it is impossible
here to enter. It is sufficient to say that it
was marked on the part of the British government by evasions, procrastinations, and vacil-
lations by no means creditable. In fact, as the
interviews followed each other, "the singular
divergencies of recollections as to facts" became
so pronounced, that Mr. Adams recorded a frank
admission that "the whole conduct of the administration here is inexplicable;" and, at last, relieved himself by declaring (to himself) that it
was "difficult to suppress indignation at the
miserable shuffling practiced throughout." In
his opinion at the time all this was attributable
to the secret machinations of the Premier: but
the real explanation was that Lord John Russell, distrustful of the good faith and ulterior
purposes of the Washington government, was
afraid of being unwarily entrapped into a position which would in some way compromise him
with respect to those responsible for depredations under Confederate letters of marque. The
British government, though it had conferred
rights of belligerency on the Confederacy, might
be called on to treat as pirates those sailing
under the Confederate colors. Again, like all
European diplomats, Lord John, or Earl Russell, as he now became, looked upon the early
recognition of the Confederacy as inevitable.

But, as events developed while the negotiation went on, recognition might well involve an armed intervention. In case of hostilities, the interests of Great Britain, as respects the four principles of the Treaty of Paris, were not altogether clear. The mercantile marine of the United States had then grown rapidly. A free hand towards it might be a good thing.

Whatever may have been Mr. Seward's objects in originally proposing the adhesion of the United States to the Paris compact at that particular juncture, there can be little doubt that, as the negotiation progressed, he became sincerely interested in it. As to Mr. Adams, after mature deliberation, he made up his mind, much to the discomposure of some of the representatives of the United States at other courts, that the articles of the Declaration were " sound in principle, and that the party coming in on the basis of liberal ideas [like the new party in America] would commit itself very badly if it should turn its back on them." He proceeded accordingly.

At first the British and French secretaries endeavored to have the negotiation transferred to Washington, there to be carried on by the representatives of the two governments, acting in unison. This dangerous move Mr. Seward most adroitly checked ; and the matter was sent

back to Europe. Mr. Adams then took it up
with Earl Russell; but it soon became apparent
that the latter was more intent on the course of
events in America than on the business in hand.
Hence resulted strange misunderstandings and
"divergencies of recollection"; but little progress towards a result. The real trouble was at
Washington, whence Lord Lyons was writing to
Earl Russell cautioning him against permitting
anything to be done without an explicit understanding as to "the effect which [the acceptance
of the Declaration by the American government
was] intended by them to have with regard to
the seceded States." Puzzled, and a little irritated, by Earl Russell's parleys and procrastinations, Mr. Adams at last determined to force
an issue; so, acting under instructions from
Washington, he notified Earl Russell of the
wish of the United States to accede to the principles of the Treaty of Paris in their entirety,
"pure and simple." This, under the terms of
the Treaty entitling other countries to become
parties to it merely on notice, would have ended
the matter in the case of any country other than
the United States; but, in the case of the United
States, the compact, being with foreign powers,
was in the nature of a treaty, and such had
to be submitted to the Senate for approval. To
meet this constitutional difficulty, the notice

of adhesion had to take the form of a convention; and a form of such a convention Mr. Adams submitted. Had Earl Russell been a statesman of the first class, as quick-witted as he was far-seeing, he would now, overlooking all immediate and petty considerations, have seized the opportunity, and committed the United States, once for all, to the new principles of belligerency. Immediate complications might have grown out of the American civil war, and those he could in some way have met as they presented themselves; but, so far as the larger and more remote interests of Great Britain were concerned, the case was clear, and he had the game in his hands. The adhesion of the United States to the new principles would be a great point gained.

Earl Russell was not equal to the occasion. Instead of meeting Mr. Adams squarely, he now had recourse to methods crab-like in the extreme. He asked for a clause to be inserted in the convention, expressly providing that it should have no bearing "direct or indirect on the internal difficulties now prevailing in the United States." Mr. Adams, of course, then closed the negotiation; and, much to the subsequent embarrassment of Great Britain on several occasions, the United States has never yet become a party to the Declaration of Paris. That Mr. Adams erred at the time in attributing the course of Earl Russell to the secret promptings of Lord Palmerston, has already been intimated. It was unquestionably due to the misgivings of Lord Lyons, prompted by his confirmed distrust of Mr. Seward; and to an inability on the part of the British foreign secretary himself to understand the real significance of events then taking place in America.

Thus ended the first of the long succession of diplomatic struggles between Lord Russell and Mr. Adams. In itself it resulted in nothing; but not for that was it unfruitful of consequences. The British minister could not but have felt, as he emerged from it, that he had been driven into an equivocal position. His language was on this point silently significant. The directness of his adversary, moreover, appealed to him; for in Parliament he had been through a lifetime accustomed to give and receive blows, and he liked a straightforward, hard-hitting opponent. When Mr. Adams reached London Lord John, so far as the Foreign Office was concerned, had fixed his position as the representative of half an empire, and he had proposed to hold Mr. Adams in the position thus in advance assigned to him. He was fast finding the task more difficult than he had supposed it would be. So he ever grew more cautious, and more wary of his opponent. Meanwhile Mr. Adams, though disappointed and puzzled, had kept his temper and carried his point ; but, so far as the assumed friendliness of Earl Russell to the United States was concerned, the scales had fallen from his eyes. His faith in the straightforwardness of any portion of the Palmerston-Russell ministry was gone. He had only himself, and the shifting fortunes of war, to rely on in future ; and, so far as the latter were concerned, the recent experiences at Bull Run, though fresh in memory, were the reverse of assuring. The autumn of 1861 was not a cheerful period in the rooms of the American legation at London.

CHAPTER XII

THE TRENT AFFAIR

DURING the month of November especially events of importance followed one close upon another. The plot thickened fast. On the 8th of that month the Confederate defenses at Port Royal, in South Carolina, were captured by a combined naval and military expedition sent out for that purpose; and on the 19th the Confederate steamer Nashville gave notice to the world, dramatically enough, that the flag of the Confederacy was on the ocean, by capturing in the British Channel the American merchant vessel Harvey Birch, and burning her within sight of the English and French shores. Greatly annoyed by this last incident, Mr. Adams in his diary admitted that, in his exultation over the news from Port Royal, very distinct "tremblings" were perceptible as to what tidings of another nature might be in store for him. His apprehensions, though undefined, were prophetic. On the very day upon which General Sherman was occupying the hastily abandoned works at Hilton Head, Captain Wilkes, in com-

mand of the United States steam sloop-of-war
San Jacinto, some five hundred miles to the
south and west, was bringing-to the British steam-
packet Trent, then on the high seas, bound from
Havana, a Spanish harbor, to the island of St.
Thomas. He then forcibly took from her Messrs.
Mason and Slidell, two accredited Confederate
emissaries, — passengers on their way from one
foreign port to another. It is curious to look
back on this performance from the standpoint of
forty years later; for, though the over zealous
naval officer is proverbially the international
enfant terrible, it is questionable whether in
modern times any naval officer has ever been
guilty of a more ill-considered and thoroughly
unjustifiable proceeding. Yet, at the moment,
it made of Captain Wilkes a hero and popular
idol throughout the loyal States of the Union;
while for a brief space of time, without possibility of any advantage to be derived therefrom,
it caused the issue of the struggle for national
existence to tremble on the verge of irretrievable disaster. Already in a most excitable
mood, the occurrence fairly swept the American people off their feet. The entire community was dissolved into a declaiming, hysterical
mob, wholly forgetful of the national contentions through seventy years; a mob to which
high officials, grave magistrates, and counsel

who professed to be learned in the law, vied with each other in ill-considered utterances, as if eager to get themselves into positions from which extrication would be at best extremely difficult. They certainly accomplished that result with marked success.

That the high-handed proceeding of Captain Wilkes was altogether unjustifiable, no American will now deny. That it was in manifest violation of the principles of international law for which the United States had from the beginning stoutly contended, was admitted at the time. That, after 1815, the United States, the case being reversed, would before the Trent affair, at the moment of it, or at any time since, have submitted to similar treatment, no one would even suggest. But the really singular feature of the situation is the utter absence of common sense and business judgment apparent in the national estimate at the time of any advantage to be gained through Captain Wilkes's act, as offset by the risks thereby incurred. Messrs. Mason and Slidell, as the event afterwards showed, were not magicians, or in any way more potent for harm than Messrs. Yancey, Rost, and Mann, already for months at work in Europe. Yet at the moment throughout the loyal States it was by every one assumed as indisputable that some great advantage had been secured for the cause of the Union, — some awful peril averted, — when a certain dull-witted Virginian and a certain acute, intriguing Louisianian were prevented from getting across the Atlantic. So far as any increased danger, likely to result from their presence in London or Paris, was involved, they might perfectly well, as was subsequently seen, have been given their passports through New York, and contemptuously had their passages on a Cunarder paid to Liverpool. Nor, curiously enough, was this hallucination over the importance of two insignificant individuals confined to those who secured forcible possession of their persons. They absolutely shared it themselves. They were on their way across the Atlantic commissioned to embroil the United States with the two great maritime powers of Europe, if they could; and now, by an almost miraculous interposition due to luck and indiscretion combined, the object of their mission was, at its very threshold, being accomplished through them to an extent they could in their wildest imaginings never have ventured to hope. James M. Mason was a coarse, unintelligent man, and that his sodden brain should not instantly have taken in the significance of what was going on is perhaps no occasion for surprise. Not so John Slidell. His head was clear; his mind alert and logical. Greatly ad-

dicted to games of chance, he was quick to catch
the bearing of men's thoughts and acts. It is
hard to believe that his heart at least did not
swell with secret exultation when, forced over
the side of the Trent, he felt that his antagonist
was playing his hand for him as he never could
have played it himself. Yet the evidence is all
the other way. Even Slidell seems to have
labored under the well-nigh inconceivable mental delusion that he could be of greater service
to the Confederacy in Paris than within the
walls of Fort Warren. At the time the performance just failed of being terribly tragic;
looked at now, it had in it many elements of
the *opera bouffe*. But, for some weeks subsequent to the arrival of the news of the seizure,
these latter elements were not conspicuously
apparent from the point of view of the United
States Legation in London.

Up to this time, though Mr. Adams studi-
ously ignored the fact, his treatment in England had been the reverse of cordial. Socially,
he had been recognized, so to speak; and nothing more. The sympathies of the aristocracy
were distinctly on the side of the slaveocracy of
the South, as against the democracy of the
North; and this the American minister had
been caused to feel with a distinctness almost
peculiar to London, where the shades and phases

of social coldness and incivility have long since
been perfected into a science. Fortunately, Mr.
Adams, by nature and bearing, was in this respect exactly the man the occasion called for.
When the Englishman was cold and reserved,
Mr. Adams was a little colder and a little more
reserved than the Englishman. He thus played
well the game to which he found himself called,
for the very good reason that the game was
natural to him.

The English country season was now come;
and, under ordinary circumstances, or at a later
period in Mr. Adams's own residence there, he
would have been overwhelmed with invitations
to the great houses: but in the autumn of 1861
such was far from being the case. A few officials bethought themselves of the American
minister and Mrs. Adams; but, as a rule, their
company was not desired, for their presence was
obviously a restraint on the freedom of conversation, then largely made up of ill-natured and
hostile, when not contemptuous, references to
America and all things American. Among
those whose social standing in London was unquestioned, Mr. Richard Monckton Milnes, two
years later created Lord Houghton, was one of
the very few whose sympathies were throughout
strongly enlisted in favor of the United States;
and he, from the beginning, showed a disposi-

tion to be civil. He had accordingly invited Mr. and Mrs. Adams to Frystone, the Milnes country seat in Nottinghamshire. Thither, little suspecting what tidings the St. Thomas steam-packet, then fast nearing the English coast, was to precipitate upon them, Mr. and Mrs. Adams betook themselves, leaving London on Monday, November 25th.

As he left the legation Mr. Adams noted that, almost for the first time since he had been in England, the mail from America brought only agreeable news. The party at Frystone Hall was large and pleasant; and the presence of William E. Forster gave evidence of care in its selection, in view of the all absorbing topics of the day. On Wednesday, the 27th, an excursion had been arranged to visit the ruins of Pomfret Castle, famous in English annals as the scene of the murder of Richard II. It was a sodden, dull day of the English November type; and just as the party was entering the ruins, to quote Mr. Adams, " a telegraphic dispatch was put into my hands from [the legation] an-nouncing the startling news that Messrs. Slidell and Mason had been taken by force out of a British steamer in the West Indies by one of our steam frigates. The consequences rose up very vividly in my mind, and prevented me from thinking much of historical associations." Re-

ferring to the incident, Mr. Forster the next
day wrote to his wife : " Just as we got into
Pomfret Castle, Adams said, in his cool, quiet
way, ' I have got stirring news,' which indeed
was a telegram with the story." Mr. Milnes, as
well as Mr. Forster, was a good deal impressed
by his guest's composure under such very trying
circumstances. The moment he knew the nature
of the information contained in the telegram, he
naturally at once arranged for Mr. Adams's return to London. " With characteristic coolness," as Mr. Reid, Lord Houghton's biographer, says, "the American minister remained
quietly at Frystone," intimating that London
was about the last place to which, under existing conditions, he felt any inclination to go.

He was entirely right. A more impulsive,
less deliberate man would probably have felt
either a desire or an obligation to get to his
post. In reality, both he and the interests he
had in charge were the better for his absence
from it. Most fortunately there was then no
Atlantic cable. Not for five years yet did one
exist. Had there been such a means of instan-
taneous communication in 1861, the Trent affair could hardly have failed to involve the two
nations in war. As it was, it required from
sixteen to twenty days to send a message from
London to Washington and receive a reply to

it. Sixteen days as a minimum afford a good
deal of time in which a popular craze or sentimental effervescence may subside ; and when
those sixteen days are doubled, or trebled, by
the necessity of yet further correspondence,
there is a very good chance that reason may resume its sway. It proved so now.

When he received his first telegram at Pomfret Castle, Mr. Adams knew only that he was
wholly without information or instructions from
Washington for his guidance. The news of the
seizure was brought to England by the La Plata.
It reached London on November 27th, eighteen
days after the event. The San Jacinto, with
Messrs. Mason and Slidell on board, made Fortress Monroe on the 15th. The seizure, therefore, was known in America twelve days before
it was known in England. Meanwhile Mr.
Adams was in a state of complete ignorance in
regard to how it had come about. The natural
inference was that Captain Wilkes had acted
under instructions. To an ordinary, well-regu-
lated intellect, it was hardly conceivable then,
as it would not be now, that a naval officer, in
command of a ship-of-war on its way home from
a distant station, should, out of his own head
and acting on newspaper information, venture
on such a performance. As Mr. Adams at this
time wrote referring to other experiences he was

then undergoing: — "These naval officers are bad, when too sluggish, like Marchand; and worse, when too active, like Wilkes." But if the Wilkes seizure had been directed from Washington, the first and natural conclusion of Mr. Adams would be that it was in furtherance of the aggressive policy outlined in Secretary Seward's dispatches of April 27th and May 21st, and that a foreign war was to be provoked. Under such circumstances, bewildered as he could not but be at the darkness in which he had been left, the chief thing for a diplomatic agent to guard against was any hasty action or ill-considered utterance. He could safely infer nothing, assume nothing, imagine nothing. He must possess his soul in patience, be enigmatical — and wait! The situation, altogether inexplicable, might be trying in the mean while, but the Washington oracle must at last speak. In the mean time, silence.

It so chanced, however, that the very exigency thus unexpectedly arisen had already been discussed as a possibility by Mr. Adams with no less a person than the Prime Minister himself. The incident was curious and interesting; besides being characteristic of Lord Palmerston, it throws a not unfavorable light on his attitude at that time towards the American struggle. He plainly did not want to have Great Britain in-

volved in it through any untoward accident.
So far from seeking a pretext for quarrel, he
was anxious to avoid one. Up to this time,
there had been no personal intercourse between
Mr. Adams and the Premier. They had both
been present, and both had spoken, at the Lord
Mayor's dinner on the 9th of November; and
Mr. Adams on that occasion had evidently been
somewhat relieved at the tenor of the Prime
Minister's remarks. They were, he wrote, characterized by "his customary shrewdness. He
touched gently on our difficulties, and at the
same time gave it to be clearly understood that
there was to be no interference for the sake
of cotton." Three days later, on the 12th of
November, Mr. Adams was a good deal surprised by receiving "a familiar note" from
Lord Palmerston asking him to call at Cambridge House, in Piccadilly, the town residence
of the latter, and see him at an hour named in
the note. Mr. Adams could not imagine why
he was thus summoned; but, of course, kept
the appointment. "His reception," he wrote,
"was very cordial and frank."

Lord Palmerston did not then fully explain
his reasons for this unusual interview; in fact
they were highly creditable to him. He was
going out of his way to give the American minister an intimation of possible impending diffi-

culty with a view to obviating it. It was then well known that Messrs. Mason and Slidell were on their way to Europe. They were at first supposed to be on the Nashville; but afterwards their arrival at Havana was announced, and it was then correctly assumed that they would sail on the Trent. It was further surmised that the government of the United States had issued orders for intercepting any vessel on which the envoys might take passage, and seizing them. Finally, the James Adger, a United States ship-of-war under command of Captain John B. Marchand, had recently arrived on the English coast, and was at Southampton, the home port of the Nassau steam-packet line. The times were troubled; the circumstances suspicious. Earl Russell submitted the facts to the crown lawyers, and had been advised that, under British precedents and past contentions, a United States man-of-war falling in with a British mail-steamer would have the right to board her, open her mail-bags, examine their contents, and, if the steamer should prove liable to confiscation for carrying dispatches from the enemy, put a prize crew on board, and carry her to a port of the United States for adjudication. In that case the law officers thought the captor might, and in their opinion ought to, disembark the passengers on the mail-steamer at some convenient port. But, they added, "she would have no right to remove Messrs. Mason and Slidell and carry them off as prisoners, leaving the ship to pursue her voyage." [1] Obviously, if this was the law as deduced from British precedents, a very ugly question was impending, and Her Majesty's government might find itself in an awkward position. It would require a great many precedents to make palatable the fact of an American man-of-war steaming out of Southampton and stopping, searching, and seizing a British mail-packet in the British Channel, and in sight of her home port. So, after reflecting over the situation, Lord Palmerston had concluded that a little friendly talk in time with the American minister might be a sensible way of preventing a trouble not less unnecessary than serious. Mr. Adams at once transmitted to Secretary Seward, in a dispatch marked "confidential," and never printed, a detailed account of that unofficial talk. While the essential and characteristic portions of it are here given in full, it is only proper to say that liberal allowance should be made in the case of some references to Captain Marchand, who, while in professional alertness not fully up to the ideals of Mr. Adams, was a gallant officer, and subsequently distinguished

[1] Walpole's *Life of Russell*, ii. 356, 357.

himself under Farragut in the battle of Mobile
Bay.   There is no reason to suppose that Lord
Palmerston spoke by the letter in what he said
of him, but he certainly spoke in genuine
Palmerstonian fashion.   Mr. Adams wrote as
follows to Secretary Seward: "He [Palmer-
ston] received me in his library all alone, and
at once opened on the subject then evidently
weighing on his mind.   He said that information had come to him of the late arrival of a
United States vessel of war, the James Adger.
She had put into one or two places, and finally
stopped at Southampton, where she had taken
in coal and other supplies.   But the day before,
his Lordship had understood, the captain had
got very drunk on brandy, after which he had
dropped down to the mouth of the river as if
about to sail on a cruise.   The impression was
that he had been directed to keep on the watch
for the steamer expected to arrive Thursday
from the West Indies, in order to take out of
it by force the gentlemen from the Southern
States, Messrs. Mason and Slidell, who were
presumed to be aboard.   Now he was not going
into the question of our right to do such an
act.   Perhaps we might be justified in it, as the
steamer was not strictly a public vessel, or perhaps we might not.   He would set the argument
aside for those whose province it was to discuss

it. All that he desired to observe was, that such a step would be highly inexpedient in every way he could view it. It would be regarded here very unpleasantly if the captain, after enjoying the hospitality of this country, filling his ship with coals and with other supplies, and filling his own stomach with brandy (and here he laughed in his characteristic way), should, within sight of the shore, commit an act which would be felt as offensive to the national flag. Neither could he see what was the compensating advantage to be gained by it. It surely would not be supposed that the addition of one or two more to the number of persons, who had already been some time in London on the same errand, would be likely to produce any change in the policy already adopted. He did not believe that the government would vary its action on that account, be they few or many. He could not therefore conceive of the necessity of resorting to such a measure as this, which, in the present state of opinion in England, could scarcely fail to occasion more prejudice than it would do good."

It is not necessary here to give the rest of this interesting but somewhat lengthy dispatch, covering as it did a half hour's rapid and desultory talk. Mr. Adams explained the orders under which Captain Marchand was acting, and

told his Lordship that the James Adger had
come out looking for the Nashville, and was now
watching the Gladiator, and not lying in wait
for the Confederate emissaries or a British mail-
steamer. As for the Gladiator, then being fitted
out to run the blockade with a cargo of arms
and munitions for the Confederacy, Mr. Adams
frankly told Lord Palmerston that he " had advised Captain Marchand to keep on the track
of her, and, the very first moment he could form
a reasonable conviction of her intent to land
anywhere in the United States, to snap her up
at once." He wholly disavowed, however, in
the case of the James Adger, the existence of
any orders from his government of the nature
of those taken for granted by Lord Palmerston.
This conversation took place on the 15th of
November, and the very thing Lord Palmerston wished to prevent happening off the harbor
of Southampton actually had happened six days
before in the Old Bahama channel. It was a
mere question of distance : apprehended within
forty miles of Southampton, it happened within
four thousand. In the absence of definite information to the contrary, the inference was
natural, as well as almost irresistible, that the
captain of the San Jacinto had acted in pursuance of orders such as Lord Palmerston had assumed to exist in the case of the James Adger,

but which Mr. Adams had denied. This was the essential point, and the situation was greatly complicated. Captain Wilkes had done just what Mr. Adams had assured the Prime Minister Captain Marchand was not instructed to do, and had no idea of doing. The thing did not have an honest aspect.

Mr. Adams returned to London with the recollection of this unfortunate talk very fresh in his mind. It had taken place only a fortnight before. Getting back on the evening of the 28th, the city was in a state of much excitement, while in the face and bearing of Lord Russell, from whom he found a summons awaiting him, he noticed "a shade more of gravity, but no ill will." Mr. Adams could only say to the foreign secretary that he was wholly unadvised both as to the occurrence and the grounds of the action of Captain Wilkes. Nor did Mr. Seward seem in haste to enlighten him; for ten days later he wrote: "The dispatches came, but not an allusion to the case of the Trent. Mr. Seward's ways are not those of diplomacy. Here have I been nearly three weeks without positively knowing whether the act of the officer was directed by the government or not. My private letters made me anxious. Strange to relate, the uniform tone is to sustain the action of Captain Wilkes." On the

14th, in the midst of the turmoil, Prince Albert died ; a lamentable occurrence, but for the moment it served as a fortunate distraction. Three days later, on the 17th of December, in the midst of the mourning, a dispatch at last came bearing indirectly on the momentous issue. Dated on the 30th of November, fifteen days after the San Jacinto had reached Fortress Monroe, it related mainly to other subjects ; but, at its close, the secretary spoke of the seizure of Messrs. Mason and Slidell, referring to it as a " new incident," which was " to be met and disposed of by the two governments, if possible " in a spirit of mutual forbearance. But it was further significantly intimated that " Captain Wilkes having acted without any instructions from the government, the subject is free from the embarrassment which might have resulted if the act had been specially directed by us. I trust," the secretary then added, " that the British government will consider the subject in a friendly temper, and it may expect the best disposition on the part of this government." Two days later, on the 19th, Mr. Adams went by appointment to the Foreign Office and had a long interview with Earl Russell, in the course of which, after repeating the tenor of the dispatch, he read it in full, and the two discussed its bearing in a friendly spirit, reaching the con-

clusion that an adjustment could be arrived at
with no great difficulty. The tone of the papers, especially the " Post," supposed to be the
personal organ of Lord Palmerston, was, however, then so bitter and uncompromising that
Mr. Adams was especially anxious to ascertain
whether in any influential quarters war was
intended. He, therefore, pressed his inquiries
closely as to the probable action of the government in case, the demands of Great Britain
not being complied with, Lord Lyons broke off
diplomatic relations at Washington. Lord Russell, in reply, intimated that in such event hostilities would not necessarily at once ensue.

One passage in this interview afforded, however, good evidence of the friendly relations
which, notwithstanding the unsatisfactory result
of the negotiation over the Declaration of Paris,
had now come to exist between the minister and
the foreign secretary. Referring, as the talk
went on, to the precedents in cases similar to
that of the Trent, Mr. Adams observed that
" the French government had always been very
consistent in maintenance of the rights of neu-
trals ; but," in quoting Mr. Adams's language,
Lord Russell went on to say, " he added that
he could not pay our government the same com-
pliment." Meanwhile, in his turn, Mr. Adams
reports that, when certain English precedents

were cited, Lord Russell quietly observed that
" there were many things said and done by them
[the English] fifty or sixty years ago, which he
might not undertake to enter into the defense
of now." All which things, as Mr. Adams remarked in reporting the conversation, " were
said pleasantly on both sides." Finally, sum-
ming up the grand result of the interview, Mr.
Adams wrote, " On the whole I inferred that
his Lordship did not desire war; but that he
was likely to be pushed over the precipice by
his desire to walk too close to the edge. We
talked of the merits of the question very calmly.
Finally I took my leave ; at the door he said
that, if all matters were left between us, he
had no doubt we should soon agree; to which
I expressed my assent."

Strange as it now seems, three entire weeks
were yet to elapse before the tension came to an
end, and the surrender of the emissaries was
announced. During those weeks nothing more
was heard in London from the Washington
oracle. Nothing, in fact, could very well be
heard, inasmuch as, to the oracle itself, the
policy the United States might in the end pursue was up to the last moment matter of the
utmost uncertainty. Into the details of what
then took place in President Lincoln's Cabinet
it is not necessary here to enter; but, so far as the

legation in London was concerned, the outward
indications did not favor a peaceful solution of
the trouble. The course pursued by the English
government at this time has since been criti-
cised,[1] and it has been claimed that the tenor of
the dispatch of November 30th and of the interview between Earl Russell and Mr. Adams
was carefully concealed from the British public,
lest the assurance of a willingness in Washington to settle the question in a peaceable manner
would destroy the warlike enthusiasm which
then pervaded the British islands. Indeed the
"Post," on the 21st of December, published a
formal contradiction, supposed everywhere to be
inspired, of a rumor which at once got in circulation, of the conversation of December 19th. In
view of the revelations since made of the debate
then going on in the Cabinet at Washington
this criticism can hardly be accepted as sound.
It is now known that the course the United
States was to pursue long trembled in the balance. Members of the Cabinet, as of both
Houses of Congress, had noisily committed
themselves to a policy which, under the circumstances, could end only in war. Such had to be
brought into line. That they would be brought
into line, and no matter with what groans, pro-

[1] Dana's *Wheaton*, § 504, note 228 (p. 507). Harris's *The
Trent Affair*, 134, 135, 274–277 ; Rhodes, iii. 534.

testations, and grimaces, eat their own scarcely
uttered words, was to the last moment questionable ; and, until it was certain, Her Majesty's
government, from the British standpoint, had
but one course to take. Those composing it,
whatever individually or in private they may
have intended or wished, must evince an inflex-
ible determination, an unchangeable purpose.
Secretary Seward, it is to be remembered, at
this time commanded the confidence of no European foreign secretary. It is wholly immaterial
whether the distrust of him then so prevalent was
or was not well founded ; that it existed is indisputable, and, in this connection, enough. He
was deemed unreliable, — in a word, "tricky."
The story of the Newcastle insult also was current, and was undenied ; yet the Duke of Newcastle was a member of the Palmerston-Russell
ministry. Moreover, while Secretary Seward
was penning his conciliatory dispatch of November 30th, Dr. Russell was writing to the
" Times : " " In the present temper of the American people, no concession can avert serious complications very long, or the surrender [by Great
Britain] of all the boasted privileges of the Civis
Romanus. . . . I believe the government will
retain [Mason and Slidell] at all risks, because
it dare not give them up, not being strong
enough to do what is right in face of popular

sentiment." In the same journal, in its issue of
December 10th, there was another letter from
Dr. Russell, in which, referring to a rumor current in Washington when he wrote that Mason
and Slidell would be given up, he went on to
say: "If it be true, this government is broken
up. There is so much violence of spirit among
the lower orders of the people, and they are so
ignorant of everything except their own politics
and passions, so saturated with pride and vanity,
that any honorable concession, even in this hour
of extremity, would prove fatal to its authors."

Such were the most authentic advices from
America, and, only five days before Mr. Adams
read to Earl Russell the dispatch of November
30th, the "Times" editorially referred to "a
general persuasion that upon his ability to involve the United States in a war with England
Mr. Seward has staked his official existence, and,
whatever may be the consequences to America
of a war with this country, to him it has become
an article of the very first necessity." As if to
emphasize this "persuasion," and wholly to discredit the pacific assurances of the secretary,
Congress met on the 2d of December, and the
same steamer which brought Mr. Seward's dispatch brought news also of the official approval
of Captain Wilkes's act by the secretary of the
navy, and the unanimous passage of a vote of

thanks to him by the national House of Representatives. As the record is gone over now, the nation seems to have been demented. Unquestionably it so impressed European observers.

Mr. Thurlow Weed was then in London, and a carefully considered letter from him had appeared in the "Times" of December 14th. Mr. Adams, to whom Mr. Weed submitted the letter before sending it, thought it "a little too smooth and deprecating," and told Mr. Weed "it would conciliate no favor." In it the writer tried to smooth over the Newcastle story, merely asserting that "by all Americans the badinage of Mr. Seward would have been readily understood;" which, as an explanation, left much to be desired: but he further intimated that the Trent affair might best be disposed of through a protracted negotiation, entered into in "a neighborly spirit." The inference was inevitable that Mr. Weed reflected in this suggestion the purpose of Mr. Seward, and the latter thus had in view a long paper discussion when he expressed the hope that the British government would "consider the subject in a friendly spirit." However much Senator Sumner or even President Lincoln might incline to it, the government and people of England did not propose to have that particular affair made the subject of a long paper controversy, resulting in an arbitration. There can be no possible question that, under similar circumstances, the American people would even now evince a similar disinclination not less pronounced.

Thus in London, between the 19th of December, 1861, and the 8th of January, 1862, it was not clear what Secretary Seward had in mind when he wrote the dispatch of November 30th; while grave doubts were not unfairly entertained as to whether he really desired to maintain the peace, or, if he did so desire, whether it was within his power to control the American situation. Indeed, as matter of fact, when the secretary of state penned his " confidential " dispatch he did not voice the sentiments of the Cabinet at that date, much less those of Congress, or the press, or the American people. Thoroughly to sober these, they needed to look the certainty of a foreign war full in the face. Under such circumstances, it seems somewhat hypercritical to hold to a strict ethical account those English statesmen who were responsible for great practical results. As Earl Russell not unjustly at the time remarked to Lord Palmerston, " the United States government are very dangerous people to run away from; " and when peace is the end in view, that end is not always best secured by evincing an over-conciliatory spirit. Such is apt to be construed as a disposition to

"run away," especially by an over-excited opponent who happens to be thoroughly in the
wrong. Certainly when thirty years later, during the administration of Benjamin Harrison,
a not dissimilar situation arose between Chili
and the United States, the latter evinced no
disposition to allow doubts to exist as to the
course it was intended in certain contingencies
to pursue. Studied in the light of that subsequent occurrence the course taken and language used by the government of Great Britain
in December, 1861, and January, 1862, stand
amply justified.

Meanwhile on December 3d, four days after
his first interview with Earl Russell on the subject of the Trent, Mr. Adams himself had written confidentially to Mr. Seward, setting forth
the situation as he saw it, and in calm, cogent
fashion pointed out the extreme undesirability
of America now placing herself "in the position which has always heretofore earned for
England the ill will of the other maritime nations of the globe, not excluding ourselves."
On December 21st this letter reached the State
Department; but even then it was in time, for
not until the 23d, two days later, was Earl Russell's leading dispatch of November 30th, de-
manding the release of the Confederate commissioners and a suitable apology, formally handed

by Lord Lyons to Mr. Seward. It nowhere
appears in how far, if at all, Mr. Adams's letter
affected the immensely momentous discussion
carried on in the Cabinet room of the White
House during Christmas Day and the day following of this year. Mr. Seward's latest biographer speaks of the missive as " warning and
very impressive," and describes Mr. Adams as
being for Mr. Seward in that emergency " a
tower of strength."

Meanwhile, in none of the discussions of the
Trent affair, many and minute as they have been,
is reference anywhere found to the " confidential " dispatch of Mr. Adams of November 15th,
or the report therein given of his interview with
Lord Palmerston of three days previous. Yet
on that occasion Lord Palmerston obviously, so
to speak, drew the American fire ; and the detailed report of what he said had reached Washington, and was lying on Secretary Seward's
table when he penned his dispatch of November 30th. It could not but have exercised a
most sobering influence, and not impossibly altered his whole tone. The contemptuous language of the British Premier regarding the two
men who at the very time when he spoke had
been seized, and about whom such a tremendous
ado was now being made, and his very direct
intimations that their presence in Europe would
in no wise affect the course of affairs, must,

nearly a month later, have furnished the presidential counselors more or less food for the saving second thought. In fact, it would seem to be quite impossible that Secretaries Chase and Welles could have listened to that statement of Lord Palmerston's views, as good-natured as they were timely and shrewd, without very unpleasant secret misgivings. Theirs was the not unusual fate of the precipitate statesman; and a thoroughly false position, never under the most favorable circumstances pleasant to contemplate, becomes especially unattractive when made suddenly apparent by the words or actions of one's opponent.

Not uninfluenced probably from this cause, the secretary of state had also within the last three months otherwise undergone a decided change of heart and of mind. Having recovered his mental poise, he saw things clearly. No longer viewing them through a distorted medium of Union sentiment in the South, Democracy, Nationality, and Americanism, instead of challenging a foreign war, he was earnestly bent on averting it. When Mr. Seward first reached this most fortunate realizing sense of the hard actualities of the situation nowhere appears. The events of July probably had much to do with his change of heart. Confronted with them, he could not but have seen that the seaboard States, from Virginia to Texas, were united as one man, and,

deaf to all sentimental appeal, could be dealt
with only by force. For this the blockade was
indispensable; and the blockade depended on
the control of the ocean. As a maritime power,
Great Britain was at that time irresistible; and
on the issue raised Great Britain was unquestionably right, excepting always her own bad
precedents; and, in the light of strenuous past
contentions, the United States was preposter-
ously wrong. Could a United States naval officer, cruising in the British Channel, stop the
Dover and Calais mail packet to take from
it Confederate emissaries? The proposition
seemed to carry its own answer. Yet, as the
"Times" in its issue of December 11th very
clearly and correctly pointed out, this, and nothing else, was claimed. However and whenever sobered, the secretary of state now saw all
this as it was, and acted accordingly, persuad-
ing the President; and, on January 8th, Mr.
Adams at last received a telegram "to the effect
that Messrs. Mason and Slidell and suite had
been surrendered. Soon after Mr. Weed came
in from the city with confirmatory intelligence,
and a later telegram put it beyond doubt. So,"
he wrote, "the danger of war is at present removed; and I am to remain in this purgatory a
while longer." He took the welcome result
very calmly, merely remarking in his diary that
the settlement left him "with an impression of

nothing to do." But it had its after-clap; for
three days later, he wrote : — " The excitement
of the times has given my situation so much
prominence that I am a sort of mark for all
classes to shoot at. The newspapers this morning are rather lively. The ' Post' insinuates
that I suppressed Mr. Seward's dispatch relating
to the Trent case in order to go into the market under cover of Mr. Peabody and speculate
in the funds. The ' News ' has a very sharp
leader putting the ' Post ' in a very awkward
position for denying, as if officially, that the dispatch had ever been communicated. It is a singular proceeding, and makes me doubt whether
that paper is so much of an organ of Lord
Palmerston after all." Finally though the reaction from the last craze had now fairly set in
and the London " Times " astonished Messrs.
Mason and Slidell, fully prepared to pose as international martyrs grateful for rescue, by saying on the day of their arrival : " We do sincerely hope that our countrymen will not give
these fellows anything in the shape of an ova-
tion," — in spite of this, the continued optimis-
tic tone of the secretary jarred upon the minister. " Our army," he wrote, " must do the
rest. I had a telegram from Mr. Seward full
of promises of what is about to be done. The
past future tense will not go down here ; and
he ought to know it."

CHAPTER XIII

A BOUT WITH THE PREMIER

"LORD PALMERSTON bounded like a boy at any cruelty or oppression. Many years later, during his second premiership, at the time when the Federal General Butler outraged public opinion by proclaiming at New Orleans that ladies who showed discontent either by their dress or demeanor would be treated like women of the town, he sent to the American minister an indignant letter of remonstrance so strong and outspoken that Mr. Adams refused to receive it, and ran off with it to the Foreign Office in the utmost consternation." [1]

With biographers, as with artists, the point of view has a great deal to do with the aspect of the matter or person under consideration. In writing the life of Lord Palmerston, Mr. Evelyn Ashley thus alluded in a passing way to an incident and correspondence, not known to many at the time it took place, and since only vaguely referred to by a few writers of diplomatic reminiscences of that period. In 1862

[1] Ashley's *Life of Palmerston*, ii. 105.

the occurrence was significant of several things:
—among others, of British wrong-headedness
and official insolence; of the strong trend of
social feeling in London during the American
struggle over slavery; of the English disposition to take liberties with those not in position
to make their resentment immediately effective;
but, above all, of the utter inability of the European public men to understand American social conditions, and their practical working.

The episode in question occurred in June,
1862. The long, depressing winter following
the adjustment of the Trent affair had worn
itself away, and the London season was now at
its height; though over it, socially, the recent
death of Prince Albert threw a deep gloom.
Parliament was in session; the war in America
was the exciting topic of the day, whether in the
club, on 'change, or at the dinner-table. From
the outset of his English experience Mr. Adams
had shared to the full in the American distrust of Lord Palmerston. This was largely
due to the well-understood fact that the London
"Morning Post" more immediately reflected the
views of the Prime Minister; and, throughout
the war, that journal was noticeable for its bitterness towards the Washington government and
the loyal cause. There was little in the way of
disparagement that could be said, which the

"Post" failed to say. Socially, and otherwise, Lord and Lady Palmerston had been rather particularly civil to Mr. and Mrs. Adams; and it has already been seen that, following the course of the "Post" closely in connection with the Trent affair, Mr. Adams had noticed certain slight indications which led him to "doubt whether that paper [was] so much of an organ of Lord Palmerston, after all." The American minister was beginning to incline more favorably towards the Premier, when suddenly the occurrence of the incident alluded to by Mr. Ashley prejudiced the former violently and permanently.

The spring had brought to Europe tidings of an almost unbroken series of Union successes, military and naval. The fall of Fort Donelson had followed hard upon the capture of Roanoke Island; and the splendidly dramatic contest at Hampton Roads between the Merrimac and the Monitor warned Europe of a complete revolution in maritime warfare. "With prudence and energy for a few weeks" longer, it seemed to Mr. Adams "by no means unreasonable to hope that we may crush the rebellion before midsummer." The tone of the newspapers of pronounced Confederate leaning was despondent, and the more prominent and influential rebel sympathizers were fast becoming satisfied that the South would collapse unless soon sustained from without. The "Post" was, if possible, more outspoken and bitter than ever. At last, on Sunday, May 11th, returning home from an afternoon walk in Kensington Gardens, Mr. Adams picked up from the hall table a telegram from Mr. Seward, forwarded from Queenstown, announcing the fall of New Orleans. "On going upstairs," he wrote, "I found Sir Charles Lyell talking with Mrs. Adams about the course of the London 'Times' on American affairs, and the singular way in which its statements are always contradicted by the event next announced. Its confidence last week as to the impossibility of accomplishing the capture of New Orleans and the Mississippi River might, for what he knew, be dissipated to-morrow. At this I smiled, and answered that I had news of the event in my hand. This seems to me the finishing stroke of the rebellion." However this may have proved in the end, the event led immediately to a sharp collision between Lord Palmerston and Mr. Adams.

General B. F. Butler's memorable order No. 28, declaring that the women of New Orleans "who insult any soldiers are to be regarded and treated as common women plying their vocation," was made public on May 15, 1862. An Englishman's idea of women of the town and the treatment accorded them, and the ideas of an American, differed greatly. As respects that class, the London of 1862 was, as nearly as a so-called civilized community could be, positively shameless. No respectable woman of ordinarily attractive aspect could venture alone in the streets. She was almost certain to be addressed; while men were invariably and openly solicited. In the United States, and especially in the cities of the South, it was in both respects altogether otherwise. In New Orleans, for instance, the deference shown to white women was well known and almost excessive. It was the custom of the country, — a custom so well understood that it had long and frequently excited the notice of travelers from Europe, and more than once been the subject of amused comment. The Southern women were, so to speak, acclimated to it. Taking it as matter of course, they often assumed upon it. Especially was this the case under the excitement of the civil war; and Pollard, the Confederate historical writer, describes the state of things in this respect then existent in terms which, to a European, would be inconceivable, as implying only one thing, and that thing a Saturnalia. " The intermingling," he wrote, " of the best ladies with the soldiers was something curious. The usual routine of social life was abandoned, and a universal interest in the war broke down the barriers of sex as well as of class. Even those ladies who were most exclusively reared, who had formerly bristled with punctilios of propriety, admitted the right of any soldier to address them, to offer them attentions, and to escort them in the street. The ceremony of an introduction was not required ; the uniform was sufficient as such." [1]

Unfortunately, when, through the fate of war, the Union soldier in his federal uniform a little later on took the place of the Confederate in those same streets, this female effusiveness assumed a quite different though not less demonstrative form. In the many accounts of a certain famous interview between Queen Louisa of Prussia and Napoleon, in October, 1806, it has never been suggested that Her Majesty began by bearing herself towards the victor of Jena as if he were a Corsican dog whose mere presence was pollution ; nor does Marbot, or any other writer of recollections of that period, anywhere mention that, after Austerlitz, high-born Viennese dames took occasion to empty the slops out of chamber windows at the moment when uniformed marshals of France were passing on the pavement below. In Spain, also, during the earlier years of the century, as in India more recently, it was

[1] *Life of Jefferson Davis*, 133.

not the custom for the women of captured cities
to demean themselves in presence of a victorious British soldiery with ostentatious contempt.
On the contrary, they generally sought a severe
seclusion, preferring for that purpose churches
and other holy places, the sanctity of which,
according to high military authority, did not
always afford them an adequate protection.
With the "ladies" of the Confederacy it was
altogether different.   Mr. Ashley innocently
suggests that they "showed discontent" by
"dress" or "demeanor."   Had they confined
themselves within those limits, at once narrow
and unobjectionable, it is quite safe to say that
the women of New Orleans would have had incomparably less grounds for outcry than, under
similar circumstances, did the females of Bada-
joz in 1812, or those of Delhi in 1857. As matter of historical fact, however, availing themselves of the habits of deference associated with
their skirts, the demeanor of the white women
of Southern cities occupied by the Union army
towards those wearing the federal uniform was,
in the early days of the war, simply both inde-
cent and intolerable.   Not content with merely
avoiding any contact with their victors, osten-
tatiously and as a contamination, they evinced
their "spirit" and patriotism in ways not
strictly indicative of refinement, or even what

is usually accepted as civility of the commonest kind. In fact the "ladies," so called, indulged in grossly insulting speech, and even spat upon the blue-clad objects of their detestation. More than this, with an ingenuity truly feline, they took advantage of the military obsequies of certain of those stationed over them who had been murdered by guerillas, and trained their children to cast more than contumely at the coffins of the dead, while they themselves in the immediate neighborhood evinced a conspicuous approval. This, as Butler truly remarked, "flesh and blood" could not long stand.

Women of the town in New Orleans were mostly mulattoes, or half-breeds ; and, when found practicing their calling in public, these were, under a municipal regulation, arrested by the police, and put with other criminals in the calaboose, or lock-up. This was the American, and altogether commendable, significance of General Butler's famous order. Under it no woman was ever maltreated ; and, in less than twenty-four hours, it brought the "ladies" of New Orleans to a wholesome realizing sense of the situation. But in London this order was construed in an altogether different way, and in accordance with the quite unmentionable practices then, and indeed still, to be witnessed in the parks and other public resorts of that city.

Altogether a delicate subject, it was one upon which the two communities spoke in different languages; and, when it was under discussion, the English simply did not understand what Americans said or had in mind. Accordingly when Butler's order No. 28, intelligible enough in America, was published in England, a storm of indignation swept through the press. No abuse of him who promulgated the order could be too strong; no denunciation of the order itself too quick or emphatic. Parliament was still in session, and apparently Lord Palmerston thought that, in this matter, it was advisable for him to make an early record.

The reported details of this obnoxious order appeared in the London papers of June 10th and were severely commented upon. Returning from an afternoon walk the following day, Mr. Adams found a note which, after hastily reading, he threw across the table to his son, who was writing on its other side, at the same time exclaiming: "What does this mean! Does Palmerston want a quarrel?" The note in question, marked "confidential," ran as follows:

BROCKET, 11 June, 1862.

MY DEAR SIR, — I cannot refrain from taking the liberty of saying to you that it is difficult if not impossible to express adequately the disgust which must be excited in the mind of every honorable man by the general order of General Butler given in the enclosed extract from yesterday's "Times." Even when a town is taken by assault it is the practice of the commander of the conquering army to protect to his utmost the inhabitants and especially the female part of them, and I will venture to say that no example can be found in the history of civilized nations, till the publication of this order, of a general guilty in cold blood of so infamous an act as deliberately to hand over the female inhabitants of a conquered city to the unbridled license of an unrestrained soldiery.

If the Federal government chooses to be served by men capable of such revolting outrages, they must submit to abide by the deserved opinion which mankind will form of their conduct.

My dear Sir,   Yrs faithfully,

PALMERSTON.

C. F. ADAMS, Esq.

In this extraordinary letter Mr. Adams apprehended a latent significance. Like Napoleon's famous reception of the English ambassador, Lord Whitworth, in 1803, it might prove to be the initial step in a far-reaching policy already decided on. As Mr. Adams wrote the next day to Mr. Seward, it was in London then very generally " affirmed with more and more confidence, that the two governments are meditating some form of intervention in our struggle. The rumor now is that M. de Persigny has come from Paris exclusively for the sake of consult-

ing on that subject. In such a connection, this
unprecedented act of the Prime Minister may
not be without great significance. I have long
thought him hostile at heart, and only checked
by the difference of views in the Cabinet. It
may be that he seeks this irregular method of
precipitating us all into a misunderstanding. If
so, I shall endeavor, whilst guarding the honor
of the government as well as my own, not to
give him any just ground of offense. It strikes
me that he has by his precipitation already put
himself in the wrong, and I hope to be able to
keep him there."

That night Mr. Adams's rest was troubled.
During the evening he drafted a reply; and,
after most careful consideration, next morning
sent it. It was designed to force Lord Palmerston's hand. If the latter's note was written in
a private capacity, it was a personal affront, and
to be resented as such; if as the head of Her
Majesty's government, it was a clear infringe-
ment on the prerogatives of Earl Russell, the
foreign secretary. In which category did Lord
Palmerston propose to place himself? The reply ran as follows : —

LONDON, 12 June, 1862.

THE RIGHT HON. VISCOUNT PALMERSTON, ETC., ETC.

MY LORD, — I have to acknowledge the reception
of your note of yesterday, making certain comments

upon what is stated to be an extract from the London "Times," which I find enclosed.

Although this note is marked confidential and private, I cannot but feel that the fact of my consenting to receive it at all must place me in a most embarrassing situation. In order that I may the better understand my duty, I will ask it as a favor of your Lordship to let me know precisely the light in which I am to consider it, — whether addressed to me in any way officially between us, or purely as a private expression of sentiment between gentlemen.

I have the honor to be, etc.

Immediately after sending the foregoing to the Prime Minister, Mr. Adams wrote to the foreign secretary, requesting an interview. This was at once accorded, and Mr. Adams then handed Lord Palmerston's note to Earl Russell, the only person connected with the government whom he officially knew ; and, remarking that it was "entirely unprecedented," asked to be informed what, if anything, it signified. "His Lordship," Mr. Adams wrote, " said that this was all new to him, and of course he could say nothing until he had seen Lord Palmerston. He hoped I would take no further action until after that."

Two days intervened, when, having heard from Earl Russell in the interim, Lord Palmerston sent the following in answer to the interrogatory contained in Mr. Adams's reply to his previous letter : —

BROCKET, 15 June, 1862.

MY DEAR SIR, — I have many apologies to make to you for not having sooner answered your letter. You are of course at liberty to make such use of my former letter as you may think best.

I was impelled to make known to you my own personal feelings about General Butler's Proclamation, before any notice of it in Parliament should compel me to state my opinion publicly.

I cannot but hope that the President of the United States will at once have given peremptory orders for withdrawing and cancelling the Proclamation.

The Federal Government are making war in order to compel the Southern States to reënter the Union, but the officers and soldiers of the Federal Government, by their conduct not only at New Orleans but as stated in private accounts which I have seen, are implanting undying hatred and sentiments of insatiable revenge in the breasts of those whom the Federal Government want to win back to an equal participation in a free Constitution.

My dear Sir,   Yrs faithfully,
PALMERSTON.

Hon. C. F. ADAMS.

To the foregoing Mr. Adams next day replied as follows : —

LONDON, 16 June, 1862.

MY LORD, — I have to acknowledge the reception

of your Lordship's note of yesterday in reply to mine
of the 12th inst. I have read it with attention, but
I regret to perceive that it inadvertently omits to
favor me with an answer to the question which I
respectfully asked in it.

Under these circumstances the painful embarrassment in which I am involved is in no way relieved.
Although it be true that the confidential character of
the first note is now taken off by your Lordship's consent, I notice that the word "private" is still at-
tached to both.

I trust your Lordship will at once understand how
impossible it is for me, with any self-respect, to entertain as private any communications which contain
what I cannot but consider most offensive imputations
against the Government which I have the honor to
represent at this Court. Imputations, too, based
upon an extract from a London newspaper on which
the most unfavorable construction is placed without
a moment's consideration of any other, or any delay
to understand the action of the Government itself.

I am quite certain that that Government did not
send me to entertain any discussions of this kind
here. It is in my view fully competent to the care
of its own reputation, when attacked either at home
or abroad. But I know it would visit with just indignation upon its servants abroad their tame submission to receive under the seal of privacy any
indignity which it might be the disposition of the
servants of any sovereign however exalted to offer
to it in that form.

Under these circumstances, I feel myself compelled, for my own relief, to the painful necessity of once more respectfully soliciting your Lordship to know whether your first note of the 11th instant was designed in any way officially, or whether it was simply a private communication of sentiment between gentlemen.

I have the honor to be, my Lord,

Yr Obedient Serv't.

The Right Hon. Viscount Palmerston, etc., etc.

Nothing further transpired in the matter until the 19th. Mr. Adams then had a further official interview with the foreign secretary on other business ; after disposing of this, he referred to the Palmerston matter which, he said, kept him embarrassed. He informed Earl Russell that Lord Palmerston " had not answered my second note, and it was now four days. His Lordship said he had written a note to his Lordship, to which no answer had been returned. He would write again. He intimated that the thing was altogether irregular, and could be regarded only as a private proceeding. This was a great relief to me, for I now saw that I had all the advantage. Another admission of his was not unimportant, and that was his belief that the rebellion was drawing to its end, at least in the open field. He referred to the motion of Mr. Lindsay, to be proposed to-morrow in the House of Commons, as one that must come to nothing. All this indicates a propitious change in the temper of the ministry, and a sign that Lord Palmerston has overshot his mark. I think it was the most kindly interview I have had."

Earl Russell's reference to the motion to be made the following day in the House of Commons probably explains the whole purpose of Lord Palmerston. He had contemplated a piece of what can only be designated as "parliamentary claptrap." Taking advantage of the loud and widespread denunciation of Butler and the order. No. 28, he meant to tell an applauding House, in true Palmerstonian vein, how he, the Premier, had given the American minister "a bit of his mind" on that subject. Unfortunately, he found that he had, in his precipitation, "overshot his mark," as Mr. Adams expressed it. On the one hand, put in a false position by the antagonist thus provoked, he had seriously compromised his personal relations with the minister of the United States ; while, on the other hand, he had been reminded, somewhat curtly it may be assumed, by his associate in the ministry, not to meddle in matters within the latter's province. Altogether, the incident was not a subject for self-laudation. It had best be silently dismissed. Mr. Adams, under the circumstances, was of the same opinion, as the following diary entry shows : —

" Friday, 20th June : — Sent a closing note to Lord Palmerston, assuming his note to be a withdrawal of the offensive imputations, and declining this form of correspondence for the future. I also sent the remainder to the government at home. My relief at getting out of the personal question is indescribable. It is not for me to become a cause of quarrel between the two countries at this crisis."

The remainder of the correspondence was as follows : —

Private.

94 PICCADILLY, 19 June, 1862.

MY DEAR SIR, — You repeat in your letter of the 16th a question which our relative positions might, I think, have rendered unnecessary, namely, whether my first letter to you should be considered as a communication between private gentlemen or as bearing an official character.

If I had been merely a private gentleman I should not have deemed myself entitled to address the Minister of the United States upon a public matter ; and if you had been here merely as a private gentleman, I should not, as Head of the Government, have thought it of any use to communicate with you upon any matter which might have a bearing upon the relations between our two countries. So much for the first part of your question.

As to the second part, it is well known that the Secretary of State for Foreign Affairs is the regular official organ for communications between the British Government and the Governments of Foreign States; but it is also well known that it is a part of the functions and may sometimes be the duty of the first Minister of the Crown to communicate with the representatives of Foreign States upon matters which have a bearing upon the relations between Great Britain and those States; and such communications are often as useful as those which take place more formally and officially between the Secretary of State and such representatives.

Now the perusal of General Butler's Proclamation excited in my mind feelings which I was sure would be shared by every honorable man in the United Kingdom, and it required no great sagacity to foresee that those feelings would not be conducive to the maintenance of those mutual sentiments of good-will between our respective countrymen, which are so much to be desired for the interest of both nations.

I conceived, therefore, that I was doing good service to both, by enabling you in such manner as to you might seem best, to let your Government know the impression which General Butler's Proclamation had produced in this country; and I thought it better that you should know that impression privately and confidentially from a person who is in a situation to judge what the feelings of the British nation may be, rather than that you should for the first time learn them in a more public manner.

I at the same time implied a hope that the United
States Government would not allow itself to be represented in such matters by such a person as the
author of that Proclamation. This hope, I am glad
to find, has proved to be well founded; for we have
learnt by Dispatches from Lord Lyons that all power
over the civil inhabitants of New Orleans has been
taken away from General Butler and has been placed
in other hands; and it appears that the new civil Governor has issued a Proclamation which, by promising
security for the *Honor* of the inhabitants of the city,
virtually and I may add *virtuously* annuls the proclamation of General Butler. We have also learnt
with satisfaction that the United States Government
have sent to New Orleans an officer specially instructed to inquire into and to redress certain out-
rageous proceedings of General Butler towards Con-
sular Agents of European Powers.

You are pleased to say in your last letter that I
have cast offensive imputations upon, and have offered
indignity to your government; I entirely deny the
charge; and assert that there is nothing in my letters
which can bear it out. My observations applied to
the Proclamation of General Butler; and the United
States Government have shown by superseding him
in his civil command that they shared the sentiments
which I have expressed, and they have thereby done
themselves honor.

I am, my dear sir, yours faithfully,

PALMERSTON.

The Hon'ble C. F. ADAMS, etc., etc.

5 UPPER PORTLAND PLACE, 20 June, 1862.

MY LORD, — In all the relations which I have had the honor to hold with her Majesty's Ministers, it has been a source of satisfaction to me to be able to say that I have met with nothing but the utmost courtesy both publicly and privately. I trust that on my part I have labored not without success to act in the same spirit. Your Lordship's note to me of the 11th instant was the first instance in which that line appeared to me to be infringed upon.

I now understand by the answer to my note of the 16th, with which your Lordship has favored me, that in writing that first note you do act as First Minister to the Crown, and that you do address me as the Minister of the United States. To that extent the case is then resolved into a public transaction.

But, on the other hand, your Lordship has put upon this apparently public act the special mark of a confidential and a private communication, thereby, so far as it may be in your power, laying an injunction of secrecy upon me, without my consent, which would seem to prevent me from construing your action as that of the Government which you represent.

I now understand your Lordship substantially to withdraw what I cannot but regard as the precipitate implications contained in your first note, so far as they relate to the Government of the United States by denying their existence. I am very happy to be able to come to that conclusion, inasmuch as it discharges me from all further responsibility in the premises. A copy of the correspondence will

be transmitted to the Government of the United
States.

It is however no more than proper to add that the
difficulties in the way of this anomalous form of proceeding seem to me to be so grave, and the disadvantage under which it places those persons who may
be serving as diplomatic representatives of foreign
countries at this Court so serious, as to make it my
painful duty to say to your Lordship that I must
hereafter so long as I remain here in a public capacity decline to entertain any similar correspondence.

I have the honor to be, my Lord,

Y'r very obed't Serv't.

The Right Hon. Viscount Palmerston, etc., etc.

Mr. and Mrs. Adams now discontinued their
customary attendance at the receptions at Cambridge House. The manner in which the wily
and really good-natured Prime Minister, acting
after his wont in such cases through the skillful
coöperation of Lady Palmerston, subsequently,
when he thought desirable so to do, renewed
social relations, was interesting and eminently
characteristic ; but to recount it is beyond the
scope of the present sketch.

CHAPTER XIV

THE COTTON FAMINE

THE European diplomatic situation from an American point of view was, in the years 1861 and 1862, sufficiently delicate without being made more so by the intervention of either the overzealous naval officer or the overbearing Prime Minister. In the Trent affair and in the Butler correspondence both these intruded themselves on Mr. Adams. In no respect was his bed one of roses. These difficulties once disposed of, the problem reduced itself to its natural elements. They were comparatively simple. It was a question whether the efforts of the moneyed, commercial, and aristocratic circles of Great Britain, stimulated by Napoleon III., to precipitate Her Majesty's government into some kind of a participation in the American war, could be held in check until either the moral, anti-slavery sentiment of England could be aroused, or the forces of the Union should assert an indisputable supremacy. To the last result an effective blockade was indispensable ; and of course an effective blockade of the Confederacy implied for Europe the almost complete stoppage of its cotton supply.

The supreme test was, therefore, to be applied at the exact point and in the way foreshadowed by B. C. Yancey to his brother, the Confederate European commissioner, at Montgomery, in February, 1861. He then, it will be remembered, advised W. L. Yancey not to go to Europe as the diplomatic representative of the Confederacy, relying solely on the efficacy of cotton to produce all desired results ; and, while so doing, pointed out that in Great Britain Cobden and Bright would certainly oppose the recognition of "a slaveholders' Confederacy." Cobden and Bright, he asserted, were the leaders of the laboring classes, and to the views and wishes of the laboring classes Her Majesty's government always in the end paid deep respect. Jefferson Davis, on the other hand, had rested the whole foreign policy, and as a result the domestic fate, of the Confederacy, on the absolute commercial, and consequently the political, supremacy of cotton. The demand for it would prove irresistible, and so compel European intervention. Six months was the period allotted, in which it was to assert its supremacy. Mr. Adams was now, as a most interested spectator, to have a chance to observe once more, on a different field and a larger scale, the struggle between Conscience and Cotton.

The parties to the contest on the side of Cotton have already been referred to. They included whatever was most in evidence in Great Britain, — birth, position, wealth, the professions, and Lombard Street. On the side of Conscience the array was meagre. B. C. Yancey had specified Messrs. Cobden and Bright only, as the leaders of the British laboring classes; and Mr. Adams so found them: but, so far as America was concerned, both these gentlemen had to yield priority to William E. Forster, only three months before elected to Parliament as member from Bradford. Throughout the struggle now impending Mr. Forster proved the most earnest, the most courageous, and the most effective friend the United States had among men prominent in English public life.[1] Mr. Adams, when he arrived in London, had absolutely no European acquaintance. Mr. Cobden he had met during one of that gentleman's numerous visits to America, dining in his company at the house of John M. Forbes on Milton Hill, in June two years before. He had

[1] When, seven years later, Mr. Adams was about to return home at the close of his mission, he requested Mr. Forster to accept from him a set of the "Works of John Adams," which he had brought out to England, and "reserved for the person whom I most esteem, as well for his stanch and unvarying support of a policy of good-will to America as for his personal qualities as I have observed them in private intercourse."

then found himself " a little disappointed in Mr. Cobden." He thought him " a man of capacity and information, but without any of the lighter graces and refinements which are only given by a first-class classical education, — a modern Englishman, of the reform school." John Bright he had of course heard of. Mr. Forster he had never either seen or heard of until, on the morning of May 14th, the day after Mr. Adams reached London, that gentleman called on him at his hotel, coming at once to talk " concerning the course of the government, and the mode of meeting " the parliamentary action already initiated by the friends of the Confederacy. " He feared that a proclamation was about to be issued which, by directly acknowledging the slave States as a party establishing its right by force, would tend to complicate affairs very considerably." In the subsequent protracted struggle, stretching over the next thirty months, Mr. Adams was in constant communication with these three gentlemen, and they rendered the United States services of inestimable value. In fact, it is not too much to say that, but for them, intervention in all probability could not have been averted, or the blockade maintained. Yet they were all in the cotton manufacturing interest, representing respectively Rochdale, Birmingham, and Bradford.

Curiously enough also, Mr. Cobden, at that time politically much the most influential of the three, was on broad general principles opposed to blockades. He considered them, like privateering, a survival from a barbarous past, and contended that in future they should, by the common consent of civilized nations, be limited in operation to arsenals, dockyards, and military strongholds.[1] He wanted the United States now to come forward and establish a precedent. So he repeatedly urged on Mr. Adams the voluntary abandonment by the United States of its blockade of the Confederacy, on the ground that it did the Union cause more harm than good. In taking this position he was doubtless influenced by his point of view as a manufacturer, and the representative of cotton-spinners; but the fact that his advice was disregarded and his commercial interests sacrificed never deflected his political action. He remained absolutely true to his fundamental principles. Temporary suffering and pecuniary loss to the contrary notwithstanding, he set human freedom and the elevation of the masses of mankind above the whir of spindles.

The European cotton famine of 1861–63, at the time a very momentous affair, is now for-

[1] Speech at Manchester, October 25, 1862. *Speeches*, 451–454. Morley's *Life of Cobden*, 575.

gotten; yet upon it hung the fate of the American Union. It has already been shown how, in the diplomatic game of the Confederacy, it was the one great card in their hand; the card sure, in their belief, to win: and, as their game grew desperate, the Confederate leaders played that card for all it was worth. Of cotton as a great commercial staple the South enjoyed a practical monopoly, and the crop of 1860, the largest on record, had gone forward in the regular way. The shipments were practically complete when the blockade of April, 1861, was declared. By the spring of 1862, the supply in European ports was running ominously low. Estimated on May 1, 1861, at nearly 1,500,000 bales, on the same date a year later it had become reduced to only 500,000. In Liverpool the stock had shrunk from close upon 1,000,000 to a little more than 360,000 bales, while the price per pound had risen from seven to thirteen pence. The shrinkage, too, was wholly in the American product; and the figures relating to that were most significant as bearing on the growing effectiveness of that blockade, which the Confederate emissaries were in the habit of referring to, with well-simulated contempt, as a mere paper pretense. But in May, 1862, the efficacy of the blockade was read in the cotton quotations; for, during the preceding six

months, the quantity received from America
had been only 11,500 bales, while in the corresponding period of 1860–61 it had been 1,500,-
000, more than one hundredfold the quantity
now received. In Manchester and Liverpool
the distress was already indisputably great, and,
moreover, obviously increasing. One half of
the spindles of Lancashire were idle, and in the
towns of Blackburn and Preston alone over
20,000 persons were dependent on parochial aid.
Of seventy-four mills in Blackburn in the early
days of September, 1862, eighteen were running full time, sixteen short time, and thirty
were entirely closed; the weekly loss of wages
amounted to one thousand pounds. Blackburn
was typical; other manufacturing communities
were in scarcely better plight. The newspapers
were full of pitiable cases of individual destitu-
tion; public meetings were held; the subject
was brought before both Houses of Parliament.
The strain on the Poor Laws was so severe that
their modification was considered; but still the
distress was not so great as had before been
known, nor were the local resources exhausted.
Meanwhile the period of six months, originally
assigned by the Confederate economical authorities as the extreme limit of European endurance,
was already long passed, and some among them
began to entertain doubts. Among these was

William L. Yancey. His observations in Europe had widened his vision ; and when returning home in March, 1862, he reached New Orleans, though in the course of a public speech made in the rotunda of the St. Charles Hotel, he intimated a belief that necessity would shortly compel a European raising of the blockade, he significantly added : "It is an error to say that 'Cotton is King.' It is not. It is a great and influential power in commerce, but not its dictator."

In the manufacturing districts the situation grew rapidly worse, — became in fact well-nigh unendurable. On the one hand, the looms which in 1860 had consumed on an average 40,000 bales of American cotton a week, now might count upon receiving, perhaps, 4000 ; on the other hand, the unprecedented price brought by the staple failed, for reasons elaborately explained, to stimulate the production of India and Egypt to the extent necessary to meet the deficiency. In May, 1862, American cotton ruled at thirteen pence per pound. It continued at about that price until July, when it rose to seventeen pence ; and thence, in August, shot up first to twenty pence, and afterwards, by speculative leaps and bounds, it went up and up, until, at last, on September 3d, it was quoted at half a crown a pound. Such

figures were unheard of; but, even at thirty
pence, the fast vanishing supply on hand at
Liverpool was depleted by shipments to Havre
and New York. The French and American
spinners were in the market at any price. Of
course none but the best equipped mills, turning out the finest fabrics, could manufacture
such costly raw material; for, in view of the
relative prices of the raw material and the coarser
manufactured fabric, it was now much more profitable to hold cotton for a rise than to turn it
into cloth. The situation was thus complicated
by a wild speculative movement, and the mill-
owner, who was fortunate enough to have a stock
of cotton on hand, shut down, because he could
make more as a speculator than as a spinner.
Meanwhile as he grew rich on an unearned
increment, the idle operatives starved. Thus
the inferior mills closed their gates, while those
of the better class ran on reduced time, — two,
three, or four days in the week. By the end
of September, out of 80,000 operatives in five
localities in Lancashire, only 14,000 were working full time, while the remaining 66,000 were
about equally divided between those working
on short time and those wholly idle. In twenty-
four unions 156,000 persons were reported as
receiving parochial relief, and the number was
then increasing at the rate of 6000 a week. As

compared with the same time in the previous
year, the war then not yet being six months
old or the crop of 1860 cotton exhausted, the
situation was deemed very bad ; the number of
applicants for relief had increased nearly three-
fold.   Before the end of October conditions
were appreciably worse.   In the same number
of unions 176,000 people were receiving relief ;
in six consecutive weeks 35,668 persons had
become paupers ; while the wholly unemployed
exceeded those working on full time by nearly
two to one.   At the beginning of 1861, the con-
sumption of cotton in Great Britain was estimated at 50,000 bales per week; at the close of
1862 it had fallen to 20,000 bales, of very inferior weight as well as quality.   The weekly
loss of wages was computed at $100,000.   The
local resources, municipal and voluntary, were
exhausted, or inadequate for the work of relief,
and a call for aid went forth.   The response
was generous.   Not only were large private
subscriptions forthcoming, but collections were
taken up throughout the United Kingdom, while
Australia, Canada, India, and even China sent
in their contributions.   Between the 9th of
June and the 31st of December the Central
Executive Committee having the work of relief
in hand charged itself with no less than £593,-
000 received from these sources.   Meanwhile,

in spite of this magnificent giving, the columns of the press teemed with instances of dire suffering.

In France the situation was no better; indeed, owing to the deeper poverty of the population at the manufacturing centres, some asserted that it was worse. At Rouen, of 50,000 operatives ordinarily engaged in spinning, weaving, dyeing, etc., 30,000 were absolutely without occupation. In the adjoining country districts, out of 65,000 hand-looms, one fifth only were at work. It was estimated that in a single district no less than 130,000 persons, aggregating with those dependent upon them a total of some 300,000 souls, were absolutely destitute, all because of the cotton famine. The editor of the "Revue des Deux Mondes" declared that a sum of twelve millions of francs was required to maintain these people for three months, even supposing that cotton would be forthcoming at the end of that time. The estimate was of course based on the supposition that immediate measures would be taken to raise the blockade.

The extraordinary feature in the situation was, however, the patience of the victims; and the organs of the Confederacy noted with ill-suppressed dismay the absence of "political demonstrations, to urge upon a neglectful government its duty towards its suffering subjects, and to enforce at once the rules of international law and the rights of an injured and innocent population." A distinctly audible whine was perceptible in their utterances. " It is," one of them said, " the great peculiarity of England that the heart of the country is thoroughly religious. The plain issue, then, between the two nations, was therefore naturally overlooked by those whose programme in America was the law of conscience overriding the law of the land ; and the prominence they gave to the slave question was especially directed to the religious public in England. And well has it answered their purpose. To this very hour the great mass of the people have no other terms to express the nature of the conflict. It is to no purpose that argument, fact, and experience have shown the utter indifference of the North to the welfare of the negro ; the complete appreciation by the slaves themselves of the sham friendship offered them ; and, still more, the diabolical preaching of the ministers of God's word, who rely on Sharp's rifles to carry out their doctrines. The emancipation of the negro from the slavery of Mrs. Beecher Stowe's heroes is the one idea of the millions of British who know no better, and do not care to know." In truth, the fundamental sin of the Confederacy had found it out. Literally, and in no way figuratively, the curse

of the bondsman was on it. Rarely, indeed, in
the history of mankind, has there been a more
creditable exhibition of human sympathy, and
what is known as altruism, than that now witnessed in Lancashire. The common folk of
England, Lincoln's " plain people," workless and
hungry, felt what the wealthier class refused to
believe, that the cause at issue in America was
the right of a workingman to his own share in
the results of his toil. That cause, they instinctively knew, was somehow their cause, and
they would not betray it. So no organized cry
went up to break the blockade which, while it
shut up cotton, was throttling slavery.

Yet not for six months, or until the close of
1862, did the distress show signs of abatement.
During those months the weekly returns of the
poor were watched with an anxiety hardly less
great than if they had been the bills of mor-
tality in a time of plague. The quotations of
cotton marked unerringly the severity of the
pressure. Touching thirty pence at the beginning of September, before the close of the year
it ruled five pence lower. A falling market
then put a stop to speculation, and cotton in
store began to find its way to the market. The
staple was no longer hoarded, and the stock on
hand was found to be materially larger than
had been supposed. In a speech made by him

at this time, Mr. Gladstone estimated that of
the entire number of persons concerned in the
manufacture of cotton fabrics, one eighth only
were at full work, three eighths were working
short time, while one half were wholly idle. Of
the unemployed and their families, 250,000 were
paupers, and 190,000 dependent to a greater or
less degree on the relief societies; the entire
charge, public and private, was £44,000 per
week. The loss of wages he computed at eight
millions sterling a year. Nevertheless, natural
causes were bringing about a gradual measure
of relief. Thus early in January, 1863, the
number of dependent persons was reported at
nearly 457,000 ; in April this number had fallen
to 364,000; and it further fell to 256,666 in
June. At the close of the year it was 180,000 ;
and, though the price of American cotton still
ruled at twenty-six pence, the supply of the
staple from all sources in 1863 was more than
twenty-five per cent. greater than in 1862. By
that time, therefore, all danger from a cotton
scarcity was over. The Confederacy had staked
its whole foreign policy on a single card ; and
the card had failed to win. Yet the failure was
due to no sudden contingencies beyond human
prevision. It was, on the contrary, a complete case of miscalculating overconfidence, —
the means were inadequate to the end. The

pressure had been applied to the full extent,
and every condition contributed to its severity.
The warehouses were bursting with manufactured
goods, the overproduction of the previous year,
which alone, through glutted markets, would
have caused a reaction and extreme consequent
dullness in the manufacturing centres. This
natural result was vastly aggravated by the
blockade, which shut off the raw material from
such of the mills as would still have kept running. The speculator, waiting for the last
farthing of the rise, then held the scanty stock
on hand unspun. The other cotton-producing
countries responded but slowly to the increased
demand, and then only with a very inferior
article, the spinning of which spoiled the machinery. Finally the Confederacy held its enemy at arm's length during five times the period
every Southern authority had fixed upon as
ample in which to establish King Cotton's supremacy. Nothing sufficed. An alleged dynasty
was fairly and completely dethroned. It was a
great game, and the leaders of the Confederacy
were skillful gamblers as well as desperate. In
that game, so lightly and confidently entered
upon, they held what proved to be a large card :
but it was not the absolutely decisive card they
thought it ; and, as is not unusual at the gam-
ing table, there proved to be in the hands

engaged other and more than counterbalancing
combinations. The bondsman and nineteenth
century self-sacrifice had not been sufficiently
taken into account. Conscience carried it over
Cotton.

One more feature in this episode remains to
be mentioned; for it was not without its influence on that deep underlying stratum of public
opinion which carried the American cause
through its crisis. By the tales of misery in
patient Lancashire, the sympathies of all Eng-
lish-speaking communities had been deeply
stirred. Contributions poured in from the re-
motest regions of the earth. Within the thirteen months ending June 30, 1863, charity provided nearly two millions sterling for the relief
of distress, in addition to £625,000 derived
from the local poor rates. Of gifts in kind.
clothing and blankets by the bale, coal by the
ton, and flour by the barrel had come in, each
in thousands. On the 6th of December John
Bright wrote to Mr. Sumner: "I see that some
one in the States has proposed to send something
to our aid. If a few cargoes of flour could come,
say 50,000 barrels, as a gift from persons in
your Northern States to the Lancashire workingmen, it would have a prodigious effect in
your favor here." As if in magic response to
the thought, there now came to the Mersey in

quick succession three food-laden " relief-ships " from New York, — the Hope, the George Griswold, and the Achilles. America then had its own burdens to bear. The amounts expended from public and private sources for the distressed of Lancashire during the fifteen months of famine were computed as reaching the amazing sum of $12,000,000, while the aggregate of loss sustained in wages alone was estimated at fifty millions. These were large amounts. They implied much suffering of a varied nature. Yet the entire contribution, great and significant as it was, would not have sufficed to cover the expenditure and waste involved on the side of the Union alone in a single month of the trans-Atlantic struggle then going on; while the sum total whether of human suffering or of pecuniary loss sustained throughout Great Britain because of the cotton famine was less than that endured each fortnight by the combined American people at home and in the field. That in the midst of such stress — carnage, wounds, and devastation — food by the cargo was forthcoming as a gift from those involved in the real agony of war to those for whom that war had occasioned distress, passing though sharp, was neither unnoticed nor barren of results.

CHAPTER XV

THE CRISIS OF RECOGNITION

MEANWHILE, in the month of September, 1862, during the severest stress of the cotton famine, the cause of the Union had in Europe passed its crisis, — that in which the full recognition of the Confederacy, and the consequent raising of the blockade through the armed intervention of Great Britain and France, were most imminent. The secret history of what then took place, giving to the course of events its final shape, has never as yet been fully revealed ; but, though nervously conscious of the imminence of danger, Mr. Adams could only watch the developments, powerless to influence them, except adversely by some act or word on his part a mistake.

All through the summer of 1862 the ministers of Napoleon III. were pressing the British government towards recognition, and the utterances of English public men of note were becoming day by day more outspoken and significant. Of these, some were of little moment ; others meant more. It did not much matter, for instance, that the honest, but ill-balanced and somewhat grotesque, John Arthur Roebuck, when addressing his constituency at Sheffield on August 8th, referred, in the presence of Lord Palmerston, to the United States as "a people that cannot be trusted," and to the Union army as "the scum and refuse of Europe." It was not much more to the purpose that he denounced the North as having "put forward a pretense," and declared that "they are not fighting against slavery," while the whole effort to reunite the country was "an immoral proceeding, totally incapable of success." Finally his appeal to "the noble Lord," then present, "to weigh well the consequences of what he calls 'perfect neutrality,'" would not under ordinary circumstances have carried much weight with the Premier. The same may be said of Mr. Beresford-Hope, who, in his address about the same time to the electors of Stoke-upon-Trent, bewailed the "unhappy infatuation" which had led the North "to venture its all upon the cast for empire, misnamed liberty," and thus to risk "its own moral degradation;" and then pledged himself to vote in Parliament to place "the Confederate States amongst the governments of the world." Nor was Mr. Lindsay of much greater moment when, at Chertsey, he declared "the question practi-

cally settled," and asked: "Is there one man in
a thousand in this country who thinks that the
broken Union can be restored?" — then proceeding to denounce "this wicked, this worthless
war." These men, and men like these, carrying
with them little weight in life, were speedily
forgotten when dead. Not so Mr. Gladstone,
who now at Newcastle, on October 7th, was be-
trayed into utterances which he was afterwards
at much trouble to explain. "There is no
doubt," he said, amid loud cheers from his audience, "that Jefferson Davis and other leaders
of the South have made an army; they are
making, it appears, a navy; and they have made
what is more than either, — they have made a
nation. . . . We may anticipate with certainty
the success of the Southern States so far as regards their separation from the North. I cannot but believe that that event is as certain as
any event yet future and contingent can be."
Mr. Gladstone was then chancellor of the exchequer; the date of the utterance was October
7th. Both time and utterance were significant;
nor did the latter pass unchallenged. In the
Palmerston-Russell ministry Sir George Cornewall Lewis held the position of secretary of
state for war. An able, an upright, and a courageous public man, Sir George Lewis, in direct
response to Mr. Gladstone, and almost imme-

diately afterwards, at a meeting at Hereford, on the 14th, while admitting that, in the general opinion of Great Britain, "the contest would issue in the establishment of the independence of the South," went on to declare that "it could not be said the Southern States of the Union had *de facto* established their independence," or were in a position to be entitled to recognition on any accepted principles of public law. It was not without reason that Mr. Lindsay, referring a few days later to this speech of Sir George Lewis's, remarked that he had "reason to believe the barrier that stopped the way [to a recognition of the Confederacy] is not any of the great powers of Europe, — is not the unanimous cabinet of England, but a section of that cabinet."

Such was the fact; and the danger was extreme. Lord Palmerston had at last made up his mind that the time had come. Accordingly, on September 14th, he wrote to Earl Russell suggesting a joint offer by Great Britain and France of what is in diplomatic parlance known as "good offices." This Earl Russell was now quick to approve. He, too, thought the occasion meet. "I agree with you," he wrote in reply to Palmerston on September 17th, "the time is come for offering mediation to the United States government, with a view to the recognition of

the independence of the Confederates.   I agree
further that, in case of failure, we ought ourselves to recognize the Southern States as an
independent state." He went on to suggest an
early meeting of the cabinet to pass upon the
question. On the 23d the Premier acknowledged the note of the foreign secretary, pro-
nouncing the plan of the latter "excellent,"
adding characteristically : "Of course the offer
would be made to both the contending parties at
the same time; for, though the offer would be
as sure to be accepted by the Southerners as
was the proposal of the Prince of Wales to the
Danish Princess, yet, in the one case as the
other, there are certain forms which it is decent
and proper to go through. . . . Might it not be
well to ask Russia to join England and France
in the offer of mediation ? . . . We should be
better without her, because she would be too
favorable to the North ; but, on the other hand,
her participation in the offer might render the
North more willing to accept it." The middle
of October was the time he suggested for action.
Naturally, the two heads of the ministry took it
for granted that their concurrence would control
its action. It proved otherwise; and hence the
great significance of Sir George Lewis's Hereford utterances in response to those of Mr. Gladstone. The difference was pronounced ; the

THE CRISIS OF RECOGNITION   283

several ministers were admitting the public into
their confidence. Lord Russell, however, per-
severed. A confidential memorandum, outlin-
ing the proposed policy, went out; and a call
was issued for a cabinet meeting on October
23d, for its consideration. The authority of the
two chieftains to the contrary notwithstanding,
the division of opinion foreshadowed by the
remarks of Sir George Lewis proved so serious
that the meeting was not held. The Duke of
Argyll and Mr. Milner Gibson were the two
most pronounced "Americans" in the cabinet;
and they received a measured support from Mr.
C. P. Villiers and Sir George Lewis. The Confederate emissaries in London had access to excellent sources of information; far better, indeed, than those at the command of Mr. Adams.
Their organ, a little later, thus referred to the
attitude of the government: "On matters of
public policy the cabinet must, in some sense,
think alike; there must be a cabinet opinion.
. . . Now, on many questions, and especially on
the American question, there prevails the greatest disunion of feeling among the members of
the cabinet. Some of them sympathize strongly
with the Confederate States. . . . Others are
devoted to the North. Others, and notably the
Prime Minister, care nothing for either party.
. . . They do not care to involve themselves in

any difficulty foreign or domestic, by siding with
the Confederates; and their only wish is to let
the matter alone. At present this party practically determines the action, or rather inaction,
of the cabinet; which is quite aware that any
attempt to have an opinion or lay down a policy
in regard to American affairs must be fatal to
the very pretense of accord, and to its official
existence. Therefore the ministry does nothing,
because nothing is the only thing which the different sections can agree to do." The question,
so far as Great Britain was concerned, thus
from this time forth became one of internal
politics, social divisions, and parliamentary majorities.

Meanwhile, following indications closely, Mr.
Adams had in July anticipated some such action
of the British and French governments as being
then in contemplation; not yet matured, he felt
sure it was in mind. "Mischief to us in some
shape," he wrote, "will only be averted by the
favor of Divine providence on our own efforts.
I wrote a full dispatch to Mr. Seward." In
that dispatch he asked for further and explicit
instructions as to the course he should pursue,
if approached by Earl Russell with a tender of
"good offices." The response reached him about
the middle of August, a few days only after Mr.
Roebuck had orated at Sheffield before his con-

stituency and the Prime Minister. So far as explicitness was concerned, the instructions now received were in no way deficient. Carrying the standard entrusted to him high and with a firm hand, the secretary bore himself in a way of which his country had cause to be proud. The paper read in part as follows : —

" If the British government shall in any way approach you directly or indirectly with propositions which assume or contemplate an appeal to the President on the subject of our internal affairs, whether it seem to imply a purpose to dictate, or to mediate, or to advise, or even to solicit or persuade, you will answer that you are forbidden to debate, to hear, or in any way receive, entertain, or transmit any communication of the kind. You will make the same answer whether the proposition comes from the British government alone or from that government in combination with any other power.

" If you are asked an opinion what reception the President would give to such a proposition, if made here, you will reply that you are not instructed, but you have no reason for supposing that it would be entertained.

" If contrary to our expectations the British government, either alone or in combination with any other government, should acknowledge the insurgents, while you are remaining without further instructions from this government concerning that event, you will immediately suspend the exercise of your functions, and give notice of that suspension to Earl Russell and to this department. If the British government make any act or declaration of war against the United States, you will desist from your functions, ask a passport, and return without delay to this capital. I have now in behalf of the United States and by the authority of their chief executive magistrate performed an important duty. Its possible consequences have been weighed, and its solemnity is therefore felt and freely acknowledged. This duty has brought us to meet and confront the danger of a war with Great Britain and other states allied with the insurgents who are in arms for the overthrow of the American Union. You will perceive that we have approached the contemplation of that crisis with the caution which great reluctance has inspired. But I trust that you will also have perceived that the crisis has not appalled us."

Ignorant of the September correspondence between the Prime Minister and the foreign secretary, but with this letter of instructions in his desk, Mr. Adams had on October 8th read the report of Mr. Gladstone's Newcastle speech. "If he," Mr. Adams wrote, "be any exponent at all of the views of the cabinet, then is my term likely to be very short." The next day came more " indications ; " and he added: "We are now passing through the very crisis of our fate. I have had thoughts of seeking a conference with Lord Russell, to ask an explanation of Mr. Gladstone's position ; but, on reflection, I think I shall let a few days at least pass, and then perhaps sound matters incidentally." Making a visit at this time to the Forsters, than whom, he wrote, " no persons in England have inspired me with more respect and regard," Mr. Adams communicated to his host "in confidence the substance of my instructions. He thought I ought to make the government aware of them, before they committed themselves." A few days later came the speech of Sir George Lewis, and Mr. Adams, still anxiously noting the situation, wrote : " I think [Gladstone] overshot the mark ; " but he rightly regarded the cabinet meeting then called for the 23d as being decisive of the policy now to be pursued. " I so wrote to the government to-day."

Exactly what passed in anticipation of this truly crucial cabinet meeting has remained a state secret. The Palmerston-Russell ministry from the beginning held office by an uncertain tenure ; it held it, indeed, through the acquiescence and silent support of a large element in

the ranks of the Conservatives, who recognized
in the Prime Minister one of themselves. He
had outlived opposition, and was now accepted
as a species of party compromise. He would
remain in office as long as he lived, provided
always he presented no strong issue, whether
internal or foreign. He understood the situation perfectly, and held parliamentary reform
in abeyance, on the one hand, while, on the
other, he did not countenance intervention.
The moral sentiment of Great Britain on the
issue of African slavery was not yet fully
aroused, and from all other sides the pressure
for recognition and the raising of the blockade
was strong. Lord Palmerston, as his correspondence with Earl Russell shows, was quite ready
to yield to the pressure, had it not involved a
break. But it so chanced that it did involve a
break; and the ministerial ranks were not strong
enough to stand a break. Sir George Lewis's
utterances, backed by Cobden, Bright, and
Forster, were very ominous. Probably considerations prevailed then similar to those which two
years later led the same two chieftains to a reluctant acquiescence in a like cautious policy
in the Schleswig-Holstein imbroglio. "As to
cabinets," Lord Palmerston then wrote to Earl
Russell, "if we had colleagues like those who
sat in Pitt's cabinet, you and I might have our

own way on most things; but when, as is now
the case, able men fill every department, such
men will have opinions, and hold to them."
However this may have been, Mr. Adams on
the afternoon of October 23d, the date fixed for
the canceled cabinet meeting, had an official
interview with the foreign secretary, at which,
after disposing of some matters of nominal
importance, he got to the " real object in
the interview."   Referring to the departure of
Lord Lyons from London for Washington, he
having in reality been detained by the government until its American policy had been decided upon, " I expressed," Mr. Adams wrote,
" the hope that he might be going out for a long
time.   I had, indeed, been made of late quite
fearful that it would be otherwise.   If I had entirely trusted to the construction given by the
public to a late speech, I should have begun to
think of packing my carpet-bag and trunks.
His Lordship at once embraced the allusion ;
and, whilst endeavoring to excuse Mr. Gladstone, in fact admitted that his act had been
regretted by Lord Palmerston and the other
cabinet officers."

Unknowingly, and with the narrowest possible margin of safety, the crisis had been passed.
Three weeks later, Mr. Adams made the following diary entry : —

" Friday, 14th November, 1862 : — Some excitement here by the publication of a letter of M. Drouyn de Lhuys, the new minister of foreign affairs in Paris, proposing to the courts of England and Russia a joint offer of mediation in the American struggle, to begin with an armistice of six months. This letter is dated on the 15th of last month, so that it has probably been already answered by both governments. The general impression here is that it has been declined. I have a letter from Mr. Dayton today, giving the substance of his conference with M. Drouyn de Lhuys, and reporting him as saying that in case of the other powers declining nothing would be done. It is nevertheless a strange move."

CHAPTER XVI

THE EMANCIPATION PROCLAMATION

In the mean time one of the great events of the century had taken place in America. On September 22d, while the British Prime Minister and foreign secretary were corresponding with a view to the immediate recognition of the "slaveholders' Confederacy," the Emancipation Proclamation of President Lincoln had been made public. Slavery as an issue in the struggle then going on could no longer be denied or ignored. It was there; and it was there to stay. The knot was cut; the shackles were knocked off.

The ultimate influence of this epochal move in Europe, especially in Great Britain, was immense; but, at the moment, it seemed to excite only astonishment, mingled with scorn and horror. It was not even taken seriously. Indeed, a reprint of the editorials of the leading English papers of that date would now be a literary curiosity, as well as a most useful *vade mecum* for the race of ready, editorial writers. An instructive memorial of human fallibility, it might preserve from many future pitfalls. Not a single one of the London journals of 1862 rose to an equality with the occasion. An event occurred second in importance to few in the development of mankind ; the knell of human bondage was sounded, and one more relic of barbarism ceased : yet, having eyes they saw not, having ears they did not hear. Purblind and deaf, they only canted and caviled. The tone varied from that of weak apology in the friendly " News," to that of bitter denunciation in the hostile " Post." The " Times " characterized the Proclamation as " a very sad document," which the South would " answer with a hiss of scorn." It was instructive merely as " proof of the hopelessness and recklessness " of those responsible for it ; while, as an act of policy, it " is, if possible, more contemptible than it is wicked." The " Morning Herald " pronounced it " an act of high-handed usurpation," with " no legal force whatever." . . . Had " Mr. Davis himself directed the course of his rival, we do not think he could have dictated a measure more likely to divide the North and to unite the border States firmly with the South." The " Post " remarked : " It is scarcely possible to treat seriously of this singular manifesto. If not genuine, the composition would be entitled to no little praise as a piece of matchless irony." The " Standard " pronounced the whole thing a " sham " intended " to deceive England and Europe " — " the wretched makeshift of a pettifogging lawyer." The " Daily Telegraph " accused President Lincoln and his advisers of having " fallen back upon the most extravagant yet most commonplace ' dodges ' of the faction that placed them in power." Meanwhile, the more kindly disposed " News " pronounced the step thus taken " feeble and halting," and gave as its opinion that the Proclamation had not " the importance which some persons in England are disposed to attach to it." These extracts are all from the issues of the leading London journals of a single day (October 7, 1862) ; but they sufficiently illustrate the tone of thought and the state of feeling in which Mr. Adams was then compelled to draw the breath of life. It was bitterly, aggressively, vindictively hostile.

It was another case of people using the same speech, and yet talking in different tongues. Even when he honestly wished so to do, the Englishman could not understand America, or things American ; and now he did not wish to. He had read General Butler's order No. 28, as he would have read a similar order governing the action of an English soldiery in India or a French soldiery in Spain. It was an invitation

to outrage. So now he saw in the Proclamation
either mere emptiness, or an incitement to servile insurrection. If not, as he believed and
hoped, an idle menace, it meant a repetition
of the horrors of the Sepoy mutiny, then only
four years gone and fresh in English memory,
or a renewal on an infinitely larger scale of the
unforgettable atrocities of St. Domingo. That
by any possibility it should prove in the result
what it actually did prove, never at the time
dawned on the average cockney brain ; nor, indeed, did the possessors of that brain welcome
the idea when at last it forced its way there.

It is, in fact, difficult now to realize the language used in 1862–63 towards the men of the
North by Englishmen who professed the most
intimate knowledge of them. For instance, a
Mr. Cowell, who had at one time lived for several years in the United States as the representative of no less an institution than the Bank of
England, but was now residing in apparent retirement at Cannes, in a pamphlet published
about this time, in reference to " points in the
Yankee national character which ought to be
borne in mind," thus delivered himself : " The
narrow, fanatical, and originally sincere puri-
tanism of their ancestors has, in the course of
six generations, degenerated into that amalgam
of hypocrisy, cruelty, falsehood, unconsciousness

of the faintest sentiments of self-respect, coarseness of self-assertion, insensibility to the opinions of others, utter callousness to right, barbarous delight in wrong, and thoroughly moral ruffianism, which is now fully revealed to the world as the genuine Yankee nature ; and of which Butler, Seward, etc., who are pure representative Yankees, afford such finished examples." And it was from the government of a community of this character that the Emancipation Proclamation of 1862 was, among those comprising certain influential classes of British society, supposed to have emanated.

To Mr. Adams, the adoption of the policy set forth in the Proclamation seemed " a mere question of time." It was emancipation through martial law ; that solution of the trouble which had been predicted by his father time and again in Congress a quarter of a century before : and now, when at last it came, as he observed the effect of its announcement on his British surroundings, his feelings found expression in that stern Puritan speech, characteristic of the stock and of the man. Communing, after his wont with himself, he wrote in his diary : " I do not pretend to peer into the future ; but this terrible series of calamities appears as a just judgment upon the country for having paltered with the evil so long. God have mercy on us, miserable offenders ! "

For a time after the news of the Proclamation reached Europe, the friends of the Confederacy seemed to have exclusive control of both press and platform. Examples of journalistic utterance have been given ; those of the average gentleman lecturer and member of Parliament were scarcely more discreet. Of the former class, Mr. Beresford-Hope energetically characterized the Proclamation as " this hideous outburst of weak yet demoniacal spite," and " the most unparalleled last card ever played by a reckless gambler." Of the latter class, Mr. Lindsay hastened to declare that : — " Instead of being a humane proclamation, it was, in fact, a specimen of the most horrible barbarity, and a more terrible proclamation than had ever been issued in any part of the world." A Mr. Peacocke, member from North Essex, towards the close of October, at a great Conservative demonstration at Colchester, went even further than Mr. Lindsay, declaring of the Proclamation that, if it " was worth anything more than the paper on which it was inscribed, and if the four millions of blacks were really to be emancipated on January 1st, then we should be prepared to witness a carnage so bloody that even the horrors of the Jacquerie and the massacres of Cawnpore would wax pale in comparison. . . . The emancipation proclamation, even if it had been in the interest of the negro, would have been a political crime; but when we reflect that it was put forth, not in the interest of the negro or of civilization, but that it was merely a vindictive measure of spite and retaliation upon nine millions of whites struggling for their independence, it was one of the most devilish acts of fiendish malignity which the wickedness of man could ever have conceived." The distress of these gentlemen should have been greatly alleviated when, at about this time, the special correspondent of the " Times," writing from the Confederacy on the effect of the Proclamation, but exercising the common capacity for self-deception to another end, gravely assured the British public that, — " Again and again the slaves have fled from the Yankee army into the swamp to escape a compulsory freedom; and there is abundant evidence that if a being so morally weak and nerveless as the African could be made to fight for anything, he would fight for slavery much rather than for liberty." [1]

A few days later, with characteristic bluntness, Mr. Bright said in a letter, " I applaud the proclamation;" and for the United States to emerge from the contest leaving " the slave still a slave will expose [it] to the contempt of the civilized world." The Confederate organ in

[1] London *Times*, December 1, 1862.

London, commenting on this letter, spoke with measurable accuracy when it announced in reply that " every organ of a considerable party " pronounced the edict " infamous," and that a similar opinion of it was entertained by " every educated and nearly every uneducated Englishman."

But, as the weeks went on they at last brought with them significant indications of a deep undercurrent of opposing sentiment; and on January 2, 1863, a gentleman from Manchester — the great city of Lancashire, and the centre of the cotton famine, then at its worst — called on Mr. Adams, bringing him a copy of an address to the President from a meeting of workingmen held on the last day of the previous year. " I was glad to seize the occasion to express my satisfaction with it," wrote Mr. Adams. " It was quite a strong manifestation of good feeling. There certainly is much sympathy felt in the lower classes, but little or none by the upper." On the 16th a committee called to present the resolutions of the British Emancipation Society on the Proclamation, which had been confirmed as finally operative by the mails of three days before. Even then, so dubious was the chairman of the organization as to the effect of the step on public opinion, that he evinced a strong disposition to defer action.

But, wrote Mr. Adams, " later in the day, [when] the committee came, it proved so numerous and respectable that I heard no more of Mr. Evans's scruple. He, as chairman, presented to me the resolutions; after which Mr. P. A. Taylor, member of Parliament from Leicester, the Rev. Baptist Noel, Rev. Newman Hall, and Mr. Jacob Bright made some remarks, all expressive of earnest sympathy with America in the present struggle. There can be little doubt that now is the time to strike the popular heart here; and the effect may be to checkmate the movement of the aristocracy." In other words, Mr. Adams was now working on the very elements in Great Britain which, two years before at Montgomery, B. C. Yancey had pointed out to his brother as fatal to the chances for recognition of " a slaveholders' Confederacy."

Soon the addresses began to pour into the Legation in a steady and ever-swelling stream. " It is clear," wrote Mr. Adams, " that the current is now setting strongly with us among the body of the people. This may be quite useful on the approach of the session of Parliament; " or, as B. C. Yancey had expressed it: " Suffrage had not then been enlarged to reach the laboring classes, but the government was scarcely less respectful of their wishes on that account." On January 29th a meeting was held in Exeter

Hall, "reported as one of the most extraordinary ever made in London," proving to Mr. Adams "conclusively the spirit of the middle classes here as well as elsewhere." For the first time since he had been in England, he had the cheering consciousness of sympathy and support. " It will not change the temper of the higher classes," he wrote, "but it will do something to moderate the manifestation of it." Four days later the delegation from the Exeter Hall meeting called to present the address. "I received them," wrote Mr. Adams, " in my dining-room, which was very full. The body seemed to be clergy; but all looked substantial and respectable. The chairman made some remarks explanatory of the difficulties previously in the way of a movement of this kind. Then came remarks from different speakers, some very good, and others quite flat; [but] there was no mistaking the tone, which was strong and hearty in sympathy with us. I think there can be little doubt that the popular current now sets in our favor. They left me with hearty shakes of the hand, that marked the existence of an active feeling at bottom. It was not the lukewarmness and indifference of the aristocracy, but the genuine English heartiness of good-will."

The organ of the Prime Minister at this time

editorially referred to the Exeter Hall meeting
as " a great disgrace to the Christian religion,
and an egregious blunder as a step towards
emancipation." [1] In so doing, it voiced the sentiments of the ruling class. Cobden voiced
those of the laboring classes ; and Cobden now
wrote to Sumner : — " I know nothing in my
political experience so striking, as a display of
spontaneous public action, as that of the vast
gathering at Exeter Hall, when, without one
attraction in the form of a popular orator, the
vast building, its minor rooms and passages, and
the streets adjoining, were crowded with an
enthusiastic audience. That meeting has had a
powerful effect on our newspapers and politicians. It has closed the mouths of those who
have been advocating the side of the South.
And I now write to assure you that any un-
friendly act on the part of our government —
no matter which of our aristocratic parties is in
power — towards your cause is not to be apprehended. If an attempt were made by the government in any way to commit us to the South,
a spirit would be instantly aroused which would
drive that government from power." The tribune of the British people and the organ of the
Prime Minister of England thus saw the thing
from different points of view. The result shortly

[1] The *Morning Post*, Saturday, 31st January, 1863.

showed which was right. From this time on nothing but an outburst of patriotic, warlike passion, provoked by some untoward incident like that of the Trent, could have sufficed to master the rising voice of English conscience. It was the final demonstration of the soundness of the advice his brother gave Mr. Yancey, two years before, so often already alluded to : — " Unless the (Confederate) government should send a Commission (to Europe) authorized to offer commercial advantages so liberal that the Exeter Hall influence could not withstand them, the British government, however well disposed, would not venture to run counter to the anti-slavery feeling by recognition of the Confederate States." Cobden and Bright, B. C. Yancey had added, were the leaders of the laboring classes ; and " Cobden and Bright would oppose the recognition of a slaveholders' Confederacy." [1]

Parliament assembled February 5th, only two days after the Exeter Hall delegation had presented the address to Mr. Adams, and six days before Mr. Cobden wrote to Mr. Sumner, setting forth its significance. " The most marked indication," wrote Mr. Adams, " respecting American affairs, was the course of Lord Derby and Mr. D'Israeli [in] the debate on the address, which decidedly discouraged movement. On

[1] *Life and Times of W. L. Yancey*, 588, 589.

their minds the effect of the President's proclamation on public sentiment here has not been
lost." Nor had its effect on that sentiment
been lost on the "Times." The utterances of
the "Thunderer" on the contrary were now
more than ever significant, and expressive of
the views of those among whom it circulated.
Read in the light of forty years after, they have
an interest still : —

"Though there is little homage to principle
in the President's proclamation, any attempt on
the part of the American government, however
tardily, reluctantly, and partially made, to
emancipate any portion of the negro race, must
have an effect on the opinion of mankind, and
tend to what we have never doubted would in
some way or other be the final result of this
war, the abolition of slavery. But our exultation is by no means without misgivings. . . .
If the blacks are to obtain the freedom he promises them, it must be by their own hands.
They must rise upon a more numerous, more intelligent, better-armed, and braver community
of whites, and exterminate them, their wives
and children, by fire and sword. The President
of the United States may summon them to this
act, but he is powerless to assist them in its execution. Nay, this is the very reason why they
are summoned. . . . Mr. Lincoln bases his act

on military necessity, and invokes the considerate judgment of mankind and the judgment of
Almighty God.   He has characterized his own
act; mankind will be slow to believe that an
act avowedly the result of military considerations has been dictated by a sincere desire for
the benefit of those who, under the semblance
of emancipation, are thus marked out for destruction, and He who made man in His own
image can scarcely, we may presume to think,
look with approbation on a measure which, under the pretense of emancipation, intends to reduce the South to the frightful condition of St.
Domingo. . . . In the midst of violent party
divisions, in ostentatious contempt of the Constitution, with the most signal ill success in war,
he is persisting in the attempt to conquer a nation, to escape whose victorious arms is the only
triumph which his generals seem capable of
gaining.   Every consideration of patriotism and
policy calls upon him to put an end to the hopeless contest, but he considers the ruin is not
deep enough, and so he calls to his aid the ex-
ecrable expedient of a servile insurrection.
Egypt is destroyed ; but his heart is hardened,
and he will not let the people go."

And thus the slave-owners, and not the slaves,
were in London, in the early days of 1863,
likened unto the children of Israel escaping

from the land of bondage; while Abraham Lincoln figured, somewhat incongruously, as the great and only American Pharaoh! As he read day by day these effusions of vindictive cant and simulated piety, it is small matter for surprise that, restrained in expression as he habitually was, Mr. Adams impatiently broke out in his diary: "Thus it is that the utter hollowness of the former indignation against America for upholding slavery is completely exposed. The motives of that censure, as for the present emotion, are jealousy, fear, and hatred. It is impossible for me to express the contempt I feel for a nation which exhibits itself to the world and posterity in this guise. It is a complete forfeiture of the old reputation for manliness and honesty."

CHAPTER XVII

THE ALABAMA AND THE "LAIRD RAMS"

CAPTAIN JAMES H. BULLOCH, formerly of
the United States navy, but later the duly accredited naval agent in Europe of the Confederacy, had at this time long been busy negotiating with the shipbuilders and shipowners of
Great Britain, and sending out to the Confederate ports large consignments of munitions of
war. Coming direct from Montgomery, he had
reached Liverpool on June 4, 1861. Through
his indefatigable efforts, the keel of the Oreto,
afterwards famous as the Florida, had, within a
month of his arrival, been laid; and, on August
1st following, he closed a contract with the
Messrs. Laird, large Liverpool shipwrights, for
the construction of the Alabama, or "290," as
she was called, that number simply designating
her order among the vessels constructed in the
Laird yards at Birkenhead. The Alabama was
not launched until the 15th of May, 1862. She
was then put in course of rapid preparation for
sea.

The purpose for which the "290" was de-

signed was at Liverpool matter of common town
talk. She was to be a Confederate commerce-
destroyer. The British Foreign Enlistment Act
had been examined by counsel on behalf of the
Confederate agent, and its provisions riddled.
There was no question whatever that the act
was designed to provide against the fitting out
of warlike expeditions in the ports of Great
Britain, and especially to prevent those ports
being made the base of naval operations against
friendly powers ; or, in the language of the en-
actment, "the fitting out, equipping, and arming
of vessels for warlike operations." Counsel
learned in the law now, however, advised that
there was nothing in the act which made illegal
the building of a warship as one operation ;
and nothing which prevented the purchase of
the arms and munitions to equip such vessel,
when built, as another operation. But the two
must be kept distinctly separate. If, then, having been thus kept separate, they subsequently
came together, this combination constituted no
violation of the law, provided the result — a
man-of-war, armed, equipped, and in every way
ready for service — was brought about in some
foreign waters more than one marine league
from the British coast. Subsequently this construction of the statute was gravely propounded
in Parliament by ministers and law repre-

sentatives of the crown, and, at last, formally laid down for the guidance of juries by
the Lord Chief Baron of the Court of Exchequer.
Obviously, the law and its administration were
together brought into contempt ; and any government official, from the Prime Minister down,
who might endeavor to enforce the manifest intent of the statute, or honestly to regard the
international obligations of the country, must do
so at his peril, and with a distinct understanding that any jury before which the case might
be brought would find heavy damages against
him. The construction of vessels, built avowedly
for war purpose, and designed as Confederate
commerce-destroyers, seemed, therefore, likely
to prove an industry at once safe and lucrative.
If a delivery to the party ordering them was
prevented, the government would have to in-
demnify every one.

Naturally, this extremely technical and thoroughly characteristic construction of the Neutrality Act failed to commend itself to the representatives of the United States in Great Britain.
That it was at the time highly acceptable to the
Parliament, the press, and the moneyed and commercial classes of that country was apparent. It
was looked upon also as an exceeding good joke.
Indeed, it had its side of broad humor. The passengers on English packets, which a little later

fell in with the Alabama, cheered her vociferously and to the echo. Was she not a Mersey-built ship, armed with English guns, manned by British sailors? She was destroying the commerce of the United States; and yet in her construction and equipment, judge, counsel, and ministers were all agreed that no law had been violated, nor had any disregard been shown to Her Majesty's Proclamation of Neutrality. The Yankee had on this occasion at least been fairly outwitted. None the less, while the shipbuilders, the lawyers, and the government officials were busy over the preliminaries of this elaborate international burlesque, and before the final perpetration of the joke, the gradual completion of the " 290 " was watched with sleepless eyes by Mr. Dudley, the very efficient United States consul at Liverpool, and Mr. Adams was kept fully advised as to her state of preparation. He, in his turn, bombarded the Foreign Office with depositions and other evidence in regard to her. These Her Majesty's government had under constant consideration; but they were uniformly advised by the crown lawyers that a sufficient case against the vessel had not been made out.

Captain Bulloch, meanwhile, was fully informed as to the movements of Mr. Dudley and Mr. Adams, and prepared to balk them. The crew of the Enrica, as the " 290 " was called, was

engaged, but not all shipped, lest their number and indiscreet talk should attract notice,
furnishing further evidence against her. She
was to meet her consort, carrying her munitions and armament, including an additional
supply of coal, in the Azores, at the Bay of
Praya. No precautions calculated to evade the
provisions of law had been omitted.

In July, 1862, heavy military reverses both in
Virginia and Tennessee had followed the Union
successes of the spring of that year, and the
spirits of those sympathizing with the Confederates, a vast majority of the English people, had
so rallied that Mr. Adams well-nigh despaired
of being able much longer to counteract the
hostile influences. "There is not," he despond-
ingly wrote, "much disguise now in the temper
of the authorities." As to the government
"authorities" at Liverpool, there was certainly
no "disguise," or pretense even of "disguise,"
so far as their individual sympathies were concerned. They were pronounced in their Confederate leanings ; though, as matter of course,
the usual protestations were made as respects the
impartial performance of what in such cases is
usually denominated "duty." Unfortunately, it
was not a question of common town talk or public notoriety ; for probably not one human being
in Liverpool who had given any attention to the

matter questioned for an instant that the war-
vessels then under forced construction at Birkenhead were intended for the service of the Confederacy. On this head the collector of the
port, Mr. S. Price Edwards, unquestionably
entertained as little doubt as either the Laird
Brothers or Captain Bulloch. When, however,
it came to evidence of the fact, the man willfully
shut his eyes, and would not be convinced by
anything possible to obtain. The imputation
and strong circumstance which led directly to
the door of proof were nothing to Mr. Edwards;
he wanted ocular demonstration, and that of
course Mr. Dudley could not furnish. It was
afterwards suggested by high authority that the
American agents should have then gone directly
to the Messrs. Laird, and asked them frankly if
they did not propose to violate the law; and, in
such case, " the high character of these gentlemen would doubtless have insured either a refusal to answer or a truthful answer." [1] This extremely ingenuous method of procedure probably
never occurred to Consul Dudley; and, on his
side, the collector would seem to have deemed
nothing short of the open admission of a criminal intent by the parties in interest as sufficient.
Imputations of corruption were subsequently

[1] Opinion of Sir Alexander Cockburn in the Geneva arbitration. *Papers Relating to the Treaty of Washington*, iv. 453.

current, involving Mr. Edwards; and it was
even whispered that he was the "private but
most reliable source" from which the Confederate agents received the confidential intimations which enabled the Alabama to escape detention.   There is no evidence whatever that
such was the case.   On the contrary, Mr. Collector Edwards would appear to have been simply
an honest but obtuse man, of decided Confederate proclivities, who thought to protect himself against official responsibility by insisting
on the impossible.   It is doubtful, however,
whether even he could have had the effrontery
to propose to the American consul the unique
method of securing evidence afterwards suggested by Lord Chief Justice Cockburn. While
the statute law of the realm was unquestionably
being turned into a manifest farce, everything
was done gravely and in an orderly way; and it
would have been manifestly unbecoming to in-
ject into the performance at its then stage
broad practical jokes of a distinctly side-split-
ting character.

It is not necessary here to enter into a detailed
account of what now took place, and the efforts,
strenuous and sustained, put forth by Mr. Adams
to induce the British government to respect its
own laws and its treaty obligations. The ground
has since that time been most thoroughly trav-

ersed, and the printed matter relating to it amounts to a literature in itself. It is sufficient to say that not only did British ministries representing both parties in the state subsequently concede that the course then pursued by those responsible for the government could not be justified, but Earl Russell himself within a year, and while still foreign secretary, admitted to Mr. Adams that the case of the Alabama was a "scandal," and, " in some degree, a reproach " to the laws of Great Britain. Finally, while as a history the work of James F. Rhodes is marked by a sobriety of tone not less commendable than the good temper and thoroughness of research throughout evinced in it, yet when he came to making a summary of the performances connected with this incident, that grave author felt moved to remark that, while to do justice to them " completely baffles the descriptive pen of the historian," they would have been most useful and suggestive "to the writer of an opera-bouffe libretto, or to Dickens for his account of the Circumlocution Office." [1]

It is sufficient here to say that after representation on representation, accompanied by endless documents and affidavits, designed to prove that which every one knew, had been for months forwarded to the Foreign Office, and there pro-

[1] *History of the United States*, iv. 88.

nounced defective or inadequate, the American minister on July 23d " addressed another communication to Lord Russell, so that the refusal to act may be made as marked as possible." Two days earlier, on the 21st, Collector Edwards had by letter notified the Commissioners of Customs at London that " the ship appears to be ready for sea, and may leave at any hour she pleases." Directly appealed to by the American consul, the Commissioners of Customs, on the 23d, with this letter of their Liverpool subordinate before them, declined to act. This was on Wednesday. Before the close of the week the papers from the Foreign Office relating to the case, covering " evidence strong and conclusive " in the words of Mr. Adams, and backed by " a still stronger opinion " of leading English counsel, had, in the bandying process, reached the table of the Queen's advocate, Sir John Harding. He just then broke down from nervous tension, and thereafter became hopelessly insane. His wife, anxious to conceal from the world knowledge of her husband's condition, allowed the package to lie undisturbed on his desk for three days, — days which entailed the destruction of the American merchant marine ; and it was on the first of these days, Saturday, July 26, 1862, that Captain Bulloch, at Liverpool, " received information from a private but most reliable source that it

would not be safe to leave the ship at Liverpool
another forty-eight hours." On the following
Monday accordingly the Alabama, alias the
" 290," alias the " Enrica," was taken out of
dock, and, under pretense of making an additional
trial trip, steamed, dressed in flags, down the
Mersey, with a small party of guests on board.
It is needless to say she did not return. The
party of guests were brought back on a tug,
and the Enrica, now fully manned, was, on the
31st, off the north coast of Ireland, headed sea-
ward in heavy weather. A grave international
issue had been raised, destined to endure and
be discussed throughout the next ten years.

Shortly before the " 290," subsequently world-
renowned as the Alabama, thus evaded the extremely sluggish crown officials, instructions had
reached Captain Bulloch from the Confederate
naval department forthwith to contract for two
ironclad ships of war, of the most formidable
description then built; and the sum of one mil-
lion dollars in cash had been placed at his disposal to be used in payment for the same. This
sum, it was promised, should, later on, be increased by an equal amount. Contracts were
at once closed with the firm of Laird Brothers,
and by the middle of July, 1862, work on both
ships had fairly begun. Fully equipped for sea,
but without batteries or munitions of war, these

ships were to cost £93,750 each, and they were
to be ready, the one of them in March and the
other in May, 1863. Naval architecture at that
time was developing rapidly. Five years later,
in July, 1867, Mr. Adams attended the great
naval review at Portsmouth in honor of the
Sultan of Turkey, and, among the ironclad, tur-
reted leviathans there arrayed, one of the two
famous "Laird rams" was pointed out to him.
Her day was already gone; "as I looked on
the little mean thing," he wrote, "I could not
help a doubt whether she was really worthy of
all the anxiety she had cost us." None the less,
built on the most approved models of that time,
and designed to be equipped with formidable
batteries and every modern appliance of war,
the Laird rams were naval creations with which
neither steam wooden ships nor the monitors
in use in 1863 could successfully cope. With
the rams, acting in concert, it was intended to
break and raise the blockade of the Southern
ports, and thus secure for the Confederacy foreign recognition. If necessary to secure this
result, New York and Boston were to be in-
vaded, and those cities put under requisition.
This scheme, as feasible apparently as it was
dangerous, it devolved on Mr. Adams to balk, if
in any way possible. Its success involved a foreign war.

Meanwhile the experience of the Alabama showed how difficult the task before him was, and the agents of the United States were in a condition of complete discouragement. The Queen's proclamation to the contrary notwithstanding, parties in Great Britain were engaged in both constructing and equipping a formidable Confederate navy. Nevertheless, though the life had been construed out of the statute, and the agents of the United States were in a demoralized condition, these last kept Mr. Adams well advised of everything going on, and the consequent pressure brought steadily to bear on the Foreign Office was by no means unproductive of results. In 1863 the Alabama was in her full career of destruction, and so much of the American merchant marine as was not sent in flames to the bottom was fast seeking protection under foreign flags. With a view to increasing the pressure, therefore, Mr. Adams now formally opened his long and memorable Alabama correspondence with Earl Russell. While work was actively going on in the Birkenhead yards, the receipt of controversial dispatches served as a constant reminder to the Foreign Office, both of its proven shortcomings in the past and its possible future delinquencies. As to neither was Earl Russell to be given rest. In March, 1863, this correspondence was published in the London papers, and much commented upon. That Great Britain should be asked to pay for the ruin wrought by the commerce-destroyers let loose on a friendly nation through her lax administration of her own laws, was a new view of the subject, — a view also which, at this stage of proceedings, savored, to the average British mind, of what they loved to refer to as "Yankee" impudence and "cuteness." A huge joke, even Captain Raphael Semmes, C. S. N., commanding the Alabama, stopped in the midst of his burnings to enjoy a quiet laugh over it. "That 'little bill,'" he wrote from Bahia to Captain Bulloch, on May 21, 1863, "which the Yankees threaten to present to our Uncle John Bull, for the depredations of the Alabama, is growing apace, and already reaches $3,100,000." The "Yankee" has not generally been deemed deficient in a sense of humor; but this joke, of an intensely practical kind, he failed to appreciate; and so war between the two countries was now regarded as imminent, and the great mercantile houses of London were taking precautions accordingly. Mr. Adams, however, did not despair. "I shall," he wrote, as he noted down the gathering indications, "do my best to avoid it." It was the dark hour of the long night; but, for him, it preceded the dawn.

The pinch now came. More and more clearly the issue of the American struggle depended on the blockade. On the other hand, the machinery for breaking the blockade was almost perfected. Owing to delays in construction at first, and later to complications growing out of legal proceedings instituted by Mr. Adams in other similar cases, the first of the two rams was not launched until July 4th, instead of in March, as had been originally agreed; and the other was delayed until the end of August. Early in September Mr. Adams forwarded fresh representations. The work for which the vessels were designed was matter of notoriety; but still the government "could find no evidence upon which to proceed in stopping" them. How much the government of Jefferson Davis counted on the shrewd stroke thus in preparation for the "Yankee," and the importance they gave to it, — greater than that set on any victory in the field, — was shown in the references to the rams of Mr. S. R. Mallory, who in the Richmond cabinet held the position of secretary of the navy. Writing to Mr. Slidell, in Paris, on the 27th of March, 1863, Mr. Mallory said: "Our early possession of these ships, in a condition for service, is an object of such paramount importance to our country that no effort, no sacrifice, must be spared to accomplish it. Whatever may be

the conditions of placing them at our command
will be promptly met." A year later, when
the action of the British government in detaining the rams proved to be final, Mr. Mallory
wrote concerning the event to Captain Bulloch
in language which sounded like a wail. He
referred to it as " a great national misfor-
tune," and spoke of his own hopes, " shared by
thousands around me," as " prostrated by the
intelligence." He then dwelt on " the bitterness
of his disappointment." Had the Confederate
government, President Davis in his turn declared, been successful in getting those vessels
to sea, " it would have swept from the ocean the
commerce of the United States [and] would
have raised the blockade of at least some of our
ports."

Those in charge of the navy of the Union and
coast defenses of the United States were correspondingly alarmed. As the result of careful
inquiry, they described the two ships as " of the
most formidable character, and equal, except in
size, to the best ironclads belonging to " the
British government. So urgent was the occasion deemed that two private gentlemen of high
character and reputation for business and executive capacity were secretly sent out to England
at the shortest possible notice to outbid the
Confederacy, if possible, and buy the ships for

the United States. Ten millions of dollars in
freshly issued government bonds were put in
their hands to be used as they saw fit for this
purpose. Diplomatically, it was a most dangerous course, as the United States now proposed
secretly to do just what its accredited representative in Great Britain was strenuously
claiming that the Confederacy had no right to
do. The emergency alone could justify the
proceeding; but the emergency was thought
to be extreme. "You must stop [the Laird
rams] at all hazards," wrote Captain Fox, the
assistant secretary of the navy, " as we have
no defense against them. Let us have them for
our own purposes, without any more nonsense,
and at any price. As to guns, we have not one
in the whole country fit to fire at an ironclad.
. . . It is a question of life and death." Nothing came of this dangerous mission, as the
two emissaries, being shrewd and practical men,
soon became satisfied that to " offer to buy the
ironclads without success, would only be to
stimulate the builders to greater activity, and
even to building new ones in the expectation of
finding a market for them from one party or
the other." They therefore, like the American
officials in Europe, quite discouraged, returned
home before the ironclads were launched,
bringing with them the greater part of their

ten millions of bonds, which were taken back to Washington "in the original packages, with the seals of the Treasury unbroken." [1]   Mr. Adams was prudently kept uninformed as to the errand of these gentlemen and the steps they took in pursuance of it.

His own instructions from the State Department were at this crisis explicit. As respects also the course the United States government proposed in certain contingencies to pursue, they left no room for doubt. In line of thought and even in expression, they followed closely the memorable dispatches Nos. 4 and 10 of April and May, 1861. " If the law of Great Britain . . . be construed by the government in conformity with the rulings of the chief baron of the exchequer, then there will be left for the United States no alternative but to protect themselves and their commerce against armed cruisers proceeding from British ports, as against the naval forces of a public enemy. . . . Can it be an occasion for either surprise or complaint that, if this condition of things is to remain and receive the deliberate sanction of the British government, the navy of the United

[1] Hughes, *Letters and Recollections of J. M. Forbes*, ii. 1–66 ; Chittenden, *Recollections of President Lincoln*, i. 194–211 ; *Proceedings of Massachusetts Historical Society*, Second Series, xiii. 177–179.

States will receive instructions to pursue these enemies into the ports which thus, in violation of the law of nations and the obligations of neutrality, become harbors for the pirates? The President very distinctly perceives the risks and hazards which a naval conflict thus maintained will bring to the commerce and even to the peace of the two countries. . . . If, through the necessary employment of all our means of national defense, such a partial war shall become a general one between the two nations, the President thinks that the responsibility for that painful result will not fall upon the United States."

With dispatches of this character on his table Mr. Adams, as the weeks rolled by, watched anxiously the dreaded vessels nearing completion. Work in the yards of the Laird Brothers had been pushed steadily forward all through the winter, sheds lighted with gas having been erected over the rams so as to insure additional hours of labor upon them. But, alarmed by the depredations of the Alabama and the demands of the United States government on account thereof, the British officials were now exercising a degree of surveillance which caused Captain Bulloch much anxiety; and, before the close of 1862, he expressed himself as apprehensive of great difficulty in getting the vessels out of British jurisdiction. This apprehension increased steadily. The object for which armored ships, provided with formidable steel beaks, must be intended, was too evident to admit of disguise ; and Captain Bulloch, confessing himself " much perplexed," became satisfied at last that the government was prepared to resort to an order in council to override the ordinary rules of law. So great was the sympathy in Liverpool and vicinity that he felt quite confident of his ability to overcome " all ordinary opposition ; " and he assured the Confederate secretary that " no mere physical obstruction could have prevented our ships getting out, partially equipped at least." But Earl Russell had been irritated by the evasion of the " 290," of which it had even been asserted that he was cognizant in advance ; and he now let it be known that he did not propose to have that performance repeated. So, unless a change should take place in the political character of the ministry, Captain Bulloch was obliged to " confess that the hope of getting the ships out seems more than doubtful, — indeed, hopeless." This was towards the close of January, 1863, — six months nearly before the first of the rams left the ways.

Messrs. Mason and Slidell at this point became factors in the course of proceedings. They shared in the views of Secretary Mallory, deeming the early possession of the ships of " paramount importance," — a result for the attaining of which "no effort, no sacrifice, must be spared ; " and now the European plan of campaign, in coöperation with that which was to take place in America, gradually assumed shape. John Slidell was its originating and directing mind, and throughout it was marked by his peculiar characteristics. Mr. Slidell acted, of course, in coöperation with James M. Mason, and of Mr. Mason something will presently be said ; but at this stage of proceedings Mr. Slidell came distinctly to the front. The field of final operations was in Great Britain ; but there Mr. Slidell, directing his campaign from Paris, was as immediately opposed to Mr. Adams as, in America, Lee was opposed to Hooker, and Meade or Grant to Johnston or Pemberton. The two men were in curious contrast ; for while Mr. Adams was essentially a Puritan, Mr. Slidell certainly could by no possibility be so classified ; Mr. Adams, simple, direct, cool and reticent, in manner chill and repellent, was incapable of intrigue ; Mr. Slidell, adroit and no less cool, friendly in manner and keenly observant of men, was at intrigue an adept.

It is not probable that either Mr. Slidell's papers or those of Mr. Mason will ever see the light, and the fact is on every ground much to

be regretted; for Mr. Slidell now evinced great
diplomatic skill.   In the Senate of the United
States he had, in the years immediately preceding
the Rebellion, been accounted one of the ablest
of the Southern leaders.   Dr. Russell, of the
" Times," met him in New Orleans in May, 1861,
and was much impressed.   " I rarely," he then
wrote, " have met a man whose features have
a greater *finesse* and firmness of purpose than
Mr. Slidell's ; his keen gray eye is full of life ;
his thin firmly set lips indicate resolution and
passion. . . . He is not a speaker of note, nor
a ready stump orator, nor an able writer ; but he
is an excellent judge of mankind, adroit, perse-
vering and subtle, full of device, and fond of intrigue ; one of those men who, unknown almost
to the outer world, organizes and sustains a
faction, and exalts it into the position of a party,
— what is called here a ' wire-puller.' "   In the
European field Mr. Slidell now not only sustained the reputation he had gained in the United
States Senate, but he also made good in all its
details Dr. Russell's pointed characterization.
Having, in January, 1863, been a year on the
ground, he had become familiar with it, skillfully ingratiating himself with influential circles
in France, social as well as political.   He apparently had access everywhere.   In the utter
absence of his correspondence or of any authen-

tic memoir of him, the scheme he now devised can be traced only in outline ; but a careful study of Mr. Adams's papers, taken in connection with the public documents and what elsewhere appears, sufficiently discloses its main features. A far-reaching, formidable conception, it was well designed to accomplish the ends the Confederate authorities had in view, and neither in its formation nor development did Mr. Slidell fail apparently to avail himself of any condition or circumstance which seemed likely to contribute to success.

That the scheme was large and partook of the character of a complicated intrigue, success in which depended on many contingencies and much individual coöperation, is undeniable. Had it been otherwise, it would not have commended itself to John Slidell ; but, in this case, it was so from necessity. The situation was neither compact nor simple. Men and events in Europe waited on events and men in America ; and, from necessity himself located in France, the Confederate envoy had to operate through French instrumentalities on England. The conditions were not of his selection. They were imposed upon him. The cards were dealt to him ; it was for him to play a hand in the game. He failed, and failed completely, partly because of the skill and conduct of his opponent, partly from the course of events beyond his power to control; but the game was a great one, and it nowhere as yet appears that he played his hand otherwise than skillfully, and for all it was worth.

In the present sketch, it is only possible to outline what the Confederate agents now attempted. While, in the absence of authentic information, much would in any case have to be surmised, space does not suffice for the full use of even such material as is now accessible. The ends Mr. Slidell had in view are obvious. They were twofold, — the recognition of the Confederacy by England and France acting in unison, and the breaking of the blockade. To bring about the recognition of the Confederacy, he had to force the hand of the Palmerston-Russell ministry through the action of a strongly sympathetic Parliament, compelling the resignation of Earl Russell as foreign secretary. To insure the consequent breaking of the blockade, in case recognition fell short of intervention, he had to prevent any interference by the English government with the Laird rams. To this end he was forced to resort to every conceivable device calculated to cover up their ownership. His mind was fertile in expedients; and he had now assured himself of the efficient coöperation of the Emperor, an immense point in favor of the Confederacy. Secure in this quarter, and with more than mere intimations of protection, he early in the year summoned Captain Bulloch to Paris, and there arranged for the transfer of the rams to foreign ownership. Thereafter the Lairds were to know as their principals only the Messrs. Bravay & Co., a French firm, supposed to be acting for the Pasha of Egypt, or other unknown governments. The papers were formal and complete, the transfer legal in all its details ; the real fact being that the Messrs. Bravay bought the ships for a specified amount, and then privately engaged to re-sell them beyond British jurisdiction for another amount, which should include a handsome commission for their house. The Laird Brothers themselves seem to have been imposed upon by this transaction. They, too, received a commission, amounting to some £5000, on account of the transfer.

This matter disposed of, Mr. Slidell next, through the house of Erlanger & Co., negotiated a Confederate cotton loan. Bonds to the amount of £3,000,000 were floated at ninety per cent, putting some twelve or thirteen millions of dollars in cash at the disposal of the Confederacy. The sinews of war were thus supplied. So far all went well. Much was accomplished ; but the last and most difficult portion of the far-reaching programme was yet to be carried out.

An aggressive American policy was to be imposed upon the British government, and recognition compelled. To this end Earl Russell was to be driven to resign from the ministry. Here the adroit, secret management of Mr. Slidell came in sharp contrast with Mr. Mason's bungling methods of procedure. In the skillful hands of the Confederate envoy at Paris, the Emperor and his ministers now seem to have become hardly more than manikins. The touch of Slidell could everywhere be traced. Two members of the English Parliament were at this juncture conspicuous for their advocacy of the Confederate cause, — John Arthur Roebuck, of the Sheffield " scum of Europe " speech of August, 1862; and W. S. Lindsay, of " this wicked, this worthless war " speech at Chertsey. Curiously enough, Mr. Lindsay was a friend of Richard Cobden ; while Roebuck only a few years before had, with characteristic savageness of speech, denounced Napoleon III. as a " perjured despot." None the less, in view of the great parliamentary campaign now in preparation, Messrs. Lindsay and Roebuck, towards the end of June, 1863, were induced to go over to Paris, where they conferred freely with the Emperor, dining at the Tuileries, and receiving assurances from him of the most outspoken character. He professed himself ripe and eager for

instant recognition; and, as both his guests as-
severated, authorized them so to state in the
House of Commons. Mr. Slidell nowhere appears, but there can be little question of his
agency behind the scene. Messrs. Roebuck and
Lindsay did not go to Paris wholly on their own
motion; the Confederate envoy was marshaling
his forces.

Then came the parliamentary demonstration.
The lead in this devolved on Mr. Roebuck.
Like Mr. Adams in other years, Mr. Slidell was
forced to do with what he had; but it is scarcely
possible that he should not have felt grave misgivings as respected the impulsive member for
Sheffield. Nevertheless, on the 30th of June,
that gentleman spoke in the Commons in support of his motion that the government be instructed "to enter into negotiations with the
Great Powers of Europe for the purpose of obtaining their coöperation in the recognition" of
the Confederacy. Into the details of this debate, and the struggle that then took place in
and out of Parliament, it is impossible here to
enter. Mr. Adams watched events coolly, but
not without anxiety. Throughout, understanding the situation well, he saw Slidell's hand.
The manipulation bespoke the master. The
drive was at Earl Russell, and at one time
his resignation was rumored; London was pla-

carded with representations of the conjoined
Confederate and British ensigns; fully three
quarters of the House of Commons were avowedly in sympathy with the Rebellion; on the 4th
of July, before a large company at Lord Wyn-
ford's table in London, Mr. Mason oracularly
announced the absence of any doubt in his own
mind that General Lee, then in reality shat-
tered at Gettysburg, was in possession of
Washington.

Unfortunately for Mr. Slidell, most fortunately
for Mr. Adams, Mr. Roebuck handled his cause
wretchedly. He made to the House an avowal
of amateur diplomacy which forced the ministry
to array itself solidly against him, and brought
upon him not only a measured rebuke from Palmerston, but an exemplary castigation from John
Bright. "The effect of Tuesday night's debate," wrote Mr. Adams to Mr. Seward, "was
very severe on Mr. Roebuck. His extraordinary
attempts to influence the action of the House by
the use of the authority of the Emperor of the
French, as well as his presuming to make himself the medium of an appeal to Parliament
against the conduct of the ministry, have had
the consequences which might naturally be expected by any one acquainted with the English
character. Thus it happened that Mr. Roebuck, though addressing an assembly a great

proportion of whom sympathized with him in
his object, demolished his cause; whilst, on the
other hand, Mr. Bright, even whilst running
counter to the predisposition of most of his
hearers, succeeded in extorting a general tribute
of admiration of his eloquent and convincing
reply." This whole episode was one which Mr.
Roebuck's biographer afterwards thought it expedient to pass over very lightly. Referring
to the dinner at the Tuileries and the subsequent debate, Mr. Leader says: "The inevitable result of amateur diplomacy followed.
None of the parties to the interview agreed as
to what actually took place. The Emperor disavowed, or declined to be bound by, the version
Mr. Roebuck gave to the House of Commons of
the conversation. The amazement and amusement, with which this mission to the 'perjured
despot' of a few years ago was received by the
general public, were expressed in very pregnant
sarcasm by speakers like Lord Robert Montagu
and Mr. Bright;" so that, thoroughly discomfited, Mr. Roebuck on the 13th of July "very
reluctantly" withdrew his motion without insisting on a division. The carefully nurtured
movement of Mr. Slidell had failed, and Earl
Russell remained at the head of the British Foreign Office.

But Mr. Slidell was none the less a dangerous opponent. He neglected no opportunity for attack, as Mr. Adams himself had occasion to realize. The episode of the Howell-Zerman letter now occurred. Altogether a very entertaining and characteristic incident, the letter referred to caused at the moment great commotion, and for a brief space threatened gravely to compromise Mr. Adams; but the affair soon passed over, leaving no trace behind. Reference only can be made to it here. Mr. Slidell, however, did not fail to avail himself of it as a possible element of discord; and again the imperial manikins went through the requisite motions in obedience to the skillful touch of Russell's adroit "wire-puller." Representations from the French Foreign Office were received at the State Department in Washington, indicating the grave displeasure of the Emperor at the spirit shown by Mr. Adams in regard to the former's proceedings in Mexico; and English newspaper correspondents from New York, of Confederate leanings, dilated on the latter's "extraordinary stupidity," and the "really clever ability of all the rebel agents." Again Mr. Slidell's blow fell short; but it was well directed, and its origin was plain, at least to Mr. Adams.

The first of the Laird rams took the water at Birkenhead on the 4th of July; Mr. Roebuck withdrew his motion for recognition on the 13th;

on the 16th arrived news " of a three days' battle at Gettysburg ; " and on the morning of the
19th Mr. Adams wrote : " When I came down
I found on my table a private telegram, which,
as usual, I opened with trepidation. It proved
to be an announcement from Mr. Seward that
Vicksburg had surrendered on the 4th. Thus
has this great object been accomplished. . . .
Our amiable friends, the British, who expected
to hear of the capture of Washington, are correspondingly disappointed." In London, the
disappointment was, indeed, intense, and only
exceeded by the surprise. That whole community — social, commercial, political — had settled down into a conviction that the Confederate
arms were on the verge of a triumph not less
decisive than brilliant, and that Lee, scarcely
less of a hero in London than in Richmond,
was in firm possession of the national capital.
Why then, they argued, intervene ? Had not
the South worked out its problem for itself ?
The first revulsion of feeling was angry. " Perhaps," wrote Mr. Adams, " the most curious
phenomenon is to be seen in the London newspapers, which betray the profound disappointment and mortification of the aristocracy at the
result. . . . The incredulity is yet considerable.
It is the strongest proof how deep-seated is the
passion in the English breast. . . . The Eng-

lish are almost up to the pitch of yielding active aid. Luckily, the aspect of affairs on the
Continent [in the Polish insurrection] is so
threatening that the government is disposed to
act with much prudence and self-restraint as to
embroiling us."

That the elaborate plan of operations of Mr.
Slidell had now received a serious setback was
apparent, but still there was one feature in it
left. The Laird rams were French property,
and, as such, rapidly nearing completion. A
great card, they at least were still in reserve.
They constituted a card also which might well
win the game. Mr. Adams, on the other hand,
not unduly elated by the tidings from across the
Atlantic, watched his opponent coolly and warily. He was at his best. Lord Russell —
high-toned, well-intentioned, cautious, even hesitating — held the key of the situation. It was
he who must be worked upon. Fortunately
Mr. Adams's immediate opponent, Mr. Mason,
having none of the *finesse* of Slidell, now played
directly into the American minister's hands.
Mr. Mason was a thorough Virginian of the
mid-century school, — " that old slave dealer,"
as Cobden contemptuously described him. Obtuse, overbearing, and to the last degree self-
sufficient and self-assertive, he was a poor in-
strument with which to work. Still, he was

there; and Slidell was forced to use the tools he
had. The whole effort of Mr. Mason now was,
in the language of Mr. Adams, " to concentrate the attacks upon Lord Russell, as if he
were the chief barrier to the rebel progress in
the cabinet. To that end the labors of the
presses conducted by rebel sympathizers have
been directed to casting odium upon his Lordship as acting too much under my influence.
This is doing me far too much honor. Lord
Russell is too old and skillful a politician not to
understand the necessity, for his own security,
of keeping the minds of his countrymen quite
free from all suspicion of his being superfluously
courteous to any foreign power." Mr. Adams
then added, with a touch of humorous sarcasm
not usual with him: " From my observation of
his [Russell's] correspondence since I have
been at this post, I should judge that he seldom
erred in that particular."

Wiser than Mr. Mason, better informed, and
far stronger in his simple directness than Mr.
Slidell, Mr. Adams, unconsciously to himself,
now braced up for the final and vital grapple.
To that end he quietly assumed control of operations. The instructions from Secretary Seward,
already referred to, were on his table. They
were to the last degree rasping and minatory.
Mr. Adams put them in his pocket, and kept

them there. He simply advised the secretary,
in most courteous and diplomatic terms, that,
as minister and on the spot, he thought he
understood the men and the situation best, and
accordingly he would assume the responsibility
of acting on his own judgment and as circumstances might seem to require. Most fortunately, there was no Atlantic cable then.

The days now passed rapidly on, and the
rams were as rapidly made ready for sea. In
the language of Mr. Gladstone the year before,
the rebels were "making, it appears, a navy."
Very courteous but very firm in his communications with Earl Russell, Mr. Adams carefully
abstained from anything which could be construed into a threat. Outwardly his communications breathed the most abiding faith in the
good intentions of the government; while in
private he impressed upon Mr. Cobden his
sense of "the very grave nature of this case,"
and his conviction "that it would end in war
sooner or later." Then he added in his diary:
"Mr. Cobden is really in earnest in his efforts,
but the drift is too much for him." Through
Mr. Milner Gibson, Mr. Cobden was, however,
in close communication with the cabinet.

Mr. Adams next visited Scotland, for it was
now August, and the dead season in London.
He was there the guest of Mr. Edward Ellice,

as also was Mr. Mason at about the same time.
His host was a very old man, and a Confederate
sympathizer. "Mr. Ellice," Mr. Adams wrote,
"talked as fast as ever, occasionally running
full butt into American affairs. I met him
there with profound silence. This is my only
safeguard." A few days later Mr. Adams was
the guest of the Duke of Argyll, at Inverary.
The Argylls throughout those trying times were
true well-wishers to the Union; but it shows
how well Mr. Slidell had covered up the Confederate tracks, that the Argylls now were almost persuaded that the rams were really being
built on French account; and only a few days
before, the Duchess had intimated as much in
a letter to Mr. Sumner. The Duke was a member of the cabinet, and Mr. Adams availed himself of this opportunity to impress on his grace
his sense of the situation "as grave and critical;"
and he further intimated that his "instructions
on the subject [were] far more stringent than
[he] had yet been disposed to execute." That
evening the Duke was much absorbed in letter-
writing, and Mr. Adams could not help wonder-
ing whether the foreign secretary was among
those to whom the letters were addressed.

Meanwhile Earl Russell was in great per-
turbation of mind. An honest, high-minded
gentleman, he wished to do right; he was vexed

by the course of the rebel emissaries, and mortified as well as irritated by the recollection of his treatment in the case of the Alabama; but he was staggered by the confident assertion of French ownership of the vessels, which the Lairds corroborated, — perhaps not dishonestly, — and moreover the law, as expounded in the Court of Exchequer, was plainly against interference. If it acted, the government must do so on grounds of prerogative, against public opinion, regardless of the advice of counsel, and prepared to be heavily mulcted by a jury. The situation was certainly trying; and yet it is now manifest that Earl Russell earnestly desired to do his duty to the crown, and whatever international obligations demanded. Like Shakespeare's noble Moor, he was, "being wrought upon, perplexed in the extreme."

Assuredly, so far as Mr. Adams was concerned, Lord Russell was now sufficiently "wrought upon." At six o'clock on the morning of September 3d, being, as he did not fail at the time to note, the thirty-fourth anniversary of his wedding day, Mr. Adams, just from the Westmoreland lake region, found himself on the steps of his house in London. He was anxious. The government could not be got to act, and the rams were now almost ready to steam down the Mersey, — of course, like the Alabama, only on a trial trip! "After long wavering and hesitation," he wrote, "there are signs that the ministry will not adopt any preventive policy. Their moral feebleness culminates in cowardice, which acts like the greatest daring. It precipitates a conflict. My duty is therefore a difficult one. Without indulging in menace, I must be faithful to my country in giving warning of its sense of injury. Nothing must be left undone that shall appear likely to avert the danger. To that end I addressed a note to Lord Russell at once. The attack on Charleston [Gilmore's 'swamp angels'] is going on with great vigor, and the cries of the Richmond press indicate success. Barring the conduct of foreign powers, I should say the rebellion would collapse before New Year's, but the pestilent malignity of the English and the insidious craft of Napoleon are not yet exhausted."

The diary written at the time tells what now ensued far more effectively than would be possible for any biographer : —

"Friday, 4th September : — A notice from Mr. Dudley that the war vessel was about to depart compelled me to address another and stronger note of solemn protest against the permission of this proceeding by the government. I feared, however, that it would be of little avail, and my prognostications proved but too true ; for I re-

ceived at four o'clock a note announcing that
the government could find no evidence upon
which to proceed in stopping the vessel. This
affected me deeply. I clearly foresee that a
collision must now come of it. I must not, however, do anything to accelerate it; and yet must
maintain the honor of my country with proper
spirit. The issue must be made up before the
world on its merits. The prospect is dark for
poor America. Her trials are not yet over.
Luckily the difficulties do not all come together.
A telegram received to-night announces the
destruction of Fort Sumter, and the shelling of
that pestilent nest of heresy, Charleston. This
will produce a great effect in Europe. It may
go so far as to save us from imminent danger
pressing both here and in France. I had a
visit from Colonel Bigelow Lawrence, who is on
his way to America; but I fear I was not in a
mood for easy talk."

The following day it was that, after a night
of anxious reflection over what yet might by
possibility be done, he wrote and forwarded to
Earl Russell, then in Scotland, the dispatch of
September 5th, which contains his single utterance since borne in memory. It was the dispatch containing the expression afterwards so
famous: "It would be superfluous in me to
point out to your lordship that this is war."

The heavy sense of responsibility and utter dreariness of spirit under which he penned this dispatch, almost unique in diplomatic correspondence, — exactly fitting to the occasion, — appears in his corresponding diary record made the evening of the day he transmitted it : —

" Saturday, 5th September : — My thoughts turned strongly upon the present crisis, and the difficulty of my task. My conclusion was, that another note was to be addressed to Lord Russell to-day. So I drew one, which I intended only to gain time previous to the inevitable result. I have not disclosed to Lord Russell those portions of my instructions which describe the policy to be adopted by the government at home, because that course seemed to me likely to cut off all prospect of escape. Contenting myself with intimating [their] existence, I decided upon awaiting further directions. This will give a month. After I had sent the note, I received one from his lordship, in answer to my two previous ones of Thursday and Friday, saying that the subject of them was receiving the earnest and anxious consideration of the government. There is, then, one chance left, and but one.

"Tuesday, 8th September : — In the ' Morning Post ' there was a short article announcing that the government had decided on detaining the vessels, in order to try the merits in court. It

had an official aspect; and yet I could scarcely
put faith in it, while I had no notice myself.
Later in the day, however, a brief notification
came from Lord Russell to the effect that orders
had been given to prevent their departure. I
know not that even in the Trent case I felt a
greater relief."

CHAPTER XVIII

THE YEARS OF FRUITION

MORE than twenty-three years later, referring to the events just narrated, of which he was very competent to speak, James Russell Lowell said of Mr. Adams: — "None of our generals in the field, not Grant himself, did us better or more trying service than he in his forlorn outpost of London. Cavour did hardly more for Italy.

> " ' Peace hath her victories
> Not less renowned than war.' "

Certainly no victory ever won by Grant was more decisive — and Grant's victories were numerous, and many of them most decisive — than that won by Mr. Adams, and recorded so quietly in the diary entry just quoted in full. There is no more unmistakable gauge of the importance of any movement made or result gained in warfare than the quotations of the stock exchange. The deadly character of the blow then inflicted on the Southern cause was immediately read in the stock list. During the week ending the 27th of August, the bonds of Mr.

Slidell's Confederate cotton loan had been active at 79; during the week ending the 10th of September, they were lifeless at 70. The rams were officially detained on the 9th of September; they were seized by the government, and the broad arrow affixed, a month later, on the 9th of October. That action extinguished hope. The bonds then fell to 65. On the 9th of July they had been quoted at 99, having previously risen to a slight premium; the news of the repulse of Lee at Gettysburg depressed them only two points, to 97, at which figure they stood firmly. Then followed the fall of Vicksburg, the loss of the control of the Mississippi, and the withdrawal of the Roebuck motion in Parliament; all which together broke the price to 87. In other words, the combined military and parliamentary disasters of the Confederacy during July affected the barometer thirteen points; while the detention and seizure of the two vessels, still, in pursuance of a solemn farce, designated El Tousson and El Monassir, reduced it fourteen points, notwithstanding that the military news then received from America was regarded as distinctly favorable to the Confederacy. That this should have been so seems inexplicable, until it is remembered that the stoppage of the rams meant more, a great deal more, than the continuance of the blockade, — it meant the continuance of peaceful relations between the United States and the great maritime powers of Europe. The departure of the rams from the Mersey, it was well understood, would involve serious complications between the United States and Great Britain, resulting almost inevitably in the recognition of the Confederacy by the latter country acting in unison with France. This had been confidently anticipated ; and the anticipation buoyed up the cotton loan. When at last the broad arrow was actually affixed to the unfinished ironclads, the sympathizers with the Confederacy realized what that meant. The Union need no longer apprehend any foreign complication, while the Rebellion was obviously sinking under the ever - increasing pressure brought to bear upon it. It was this unexpressed conclusion which was clearly read in the quotations of the cotton loan. A decisive Union advantage had at last been secured.

Already badly deranged by the parliamentary fiasco of July, followed by the military reverses in Pennsylvania and on the Mississippi, Mr. Slidell's diplomatic programme — his great European campaign, so well conceived, so far-reaching, so carefully matured, so warily conducted — had now come to naught on the vital issue. A great lover of cards, Mr. Slidell was an adept in their use. He rarely played save to

win. But this, the great game of his life, was
now over; and he left the table a loser. Probably his knowledge of the well-known puritanic
traits of his opponent did not serve to alleviate
the bitterness of defeat.

As for Mr. Adams, though hardly a note of
exultation could be detected in his diary, much
less in his correspondence, he did not fail to
realize the momentous importance of what had
now taken place. Describing the course of
events in a familiar letter written a few days
later to his brother-in-law, Edward Everett, he
said : " Friday [September 4th] I gave up all
for lost, and made preparation for the catastrophe. On Saturday I got news of a prospect
of a change. And yesterday [Tuesday] there
came a notice that the departure of the *two*
vessels (for the other had been launched in the
interval) had been prevented. This is rather
close shaving. Even now I scarcely realize the
fact of our escape."

Notice of the detention of the rams reached
Mr. Adams on the 8th of September, 1863. On
the 18th of July, fourteen months before, William E. Forster had hurried to his house in great
distress, bringing a telegram, just received from
Queenstown and printed in the " Times," announcing that " General McClellan, with all his
army, was negotiating for a capitulation." " The

news," wrote Mr. Adams, "spread like wildfire,
and many eagerly caught at it as true. The
evident satisfaction taken in the intelligence is
one of our delectations. It almost equals the
days of Bull Run." Things had then gone
steadily from bad to worse: Pope's ridiculous
fiasco ; the disasters in Tennessee and Kentucky ;
the Confederate invasion of Maryland ; the battle
of Fredericksburg ; the repulse of Chancellors-
ville ; the failures before Vicksburg. At last,
in June, 1863, the Army of Virginia crossed the
Potomac and fairly carried the war into the
free States. On July 16th of that year, tidings
reached London of severe but indecisive fighting at Gettysburg ; yet so strong was the
tendency of feeling developed under the news
of the invasion, that it infected even friendly
Americans. " Mr. Lampson was a full believer that by this time Washington must be
taken ; and when, the other day, I exposed
the absurdity of it to him, I saw that he was not
convinced. This comes from what may be denominated the atmospheric pressure of opinion as generated in England by the London
' Times.' It is difficult even for me to put
myself above it." This was on July 17th.
Then the day broke in one great burst of light.

Exactly six weeks later, the European victory
was won. The tribulation of fourteen months

had come to an end, and thenceforth all went
well.   Mr. Adams had now established his own
position, as well as the position of his country,
at the Court of St. James; nor was either again
challenged.   The adversary even abandoned
the field; for, less than two weeks after the
detention of the rams was officially announced,
Mr. Mason, in a not undignified letter addressed to Earl Russell, shook the dust of inhos-
pitable England from his feet and withdrew to
more sympathetic Paris.   " The ' Times,' " wrote
Mr. Adams to Secretary Seward, briefly noti-
cing the occurrence, " distinctly admits this to be
a relief to the government; though I confess
myself at a loss to understand how he annoyed
them.   The selection of Mr. Mason to come
here was an unfortunate one from the outset.
I can scarcely imagine an agency to have been
more barren of results."   He was not heard
from again.   Remaining in Europe, sometimes
in France and sometimes in England, until the
close of the war, Mr. Mason then returned to
his native Virginia by way of Canada, and,
broken in spirit as in fortune, there died in 1871.
More fortunate than his Virginian colleague, in
that he had been shrewder in the transfer be-
times of a share of his worldly possessions
from the Confederacy to Europe, Mr. Slidell
never returned to America.   He was not again

heard of in the field of diplomacy, except, later in 1863, in connection with the summary seizure by the Emperor Napoleon of various war vessels, which that potentate had about a twelvemonth before encouraged the Confederates to contract for at Bordeaux and Nantes. His English defeat had followed Mr. Slidell into France. He never emerged from its shadow; but, after the final suppression of the Rebellion, transferring his residence to England, he there died in 1871, surviving his brother envoy, with whom his name will always be so closely associated, by only three months.

Having in remembrance the judgment of the Court of Exchequer in the Alexandra case, the British ministry had no hope of obtaining a favorable verdict as the outcome of a suit brought against its agents for the detention of the rams. It was futile for it to hope to prove "a valid seizure for a valid cause of forfeiture." It only remained to settle the matter on the best terms attainable. This finally was done; and, no other purchaser being found, the two rams the next year passed into the hands of the government, and were named the Wivern and the Scorpion. The sum paid for them was £225,000.

Mr. Adams remained in London until the spring of 1868, when, the war being long over, he insisted on the acceptance of his resignation.

Meanwhile, after he had achieved his great success in securing the detention of the rams, his position as respects the authorities at Washington was greatly changed. There too, as well as in Great Britain, it became assured. His experience in this matter greatly resembled, indeed, that of certain generals in the field during the civil war. It will be remembered how they were at first constantly hampered and thwarted by interference from Washington. While in this respect Mr. Adams had little, comparatively speaking, to complain of, and while his chief in the State Department never failed to give him full rein and undeviating support, yet Secretary Seward was wholly without diplomatic experience himself, and, moreover, set a politician's undue estimate on the importance of indirect means and influences. Accordingly, until Mr. Adams had thoroughly established himself in his position by success in stopping the rams, he was encumbered with a great deal of assistance with which he would gladly have dispensed. Secretary Seward failed to realize how much the irregularly accredited envoy tends to discredit the regularly accredited minister.

Fortunately, there were two sides to this annoyance; for his opponents seem to have suffered from it quite as much, or more even, than Mr. Adams. In September, 1862, for instance,

Captain Bulloch wrote thus from Liverpool to Secretary Mallory: " I do not hesitate to say that embarrassment has already been occasioned by the number of persons from the South who represent themselves to be agents of the Confederate States government. There are men so constituted as not to be able to conceal their connection with any affairs which may by chance add to their importance, and such persons are soon found out and drawn into confessions and statements by gossiping acquaintances, to the serious detriment of the service upon which they are engaged." The unfortunate experience of Mr. Slidell, as the result of the amateur diplomacy he initiated between the two itinerant members of the Commons, Messrs. Lindsay and Roebuck, and the Tuileries, has already been described.

During the early years of his mission, indeed until the autumn of 1863, Great Britain was, for reasons which at once suggest themselves, the special field of American diplomatic activity, and the minister at London was at last driven to active remonstrance. These emissaries were of four distinct types: (1) the roving diplomat, irregularly accredited by the State Department; (2) the poaching diplomat, accredited to one government, but seeking a wider field of activity elsewhere; (3) the volunteer diplomat, not ac-

credited at all, but in his own belief divinely
commissioned at that particular juncture to
enlighten foreign nations generally, and Great
Britain in particular; and (4) the special agent,
sent out by some department of the government
to accomplish, if possible, a particular object.
Messrs. J. M. Forbes and W. H. Aspinwall,
already referred to as sent out by the Navy Department in 1863, to buy the rams, were of the
last description, as also was Mr. William M.
Evarts; and they were men of energy, tact, and
discretion. Accordingly they had the good sense
to confine themselves to the work they were in
England to do, and did not indulge in a pernicious general activity. With his rare tact,
shrewd judgment, and quick insight into men,
Thurlow Weed also made himself of use both in
Great Britain and on the Continent, and relations of a most friendly and lasting character
grew up between him and Mr. Adams. Of
other diplomats, roving, poaching, and volunteer, Mr. Adams, as is evident from his diary
records, had grave and just cause of complaint;
they were officious, they meddled, and they were
to the last degree indiscreet. They were peculiarly addicted to the columns of the "Times,"
in which their effusions appeared periodically;
but not always did they confine themselves to
ill-considered letter-writing, or mere idle talk.

This annoyance reached its climax in the spring of 1863. Special emissaries of the Treasury and of the State Department then arrived in quick succession, and naturally the newspaper correspondents of Confederate leanings got scent of their missions, and set to work to make trouble. One of them, writing from New York to the London "Standard" over the signature of "Manchester," spoke of Messrs. Forbes and Aspinwall as "delegates" about to be followed by eight other men of note, "one being Mr. Evarts, all of whom would regulate our affairs abroad, and Mr. Adams is ordered to be their mouthpiece." This correspondent then proceeded as follows: "[Mr. Evarts] is a particular friend of W. H. Seward. The latter, it is well known, has lost all confidence in Mr. Adams, who, but for his name, would have been recalled long ago. Mr. Seward expresses himself on all occasions, early and late, that the real source of bad feeling in England towards the North has been caused by the extraordinary stupidity of Mr. Adams, our minister, and the really clever ability of all the rebel agents." This particular letter Mr. Adams never saw until his attention was called to it by an emphatic private denial from Mr. Seward of the statements contained in it. None the less, though outwardly he gave no sign, the regularly

accredited minister to Great Britain chafed
sorely in private over these efforts at advice and
supervision. "It cannot be denied," he wrote,
"that ever since I have been here the almost
constant interference of government agents of
all kinds has had the effect, however intended,
of weakening the position of the minister. Most
of all has it happened in the case of Mr. Evarts,
whom the newspapers here have all insisted to
have been sent to superintend my office in all
questions of international law. I doubt whether
any minister has ever had so much of this kind
of thing to contend with." Mr. Adams probably had grounds for this doubt. Meanwhile,
on the other hand, few foreign ministers at any
time, and certainly none ever from the United
States, occupied such a difficult and responsible
position at so critical a period.

After the stoppage of the rams, Mr. Adams
suffered no more annoyance from this source
than did General Grant from interference of a
similar kind after the fall of Vicksburg; and
from the same reason. But, as a mere function
of state, the position of minister had no attraction for him; indeed, its duties were dis-
tasteful. He yearned to be at home in New
England, referring continually to his prolonged
residence in Europe as an "exile." Yet in
fact no American representative, before or

since, has ever enjoyed a position equal to
that held by him during the remaining four
years of his service. He had, under trying
circumstances, won the confidence of all parties.
The cause and country he represented had,
moreover, been brilliantly successful ; and certainly not less in Great Britain than elsewhere
success counts for much.

The correspondence in relation to the so-called
Alabama claims was renewed in 1864, and carried on at great length through 1865, Earl Russell being still the foreign secretary. It attracted much attention, both in Europe and at
home, and the conduct of his share in it greatly
enhanced the reputation of Mr. Adams. Subsequently it became the basis of the American
case in the Geneva arbitration.

Later, and after the close of the civil war,
occurred the " Fenian " disturbances in Canada
and Great Britain, throwing on the London
legation a good deal of business the reverse
of agreeable. The blowing up by dynamite of
historic public edifices as well as police stations,
and the murdering of the constabulary while in
the performance of its duties as such, are
criminal acts, even when committed in Europe
by those naturalized in America. This purely
prosaic and matter-of-fact view of the case did
not, however, during the years 1865–67, altogether

commend itself to the Irish-American political element.   Consequently, though in almost every case he succeeded by judicious intercession in mitigating the severity of the British law, Mr. Adams did not entirely escape censure at home.   In certain quarters, never conspicuous for coolness of judgment or moderation in speech, it was assumed that a truly sympathetic American diplomatic representative would now make his presence in London known by demonstrations not less frequent than vociferous.   He would, in fact, claim for naturalized American citizens the inalienable right, subject to some not very material limitations, to do, in the British Isles at least, anything, anywhere, and to any one.   It is almost needless to say that Mr. Adams shared to a very limited degree only, if indeed at all, in this view of what was incumbent upon him.   His dissent also extended to the manner as well as the matter.   Hence the indignation aroused.   One ardent Congressional representative, indeed, evincing, perhaps, a certain confusion in his ideas of constitutional law, went so far as to propose the formal impeachment of the American minister near the Court of St. James.   This, however, was a mere passing episode, scarcely deserving of mention; and, as such, was wholly lost sight of in the general recognition afforded Mr. Adams, on both sides of the Atlantic, as his term drew to its close.

His own record of the long and interesting experiences he went through, social as well as political, was detailed and graphic ; and of its character no better idea could, perhaps, be given than through his description of certain occurrences which, judging by the detail of his record, seem most to have interested him. One of these was an attendance at the Sunday services held by Mr. Spurgeon, the famous evangelist preacher. Thither curiosity took Mr. Adams, himself always a regular church attendant, on the 13th of October, 1861, he having then been five months only in England.

"Sunday, 13th October, 1861 : — A clear, fine day throughout, a thing quite rare at this season. Mrs. Adams and I took the opportunity to execute a plan we have entertained for some time back, which was to go across the river to attend divine service at the great tabernacle at which the most popular preacher in London officiates. We were obliged to go an hour in advance of the service in order to get a chance of seats. As it was, crowds were in waiting at the doors. A hint had been given to me that, by special application at the side door, the police officer might admit us. There is a magic power in liveried servants in similar cases here, and we found ourselves immediately in an immense hall, surrounded with two deep tiers of gallery. The seats, however, though empty at the moment, all belonged to individuals by ticket just as rigidly as if it was a theatre, and I was beginning to despair, when a civil, plain-looking man met us and offered two seats in the front gallery, vacant by reason of the non-attendance of two of his daughters, which I accepted with pleasure. This position gave us the opportunity to see the entire audience after it was assembled, and the slow but the steady process of accumulation, until, from top to bottom, including the very highest point under the roof, not an empty place was to be found, not excepting any of the aisles or passageways. It is estimated that the house can hold seven thousand people at the lowest. The spectacle was striking, for the people were evidently almost all of the pure middle class of England, which constitutes the real strength of the nation, and yet which in religion relucts at the inanimate vacuity of the ministrations in the Established Church, and grasps at something more vigorous and earnest than forms. Mr. Spurgeon is a short, thickset man, thoroughly English in matter and manner, yet without physical coarseness, so common an attendant of the frame after youth. There was no pulpit. He stood on a raised platform under the first gallery, projecting sufficiently to admit of several rows of seats behind, and between flights of steps on each side which led down to the body of the hall. A slight railing ran before him, which continued on the stairs to the bottom. A table at one side, and a chair. This was the appearance. The service was in the usual simple form of the dissenting churches. A rather short prayer. The hymns were read aloud, and sung by the whole congregation without accompaniment. Then the sermon from the text 3 Ephesians xv., — 'Of whom the whole family in heaven and earth is named.' He discoursed upon this with great fluency, moving from time to time to one or the other side. His topics were drawn from the three significant words of his text, the link word, as he called it, which was Christ, as referred to from the antecedent in the verse before ; then the key-word, which was the family ; and lastly the password, which comprised all its members. Everything else, however, was grouped around the single centre of the family ; the head and father of the members, living and dead, recognized by the name of Christ, no matter what the superadded denomination. There was breadth and grandeur in his images, not a little heightened by the mode of singing beforehand a Wesleyan hymn developing the idea of the solemn march of the host, never breaking its ranks even in crossing the narrow river that separates this and the other world. The family con-

tinued one, going on to its reward for its faithful
devotion to its chief.   And, although professing
himself a Baptist and a Calvinist, he disavowed
all narrowness of sectarian bigotry, and compared the effect of the distinctions between them
to that produced by the prenomen among brothers and sisters.   His division was lucid, and
his treatment remarkably effective, of a few
simple ideas.   For there was no very characteristic thought nor novel reasoning.   His power
consisted in sympathy with the current of human
feeling in all ages on the solemn topic of moral
responsibility to a higher power both here and
hereafter.   During his whole address, the attention was profound, and the emotion at times considerable.   How singular is the sway of the human voice when guided by a master of its tones!
As the great multitude finally poured itself in a
quiet, orderly channel out of the edifice, I could
not but speculate upon the new view of English
society that had here been opened to me.   Here
is visible the kernel that cracked the hard outer
shell of conventional formalities in the days of
the Reformation.   Here lie, but partially awak-
ened, the elements of moral revolution whenever
the corruption of the privileged classes shall
have reached a point that renders submission no
longer tolerable.[1]   This crowded auditory is the

[1] " When the intelligence came that the emancipation policy

standing protest of the city of London against
the monotonous vacuity of the teaching of the
Established Church. Well it will be for the
safety of all if they never fall into hands more
dangerous than those of Mr. Spurgeon. I confess I was very agreeably disappointed in this
visit."

Another entry, and of a gathering of a wholly
different character, was that of Wednesday,
February, 1865. Mr. Adams had then been
nearly four years in England, and, owing to the
delicate health of a daughter, the physicians
recommended for her a winter in Italy. Unable to leave his post, for those were the closing
days of the civil war, Mr. Adams accompanied
his family only to Folkestone. It was a soft

of the President was confirmed by the supplementary proclamation of January 1st, the demonstrations of support [in Eng-
land] were greater than had been known for any movement
since the uprising for the abolition of the duties on corn. . . .
On a Sunday Spurgeon thus prayed before his congregation of
many thousands: 'Now, O God! we turn our thoughts across
the sea to the terrible conflict of which we knew not what to
say; but now the voice of freedom shows where is right. We
pray Thee, give success to this glorious proclamation of liberty
which comes to us from across the waters. We much feared
that our brethren were not in earnest, and would not come to
this. Bondage and the lash can claim no sympathy from us.
God bless and strengthen the North; give victory to their arms!'
The immense congregation responded to this invocation in the
midst of the prayer with a fervent amen." Rhodes, *History
of the United States,* iv. 350, 351.

spring day, with light vapor clouds; a gentle breeze from the west slightly rippled the surface of the Channel as he watched the receding packet from the head of the pier. "The steamer grew smaller and smaller, and I reflected that I was alone, and now — what to do next?" The solitary house in London did not seem attractive, and Mr. Adams gradually bethought himself of Canterbury. He had never visited Canterbury. So he resolved to get all the benefit he could from his trip by seeing one more cathedral town. Of the cathedral itself he wrote : " Although not perhaps so full of striking effects as some of the others, there are parts which are very imposing, and which become far more so to the visitor from the historical associations with which they are connected. The greatest of all is what is called Becket's corona. It was the blundering passion of Henry which made the fortune of the edifice where the crime of Becket's murder was committed. For many generations following, the religious heart of the Christian community continued to respond to the call made upon it in the name of the slaughtered martyr. Here was the shrine which pilgrims came from afar to visit, and to cover with the most costly of presents. The counter-clap of the Reformation came to knock it all away, so that nothing now remains but the stone to mark the site where the act was committed, and the corona built up in his honor. Here, too, is the effigy of Edward, the Black Prince, in brass, in remarkable preservation, — a slight built, youthful figure, considerably below the medium size. Henry the Fourth and his second wife are also here. There is a spacious chapter house, and cloisters which go all round the square. How imposing all this must have been five centuries ago! There are plenty of monuments of archbishops down to Cardinal Pole, the last of the Catholics, whose sarcophagus, as compared with the rest, sufficiently shows the change that the public mind had undergone. Nobody resisted the eighth Henry's ruthless desecration of Becket's holy shrine. In this day the great cathedral finds itself sadly out of place. The archbishop lives in London, and seldom pays it more than a formal visit. The town is a quiet, little, mean-looking one, strangely contrasting with the stately and spacious central structure. Its general effect is not equal to that of York or Lincoln, or even Durham.

"Having thus accomplished my object, I returned to the Fountain Hotel to dine. A quiet, country inn; but clean and good, and without any pretension. Having my evening on my hands, I inquired of the waiter if there

was any public amusement here. He answered
that a concert of the Catch Club was to be held
a few doors from there. It would be very full,
and admission could be had only through members. But if I wished to go, Mr. Fine, the land-
lord, who was a member, would pass me. I went,
and paid my shilling entrance fee without having
occasion to name Mr. Fine. The spectacle to
which I was introduced was curious, and to me
novel in this country. It was a good-sized hall,
at one end of which was a platform for the per-
formers, and at the other a gallery. The women
congregated in both places, where they sat apart
by themselves. On one side, and close to the
wall, was a small box, in which sat the chairman
and other officers. Along the body of the hall
were three rows of tables, with chairs on both
sides of each. Here were the men of Canterbury, I should think fair specimens of the middle
class of the small towns. Every man had either
a pipe or a cigar, smoking all the evening, and
before him was a glass of spirits and hot water,
which was supplied from waiters carried around
by servants. These were renewed as often as
emptied, each one costing sixpence, which was
paid on the spot. As I can take neither of
these luxuries, my position was singular, but it
elicited no remark. The music was composed
of two catches for four voices, two solos, two or

three concerted pieces for instruments, and three
ballads by Mr. McKnew, a 'nigger' minstrel fan-
tastically dressed. Among them all, the latter
incontestably carried away the honors. He was
applauded noisily, and each time called back to
sing again. But he never repeated. The buf-
foonery was poor, occasionally bordering the
coarse. A burlesque of a speech of thanks was
sheer nonsense. Yet everything was accepted
as droll, laughed at, and boisterously approved.
Yet in the midst of this steam of hot liquor
there was no disorder or irregularity of deport-
ment. The general aspect was gravity. The
conversation was from neighbor to neighbor.
No voices raised high. No appearance of undue
excitement. The brandy or rum or gin was perceptible on the surface of the outer cuticle, but
it rather dulled than stimulated the eye. These
people were evidently happy after their fashion.
But that fashion, before it was over, became so
intolerable to me that I was obliged to take my
leave of the stifling atmosphere at the cost of
missing the latter part of the entertainment. I
suppose that this is about the summit of pleasure
during the winter season to English people of
this type. I knew they drank freely, but I had
no idea smoking was so universal among them.
Went back to my hotel, and soon to bed; but
I slept very partially, hearing at intervals the

howling of the wind, as well as the raindrops
beating against the window, and I congratulated
myself on having expedited the travelers."

In curious contrast with the foregoing was an
account of a breakfast at Mr. Gladstone's, some
fifteen months later.   Mr. Gladstone was then
chancellor of the exchequer and leader of the
House of Commons in the brief Russell ministry,
following the death of Lord Palmerston.   The
Colonel Holmes referred to was Oliver Wendell
Holmes, Jr., then fresh from the army after the
close of the Rebellion; now (1899) the Chief
Justice of Massachusetts.   In June, the London
season was at its height; and the Russell ministry, in consequence of adverse majorities in
the Commons on the reform bill it had introduced, resigned on the 26th of the month.

"Thursday, 7th June, 1866 : —The other evening at the Queen's ball Mrs. Gladstone asked
me, as from her husband, to come to breakfast
this morning, at the same time that Colonel
Holmes was invited.   At first I hesitated on the
score of various engagements and arrears of
work ; but, on consideration that this was the
second time of such an overture, I decided to go.
I found no cause to regret the decision, for the
company was very pleasant. The Duke and
Duchess of Argyll, Lord Littleton, Lord Houghton, Lord Frederick Cavendish with his wife, and

one of his uncles, and several whom I did not know. I forgot Lord Dufferin. We sat at two round tables, thus dividing the company; but Mr. Gladstone took ours, which made all the difference in the world. His characteristic is the most extraordinary facility of conversation on almost any topic, with a great command of literary resources, which at once gives it a high tone. Lord Houghton, if put to it, is not without aptness in keeping it up; whilst the Duke of Argyll was stimulated out of his customary indifference to take his share. Thus we passed from politics, the House of Commons, and Mr. Mill, to English prose as illustrated from the time of Milton and Bacon down to this day and contrasted with German, which has little of good, and with French. In the latter connection Mr. G. asked me if I had read the Conscrit of Erckmann-Chatrian. Luckily for me, who have little acquaintance with the light current literature, I could say 'Yes,' and could contrast it favorably with the artificial manner of Hugo. It is a cause of wonder to me how a man like Gladstone, so deeply plunged in the current of politics, and in the duties of legislation and official labor, can find time to keep along with the ephemeral literature abroad as well as at home. After an hour thus spent we rose, and on a question proposed by Colonel Holmes respecting

a group of figures in china, which stood in a
corner, Mr. Gladstone launched forth into a dis-
quisition on that topic, which he delights in, and
illustrated his idea of the art by showing us
several specimens of different kinds. One a
grotesque but speaking figure in Capo di Monte,
another a group of combatants, two of whom
were lying dead with all the aspect of strained
muscle stiffening; and lastly, a very classical and
elegant set of Wedgwood ware, certainly finer
than I ever saw before. He might have gone
on much longer, but we were separating, and
I was obliged to hurry home in order to complete the week's dispatches. This is the plea-
santest and most profitable form of English
society. I have not met with much of it since
I have been here, and hence infer that it is rare.
It reminds me a little of my father's breakfasts
[in Washington] when he was Secretary of
State and I a boy."

The following are Mr. Adams's descriptions of
the funeral obsequies of two of the most distinguished of the public men with whom he came
in contact while in England, — Richard Cobden, the most influential of those who, during
the period of rebellion stress, sympathized
with the Union, though not more courageous or
outspoken than Bright or Forster; and Lord
Palmerston, the jaunty Premier, to whose really

strong points and attractive attributes Mr. Adams, it must be conceded, did scant justice. Mr. Cobden died on the 2d of April, 1865, the very day of the capture of Richmond and the fall of the Confederacy. Lord Palmerston, still Prime Minister at the great age of eighty-one, followed him on the 18th of October.

"Friday, 7th April, 1865 : — To Midhurst [in Sussex, some fifteen miles from the south coast of England], which we reached at noon. We all got out and walked perhaps a mile to the point at which the immediate procession would pass from the house to the church of Larington, where the body was to be buried ; here we were to fall in and follow. I saw Mr. Gladstone, Mr. Villiers, and Mr. Milner Gibson, of the ministers, and perhaps sixty members of Parliament. Lord Kinnaird, the only peer, and I walked together. Besides which there were deputations from several of the great towns of the north, Manchester and Birmingham, Bradford and Rochdale, and Liverpool. The day was lovely, and the scenery of that peculiarly quiet, English character seen nowhere but in this little island. It has not, however, that defect of flatness and over-culture which robs so many parts of all interest. There is irregularity of surface, and in a degree roughness of wood and wild to make the picturesque. We wound along a road gradually ascending until we came to a steep rise, which brought us to the little church. The site is thus high; and from it the eye wanders over a wide space terminating in a range of distant hills, all rural and quiet. Here the last ceremonies were completed. The land is thrown up in glacis, on the highest of which was the tomb into which the body was finally placed to repose. In front were the pall-bearers and nearest relatives. On one side were the members of Parliament, and at the back I stood, with many more, thus making three sides of a square, the fourth side left open at the corner of the sloping terrace. There was emotion shown by none so much as by Mr. Bright. No pageant could have touched me so much. I felt my eyes filling from mere human sympathy. The deceased statesman had fought his way to fame and honor by the single force of his character. He had nothing to give. No wealth, no honors, no preferment. A lifelong contempt of the ruling class of his countrymen had earned for him their secret ill-will, marked on this day by the almost total absence of representatives here. And, of all foreign nations, I alone, the type of a great democracy, stood to bear witness to the scene. The real power that was present in the multitude crowding around this lifeless form was not the less gigantic for all this absence.

In this country, it may be said to owe its existence to Mr. Cobden. He first taught them by precept and example that the right of government was not really to the few, but to the many. He shook the pillars of the aristocracy by proving that he could wield influence without selling himself to them, or without recourse to the arts of a demagogue. Thus he becomes the founder of a new school, the influence of which is only just beginning to be felt. In the next century the effects will become visible. Such were my meditations as I drew away from the spot, and sauntered along a quiet cross-road by myself back to the little town of Midhurst, — old, with narrow streets, but neat as possible, and substantial-looking. No dilapidation, or symptom of dirt or poverty. An aspect of complete repose, as it were Pompeii after an entombment of centuries. Presently Mr. Forster overtook me. We soon afterwards returned in the train which got to town at six. Thus passed the day. I was glad I went, for it seemed to be very acceptable. Besides which, it was an event to mark in a lifetime."

"Friday, 27th October. — According to the programme, my carriage and servants were sent at eleven o'clock to Cambridge House, to make a part of the escort of the corpse to Westminster Abbey, whilst I went directly to the Abbey

at noon. A stall in the choir was assigned to
me, from which I had a good opportunity to
see everything of the ceremony in the interior.
The Prince of Wales and the Duke of Cambridge came in successively, and each had a stall
assigned next to the desk of the subdeans.
Only Mr. Musurus, of the ambassadors, and
Messrs. D'Azeglio, Bülow, Wachmeister, Ne-
grete, and myself, of the ministers, with several
subordinates, supposed to represent their principals, and Baron Blome.   The members of Parliament, many of the Lords and other officials,
had places on a raised platform placed in the
' Poets' Corner.'   Spectators' heads were visible peering out from every arch or window base,
even to the very roof, where they looked little
dots; but it gave no idea of a great crowd.
Presently came in the usual assortment of city
organizations, with their comical livery dresses,
and the maces, which make the bathos of every
public demonstration of this kingdom. After
these had been carefully disposed of in the space
just before the altar, the choir came in, preceding
the body, and chanting the opening sentences
of the burial service, ' I am the resurrection and
the life,' and ' I know that my Redeemer liveth.'
To me, this was the most impressive moment of
the whole ceremony. The singers slowly filed
off into their places in front of me, making way

for the body, borne in apparently by the chief
members of the old cabinet, with the new Premier at the head, Lord Russell. Just in advance was a man bearing on a velvet cushion
the empty coronet, a good type of the vanity of
the bauble. Then followed the mourners and
attendant followers, who filled the remaining
seats in the choir. Of the whole mass, the only
blood relations were two persons of the name of
Sullivan, never heard of in his day of power,
and therefore probably of very modest preten-
sions in the social scale; but there were many
of his wife's descendants. The ceremony went
on in customary form until the moment for
moving to the grave. We then all filed out in
order, and made a circle around the grave. The
effect was fine in the midst of the monuments
to the great men of other times, — Chatham and
Fox and Pitt and Canning, each of whom was
a much greater man than Palmerston; yet not
so much so, but that he might properly enough
be permitted to repose at their feet. Many are
resting around him who were not half so deserving as he. Dean Stanley read the remainder of the services clearly and with effect, but
there was nothing to stir emotion. Then came
Händel's hymn, ' His body is buried in peace,'
very well sung in the midst of a sudden change
of light caused by heavy rain outside, which

gave a touch of gloom that did not form any marked feature of the ceremony before. So it ended. Imposing, but not affecting. Lord Palmerston's career was one of success which drew myriads of friends of a certain sort about him, but he was the incarnation of the passions of this world. Hence when he vanishes he leaves nothing but a historical memory. I could not but recall the moment when I stood, only a few months ago, by the grave of a greater, because a more single-hearted and truthful, statesman, and witnessed the simple but earnest tribute paid to his worth by hundreds of men who were drawn to the spot by no idea but the sole desire to sprinkle [it] with their tears. At that time I, though a stranger, felt the moisture spontaneously rising in my eyes. At this, I not only stood myself unmoved, but saw no one anywhere who looked less calm than I. The historical scene was over ; and Palmerston is no longer a word of charm for any perhaps but the widow, who served him faithfully in his days of pride, and who in his loss will daily realize the change that has come over herself and her own ambition. The mainspring is gone."

CHAPTER XIX

THE GENEVA ARBITRATION

WHEN he returned to America in June, 1868, Mr. Adams was in his sixty-first year, and much future public usefulness might have been expected of him. He was, however, not only, so to speak, out of touch with both the great political parties which divided the country, but he came back to a country quite different from that which he had left. Between the United States of 1861 and that of 1868 a great gulf intervened; and Mr. Adams was a man who adjusted himself but slowly to new conditions. Moreover, the rough, crude policy of reconstruction, inaugurated in opposition to President Andrew Johnson by the more radical element of the Republican party, now in complete ascendency, offended all his ideas both of public morality and constitutional law; on the other hand, not only was the record of the Democratic party objectionable, but he could not help seeing much to criticise in its present attitude and political methods. Still, he came back with a great reputation. Throughout the war he had

been brought in conflict with those representing
foreign nations only. Thus he was in no way
associated in men's minds with domestic strife,
and consequently he was in a strong position to
render public service. He evinced, however,
no disposition to take part in political affairs,
avoiding all public expression. While the active politicians — the workers and schemers of
both parties — looked at him somewhat askance,
regarding him as an unknown and to a degree
a questionable factor, he betook himself at once
to Quincy, and, busying himself with the family
papers, quietly resumed the life he had abandoned when he went to Washington ten years
before. Naturally, he did not find the change
healthful, or his work exhilarating. He understood at last his father's dislike, in his latter
years, to raking over "stale political excitements."

Though, at the presidential election which followed his return, Mr. Adams cast a silent vote
for the Republican candidate, General Grant,
as representing a policy of peace and restored
good feeling, he took no part whatever in the
canvass. The radical element repelled him.
After the election, however, and when the cabinet of the coming President was in discussion,
his name was much canvassed in connection with
the Department of State; but there is no reason

to think that Grant ever seriously considered
the appointment.   When Mr. Adams left for
England in 1861, the now incoming President
was a compulsorily retired captain, unknown
and quite discredited ; nor could anything have
more emphasized the change the intervening
years had wrought than, a few months after
his return, to be introduced to this personage,
become, as if by magic, the most exalted character in the land.   The two met for the first
time at a Boston dinner-table, early in December, 1869.   They doubtless each scrutinized the
other with curiosity ; it is questionable whether
on either side the conclusion was altogether favorable.

Harvard University was then looking for a
President in place of Thomas Hill, recently resigned.   Mr. Adams was somewhat in the line
of safe precedent, and the members of the cor-
poration accordingly turned towards him.   In
March, 1869, a formal tender of the position
was made.   Mr. Adams declined to consider it.
He saw in himself " no especial fitness " for
the office ; and to accept it would, as he wrote,
" involve a necessity of breaking up all my arrangements, and the abandonment of plans to
execute which I had given up public life."   The
conclusion was not less wise than clear ; and,
Mr. Charles W. Eliot being the next choice,

neither Mr. Adams nor the University had occasion subsequently to regret it.

Meanwhile the questions at issue between the
United States and Great Britain, left unsettled
by Mr. Adams, were rapidly being brought to a
head.   Mr. Reverdy Johnson, of Maryland, had
succeeded Mr. Adams at London.   A treaty,
subsequently known as the Johnson-Clarendon
treaty, had been negotiated by Mr. Johnson
with Lord Clarendon, the British foreign secretary in the first Gladstone administration,
and, in the last month of Andrew Johnson's
term, was submitted to the Senate for its approval.   Carried over as unfinished business
into Grant's first term, on April 13th it was
rejected by a vote practically unanimous.   It
was on this occasion that Mr. Sumner, then
chairman of the senate committee on foreign
affairs, introduced into the case the element of
" indirect claims."   " The practical effect of
this proceeding," wrote Mr. Adams on the day
Mr. Sumner's speech was published, " is to raise
the scale of our demands of reparation so very
high that there is no chance of negotiation left,
unless the English have lost all their spirit and
character."   A few days later Mr. Motley, then
recently appointed, and on his way to succeed
Reverdy Johnson at London, called on Mr.
Adams.   " He seems anxious to do his best,"

wrote Mr. Adams ; " but his embarrassment is considerable in one particular which never affected me, and that is having two masters. Mr. Seward never permitted any interference of the Senate, or Mr. Sumner, with his direction of the policy."

There is not space in the present work to enter in detail into the history of the treaty of Washington. Very interesting, it is replete with individual characteristics ; but Mr. Adams was concerned only in its results. He took no part in the negotiations, nor was he more than incidentally consulted as they progressed. To expect an agreement of the two sides on the numerous and intricate questions in dispute was altogether unreasonable ; and so, in the end, a series of references to arbitration was agreed on, one of which, and incomparably the most important, covered the Alabama claims. The really noticeable feature in the treaty, however, — the feature unprecedented in diplomacy, — was a confession of wrongdoing on the part of one of the contracting parties, incorporated in the preamble. Her Britannic Majesty's representatives there declared themselves authorized to " express in a friendly spirit the regret felt by her Majesty's government for the escape, under whatever circumstances, of the Alabama and other vessels from British ports, and for the depredations committed by those vessels," — an admission which, eight years before, it would have seemed to Lord Palmerston and Earl Russell well-nigh inconceivable that England ever would descend to make.

Three rules for the guidance of the arbitrators in their disposal of claims in dispute were then formulated. Through these rules the principles of international law theretofore recognized were distinctly developed and defined; and to this result the clear and detailed record, so laboriously made up by Mr. Adams in his correspondence with Earl Russell, greatly contributed. The arbitrators, five in number, were to be named: — one by each of the two nations concerned; one by the King of Italy; one by the Emperor of Brazil; and one by the President of the Swiss Confederation. Count Frederic Sclopis, the Baron d'Itajubá, and Mr. Jacob Staempfli were duly designated by the three foreign countries. Great Britain appointed Sir Alexander Cockburn, Chief Justice of the Court of Queen's Bench; Mr. Adams was appointed on behalf of the United States. It was further provided that the tribunal should meet at Geneva "at the earliest convenient day" after appointment, which was subsequently settled as some time in December, 1871. None of those with whom he thus found himself about to be associated had

Mr. Adams ever met ; Sir Alexander Cockburn
not having actively participated in English social
life during the period of Mr. Adams's London
residence.

Meeting at Geneva at the time fixed, the
Board organized by the selection of Count
Sclopis as its presiding member, and then adjourned for six months to give the several arbitrators the time necessary to master, as best they
could, the elaborate arguments already in print,
amounting almost to a literature. Being the only
one among them thoroughly familiar with the
subject in all its aspects, Mr. Adams felt himself
comparatively at leisure. Going from Geneva
to the Riviera and thence to Italy, he was meditating a trip to Egypt, when, suddenly, he found
himself recalled to America. A new and serious
difficulty had arisen in the path of the arbitration. Sir Alexander Cockburn, the British appointee on the board, had never regarded the
proposed plan of settlement with favor ; and he
left Geneva distinctly prejudiced against it. He
would have liked to find some good and sufficient pretext for bringing the arbitration to an
end ; nor, in his search for such a pretext, did he
have far to go. It was found in the American
case, under the head of " Indirect Damages."

The generically so-called Alabama claims, as
advanced originally by Mr. Adams in his cor-

respondence with Earl Russell, and as subsequently provided for in the Johnson-Clarendon treaty, included only the direct losses resulting from the depredations of such of the Confederate cruisers as, during the civil war, escaped from, or found refuge and comfort in, British ports. So many ships had been destroyed; so much damage inflicted. It all admitted of enumeration and proof; it was definite and measurable; any jury could have passed upon it, and assessed a verdict under well-established rules of computation applied in accordance with recognized principles of law. Something more than this had first been foreshadowed by Mr. Sumner in his speech, already referred to, on the rejection of the Johnson-Clarendon treaty in April, 1869. Vague, intangible, admitting neither of measurement nor of computation, this " something " subsequently became known as the claim for indirect or consequential damages. A single item only, that of diminution of tonnage in the carrying trade, was computed by Mr. Sumner in his speech at a hundred and ten millions of dollars; while he vaguely intimated that an additional two thousand millions, or thereabouts, something more or a trifle less, might be fairly chargeable in the same way on account of the prolongation of the war. Obviously, among reasonable or reasoning men, such a claim was not

entitled to serious consideration. Preposterous
on its face, the suggestion of it was calculated
to excite derision.   Even Mr. Sumner probably
did not look upon it as a thing convertible into
figures, or to be measured in pounds and pence.
His mind was then working in another direction. He meditated conjuring the British flag
out of the entire Western Hemisphere ; and
this was the spectre with which he proposed to
exorcise.[1] A result wholly visionary, except at
the close of a decisive trial of strength, was
thus to be brought about through an impossible
computation of quantities which did not admit
of ascertainment. The device was in every respect characteristic. Of course it does not need
to be said that no nation not wholly crushed and
helpless would, any more than an individual,
submit to be mulcted in this fashion. The proposal was an insult, and its discussion would be a
humiliation. The United States had but to consider what its own feelings would be if it were
insolently confronted with such a proposition.

The consequences are readily imaginable, therefore, when, on the distribution of what was
known as " the American case " at Geneva on

[1] See the extraordinary memorandum submitted by Mr.
Sumner to Secretary Fish on the 17th of January, 1871,
printed by Professor Moore, *International Arbitrations*, i. 525 ;
also, Sumner's *Works*, xiii. 127–130.

February 15th, an examination disclosed the fact
that this claim for indirect and consequential
damages had in it been advanced. In the presentation, too, there was not a sign of humor, nor
an indication of a sense of absurdity. On its
face the claim was made seriously. It is needless at this point to enter into any elaborate
discussion of why this thing was done, by whom
it was inspired, or to what end it was designed.
That it was there, was at the time both plain
and sufficient. The treaty was endangered.

The London press at once seized on the matter.
The " Morning Advertiser " opened on January
4th by asking whether it was possible that
" imbeciles and fools " could have so conducted
negotiations as to put it in the power of any
tribunal, " even by possibility, to award our national degradation and financial ruin ; " if they
had, it only remained for the nation at once to
resume a faculty it had so fatally delegated to
such " crass incompetency." The chorus then
became general ; and, in its turn, Great Britain
passed into a condition of hysteria not unlike
that experienced by the Northern communities
of the United States when they heard of the
Trent performance of Captain Wilkes.

The ministry bowed to the storm. Significantly referred to in the Queen's speech at the
opening of Parliament on February 9th, the

" indirect claims " became at once matter for parliamentary discussion and diplomatic correspondence. Mr. Disraeli, the leader of the opposition, characterized them as " preposterous and wild," equivalent to a " tribute from a conquered people; " and the Prime Minister, Mr. Gladstone, in reply, referred to this language as " rather under the mark than an exaggeration," and was loudly cheered when he went on to declare that " we must be insane to accede to demands which no nation with a spark of honor or spirit left could submit to even at the point of death." [1] The British commissioners in due time each rose in his place, whether the House of Lords, or Exeter, or the Oxford lecture-room, and expressed their astonishment at the construction put upon their handiwork; while presently Lord Granville began to exchange notes on the subject with General Schenck, now the

[1] This debate occurred in February, 1872. By the terms of the treaty of Versailles, which, in February, 1871, exactly twelve months before, brought the Franco-Prussian war to a close, France, besides the loss of Alsace and Lorraine, had been forced to submit to the payment of a war indemnity of one thousand millions of dollars. This precedent, very fresh at the time, was obviously present in the minds of those who took part in the debate. The suggestion of some enormous money payment was, therefore, less absurd than it would otherwise have seemed, and much more offensive. Great Britain was to undergo a fate similar to that of prostrate France.

American minister to Great Britain, and Sir Edward Thornton with Secretary Fish.

The really unfortunate feature in the thing lay in the discreditable turn it gave to what had up to that point been a most creditable negotiation, — one good in itself, and promising yet better in what it might lead to as a precedent. As the Earl of Derby intimated, it gave the impression on the part of the Americans of " a good deal of acuteness, — I will not call it by a harsher name," — not pleasant to contemplate. The real fact, however, would seem to be that the indirect claims were inserted in the American " case " by those who prepared it, not because of any faith in them or a hope that they might possibly be entertained, but in order to get rid of them, and as a species of political estoppel. They had been advanced by Senator Sumner and advocated by General B. F. Butler, — both factors in Washington not to be disregarded. They could not, therefore, well be abandoned, while they were certain to be overruled. They were accordingly brought into the case, and presented as clearly, fully, and vigorously as possible, with a view to forestalling home criticism. Meanwhile the British commissioners, understanding the situation of their American associates, had assumed a tacit abandonment; and the language of the treaty was intentionally so framed that, without any express renunciation of consequential damages, it could be construed so as to exclude them.[1] As a result, in order to avert a possible subsequent danger, the one side presented with all possible earnestness and apparent conviction a claim which it knew to be preposterous and intended to have overruled; while the other, taking the thing seriously, gave way to an outburst of indignation at what was assumed to be an attempt to overreach.

Passing through London in February, on his way home, Mr. Adams found the British mind in much the same condition of ferment that he recalled so vividly during the December of ten winters before. Forming a tolerably clear idea of the situation, he left for New York, arriving there on February 21st, and going at once to Washington to confer with the President and Mr. Fish. Thence he returned to Boston, where he remained until the following May, when he embarked once more for Europe.

Meanwhile a new contingency arose, and, to his own great surprise, Mr. Adams suddenly found himself a prominent candidate for a presidential nomination. The history of the movement which culminated in the Cincinnati con-

[1] This subject is very clearly and fully dealt with by Professor Moore, *International Arbitrations*, i. 629–639.

vention of May, 1872, and the nomination of
Horace Greeley as the opposing candidate to
President Grant in the canvass of that year, is
curious, and not without its humorous as well as
interesting features. It can, however, here only
be alluded to. President Grant's first administration, as it drew to its close, was not generally
regarded as a success. Many of the recognized
Republican leaders — men like Sumner, Schurz,
Trumbull, and Greeley — were in open insurrection, and they were supported by the most influential portion of the independent press. The
Democratic party was demoralized by repeated
defeat, and ready to accept any candidate who
might bring with him reasonable assurance of
success. "Any one to beat Grant" was the
cry. Under these circumstances, Mr. Schurz,
then a senator from Missouri, conceived a brilliant political *coup*. By summoning a convention of the independent elements early in the
canvass, he proposed to forestall the action of
the Democrats, and to unite the entire opposition under one generally acceptable candidate,
as against the reëlection of the President. From
every point of view, — character, experience, isolation from party, known political views, and
freedom from recent controversies, — Mr. Adams
was, as a candidate, the natural and logical outcome of such a movement. It was so intended

by those most active in it. The more influential
Democrats expected and desired it. Everything
pointed to it. When, suddenly, at the last moment, through one of those ingeniously devised
political manipulations for which New York has
from time immemorial been famous, Horace
Greeley was, as if by some sleight-of-hand trick,
substituted for Mr. Adams as the presidential
candidate of those political elements — including reformers of the civil service, free-traders,
the Jacksonian Democracy, and the remnants
of the Southern oligarchy — to which Horace
Greeley had throughout his active and prominent
career been as objectionable as any man who
could have been named. The blunder, brought
about in the idea of some supposed superior
"availability," was irretrievable, and resulted in
a political fiasco and personal tragedy. In November, the dazed and beaten opposition pulled
itself out of a slough of defeat in time to look
stolidly on while its odd and wholly uncongenial
candidate was borne to his grave. Mr. Adams
had then just returned home from the successful performance of his last public service.
He had simply been saved from either a political
defeat, or a presidency predestined from its
commencement to failure. This he fully realized.

Meanwhile it is a fact, curiously illustrative

of Mr. Adams's political isolation and the personal respect in which he was at this time held, that in April, 1872, when his name was most in discussion as the probable nominee of the Cincinnati convention, then actually gathering, direct overtures were made to him to induce his acceptance of the second place on the ticket with Grant. These emanated from no less a person than Roscoe Conkling, and in the name of the New York delegation to the Republican presidential convention, to whom was to be given the choice of a vice-presidential candidate. Mr. Adams declined to consider the proposition, and Henry Wilson was subsequently decided upon.

Mr. Adams sailed for Europe on April 24th, one week before the day fixed for the meeting of the convention at Cincinnati. The first news he heard on reaching London was of his own defeat, and the nomination of Greeley. "This," he wrote, "was odd enough. The unexpected is what mostly turns up. This completely oversets all the calculations of the original authors of the convention, for success with such a candidate is out of the question. My first sense is one of great relief in being out of the *mêlée*."

It was now very questionable whether the arbitration would proceed. The British attitude was one of distrust, — uncertainty, with a ten-

dency to defiance. A novel feature in the arbitration had been the presence in the tribunal of
a nominee of each of the high contracting parties.
The framers of the treaty probably had recourse
to this expedient in order to meet the obvious
objections to confiding a reference of such importance to a board composed of individuals
whose familiarity with the English language was
not less a matter of uncertainty than was their
knowledge of the principles of law involved. To
both parties it seemed desirable to reserve some
means of insight into the methods of procedure
of a tribunal thus made up. This expedient now
saved the arbitration. Mr. Adams, no less earnest to bring a great and novel experiment to a
successful issue than the Anglo-American controversies to a close, proved equal to the occasion. The result turned on him.

Sir Alexander Cockburn now regarded the
arbitration as dead. So confident was he of
this that he dismissed the matter from his mind,
and went back to Geneva without putting himself to the inconvenience of making a study of
the case. As he subsequently expressed it in
the conferences of the board, " he had not
known what Mr. Adams proposed to do." Mr.
Adams " proposed," somehow, to carry the thing
through ; and he did it. The British counter-
case once filed, as he told W. E. Forster, at that

time in Gladstone's ministry, when they parted in London, "my business is to go to Geneva. In case Great Britain should decline to appear there, I shall urge the other arbitrators to go on nevertheless to decide on the issues now made up." Reaching Geneva at the time appointed for the reassembling of the arbitrators, he found everything uncertain. A brief survey of the situation satisfied him that there was but one course to pursue. The knot had to be cut. "We must," he wrote, "decide upon rejecting the whole question of indirect damages; and I must set it in motion, or nothing will come of it." He proceeded accordingly.

The English counsel were then communicated with. "What," said Lord Tenterden, "does Mr. Adams want? If he means business he must go further. He must have the indirect claims rejected." Adroitly seeing his colleagues on the tribunal, one by one, Mr. Adams now arranged the method of procedure. After a prearranged formal adjournment of the board on the 17th, the five arbitrators remained together for consultation. The French of Mr. Adams's Russian childhood now asserted its value; and gradually, by a process which he described in detail at the time, the reluctant Cockburn was led up to intimating "that an extra-judicial opinion might be made, which, if satisfactory to the United States so far as to extinguish their demand, would not be disputed by Great Britain. I saw at once the opening," wrote Mr. Adams, " and asked him directly whether such a step taken here would, in his opinion, satisfy the government, and remove all obstacles to immediate progress. He said he thought it would. I said that, in that event, I was prepared to make a proposition. I should be assuming a heavy responsibility ; but I should do so, not as an arbitrator representing my country, but as representing all nations." The English member of the Board then absenting himself from its next meeting, the claim for "indirect damages" was, under the lead of Mr. Adams, summarily ruled out of consideration, as opposed to the principles of international law. This obstacle being thus removed, and the decision accepted as final by the United States, the requests for yet further delay made on behalf of the British were disallowed, and the arbitration proceeded. A few days afterwards, as Mr. Adams was leaving the Geneva *Salle des Mariages*, the chamber in which the meetings of the arbitrators were held, one of the newspaper correspondents handed him a slip from the London "Times," in which the whole success in saving the treaty was attributed to his efforts. "Thus it goes forth ; " he wrote, — " the Chief Justice only

echoed the voice of Great Britain. Well, I suppose I must take that responsibility. Such a
success is far more precious to me than any nomination or election to the place of President."
At that day's session " the Chief Justice," or Sir
Alexander Cockburn, had begged for delay in
which to prepare himself, on the ground that,
until then, he had not supposed that anything
would come of the arbitration. " He was not
in Mr. Adams's situation," he said ; " nor could
he foresee what Mr. Adams was about to do to
remove all difficulties." The victory was complete.

Into the subsequent history of the arbitration,
which, " whether measured by the gravity of
the questions at issue, or by the magnanimous
and enlightened statesmanship which conducted
them to a peaceful determination, was justly
regarded as the greatest the world had ever
seen," [1] there is not space here to enter. The
award ($15,500,000) there secured in favor of
the United States was, for Mr. Adams's public
life, what Cromwell called " the crowning
mercy." Of his judicial carriage in securing
that result, the agent of his government subsequently wrote : " I must bear testimony to the
perfect and dignified impartiality with which,
throughout the proceedings, Mr. Adams main-

[1] Moore, *International Arbitrations*, i. 652, 653.

tained his position as a judge between the two contending nations. Of him, at least, it may be said that his love of country never controlled his sense of justice, and that at no time did he appear as an advocate."

CHAPTER XX

CLOSING YEARS

THE days passed at Geneva were among the most satisfactory and happiest of Mr. Adams's life. Everything combined to cause him to enjoy them, — scenery, climate, occupation, social surroundings, and, above all, success. On the last day (September 14th) of the sessions of the tribunal, and when its presiding member had declared it dissolved, Mr. Adams wrote: "Thus closed this great experiment, with as much of success as could possibly have been expected. I walked home, musing. It is now eleven years since this mission was given to me. Through good report and through evil report, my action has been associated with its progress; and, now that it is ended, I have only to return my humble thanks to the Disposer of events for the blessing He thought fit to confer upon me in carrying the matter to its end. I may hope to consider it as an honorable termination to my public career."

On the 31st of October following, after ten days of weather than which he declared he had

never seen anything " more dismal," Mr. Adams
took his departure from London, though, " I
presume, never to see it again, with little regret." " Yet," he added, " I leave [Europe]
with no painful associations. To me it is connected with the only brilliant part of my career.
Thus it is well it should rest in my memory."

The active public life of Mr. Adams practically ended, as he had surmised it might, with
the Geneva arbitration. It had extended over
just thirteen years. It covered the whole period
of the civil war, including the process of reconstruction; and he was, in all respects, singularly
happy in the share of work allotted to him. It
was important; it was work for which he was
by nature peculiarly adapted; it was done amid
congenial surroundings; it was complete; and
it was successful. A public man could ask for
nothing more. The contentions in which he was
engaged were of surpassing magnitude, and involved momentous consequences; they extended
through a long period of time; they were carried
on wholly with foreign nations; and, in their
conduct, he came in collision with some of the
foremost of European public men. Yet his success was as final as it was complete and unquestioned. When he landed in New York on November 13, 1872, he had a right to exclaim,
as he did, " Io Triumphe! " for every issue be-

tween Great Britain and the United States growing out of the great civil war either was definitely settled, or was in course of early settlement. His work was done ; and done thoroughly.

Returning to Boston in November, immediately after the second election of Grant, Mr. Adams found the business portions of his native city a mass of smoking ruins, — the great Boston fire having occurred during the previous week. He at once resumed his former mode of life, nor was it again disturbed. He was now at just the age when his grandfather had left the presidency to rust out his declining years in the dreary monotony of a "dignified" retirement ; at just the age also when his father, rebelling at the idea of a similar fate, had flung himself into that congressional career which proved the most brilliant and active portion of his active and brilliant life. Had he been fully and keenly disposed, or had circumstances proved propitious, Mr. Adams might, in the ordinary course of nature, have yet had before him ten years at least of active public service ; years in which, aided by the experience he had gathered and the reputation he had won, he might most advantageously have influenced the course of events. In his case this was not to be.

Not that he probably would have disliked

another term of place and power; for with him
too, as he one day wrote, "public life was a
very fascinating occupation, but like drinking
brandy. The more you indulge in it, the more
uncomfortable it leaves you when you stop."
Accordingly, he would now have not been dis-
pleased to hear that unequivocal call which
would have summoned him back to activity;
but, though only just past the climacteric,
though four years younger than Lord John
Russell when they first faced each other at Pembroke Lodge, he was now an old man. Matured early, he grew old early. Even in 1875,
only three years after he got back from Geneva,
while his name was still common in men's
mouths and in the newspapers in connection
with the senatorship in succession to Sumner
and Wilson, with the governorship of Massachusetts, with the Department of State, with the
presidency itself after Grant's second term had
run out, — even then Mr. Adams was no longer
fit to bear the burdens of office. Responsibility
weighed upon him; work troubled him; trifles
worried him. His powers, physical and mental,
having long since attained their growth, had
begun to decay; and the consciousness of it
saddened him.

He had also early in life assigned to himself
a task not yet wholly performed; and once

more he turned to the family papers. Arranging old letters, and, in the evening of life, reading diaries, written by those now dead, of days long past but still remembered, is at best to no man exhilarating. So Mr. Adams now found. Immediately after the return from Geneva he had set to work on the publication of portions of his father's diary, which he entitled "Memoirs." The first volume appeared in 1874. At last, on a certain day in August, 1877, he found the final volume lying on his table. The labor imposed on himself nearly forty years before in connection with his grandmother, his grandfather, and his father was completed ; and, laying down the volume, he wrote : "I am now perfectly willing to go myself. My mission is ended, and I may rest."

Mr. Adams died in Boston on the 21st of November, 1886. Mrs. Adams outlived her husband two years and a half, dying in Quincy on the evening of June 6, 1889. Their married life covered over fifty-seven years ; and five children, four sons and one daughter, survived them.

INDEX

INDEX

ton for refusing to sign remonstrance against admission of Texas, 76–78; describes Webster's part in Massachusetts Whig Convention of 1846, 80; depressed at defeat of Conscience Whigs, 82; on Sumner's poor speech in Whig Convention of 1847, 84; realizes his lack of success as an editor, 87; grows weary of the enterprise, 88; relieved at abandoning the paper, 88.

Free-Soil Leader. Plans a bolt from Whig nomination of Taylor, 89; appointed delegate to Buffalo Convention, 90; dreads nomination of Van Buren, 90; chairman of convention, 91; nominated for Vice-President, 91; gratified at size of Free-Soil vote in Massachusetts, 92; gains a reputation independent of his ancestors, 93; sensitive to sneers on this point, 93–95; confronted with his own utterances on Van Buren, 95, 96; his opinion of Van Buren in 1848, 96; his position as supporter of Van Buren illogical, 97; turns from politics to editing the Works of John Adams, 100, 101; passes several years in privacy, 101, 102; in danger of becoming worn out as a public man, 103; mentioned to succeed his father, but supports Horace Mann, 103; defeated for Congress in 1852, 104; not supported by the Democrats, 104; opposed by native Americans, 105.

Member of Congress. Nominated in 1858 for Congress, and elected, 105; engages a house in Washington, 106; neglects Giddings's advice and fails to ask for a good appointment on committees, 111; given the merely honorary succession to his father's committee position, 111, 112; reluctant to speak in the House, 112; urged by constituents, makes

a set speech, 113; tribute of Cobb to his moderation, 113; substance of his speech, 113, 114; favors nomination of Seward, 114; depressed by nomination of Lincoln, 114; his opinion of Lincoln in 1860, 115; his part in campaign of 1860, 115; does not claim to have foreseen secession, 117; astounded when it comes, 118; later says it could have been stifled by prompt action, 128; realizes necessity for a conciliatory attitude, 129, 130; sees necessity of preventing outbreak until after March, 1861, 130, 131; favors conciliatory measures to gain time, 131; hopes to hold border states, 131; represents Massachusetts in Committee of Thirty-three, 132; not disappointed at failure of committee, 132, 133; at outset induces Southern extremists to show their plans, 134; hopes in this way to put South in the wrong, 134; does this by proposing compromise measures, 136, 137; upon refusal of South to be satisfied ceases to urge compromise, 139; sums up his course, his success, 139, 140; his speech of January 31, 140–142; his speech conciliates moderate men, 142; urged for Treasury Department, 143; not considered by Lincoln for any position, 143, 144; his appointment to English mission secured by Seward, 144; visits Seward and Lincoln to consult on instructions, 145; scandalized at Lincoln's indifference, 146.

Minister to England. On arrival in London visited by Bates, 147; surprised at proclamation recognizing Confederacy as belligerent, 148; situation on his arrival, 158; ignorant of Seward's proposed vigorous foreign policy, 167; annoyed by talk of Seward's hostility to England, 168; secures

ELECTROTYPED AND PRINTED
BY H. O. HOUGHTON AND CO.

The Riverside Press

CAMBRIDGE, MASS., U. S. A.

American Statesmen

Edited by John T. Morse, Jr.

Each, 16mo, cloth, gilt top, $1.25 ; half morocco, $2.50.
The set, 31 volumes, half levant, $77.50.

BENJAMIN FRANKLIN. By John T. Morse, Jr.

SAMUEL ADAMS. By James K. Hosmer.

PATRICK HENRY. By Moses Coit Tyler.

GEORGE WASHINGTON. By Henry Cabot Lodge.
  2 vols.

JOHN ADAMS. By John T. Morse, Jr.

ALEXANDER HAMILTON. By Henry Cabot Lodge.

GOUVERNEUR MORRIS. By Theodore Roosevelt.

JOHN JAY. By George Pellew.

JOHN MARSHALL. By Allan B. Magruder.

THOMAS JEFFERSON. By John T. Morse, Jr.

JAMES MADISON. By Sydney Howard Gay.

ALBERT GALLATIN. By John Austin Stevens.

JAMES MONROE. By President D. C. Gilman.

JOHN QUINCY ADAMS. By John T. Morse, Jr.

JOHN RANDOLPH. By Henry Adams.

ANDREW JACKSON. By Prof. William G. Sumner.

MARTIN VAN BUREN. By Edward M. Shepard.

HENRY CLAY. By Carl Schurz. 2 vols.

DANIEL WEBSTER. By Henry Cabot Lodge.

JOHN C. CALHOUN. By Dr. H. Von Holst.

THOMAS HART BENTON. By Theodore Roosevelt.

LEWIS CASS. By Prof. Andrew C. McLaughlin.

ABRAHAM LINCOLN. By John T. Morse, Jr. With
  Portrait and Map. 2 vols.

WILLIAM H. SEWARD. By Thornton K. Lothrop.

SALMON P. CHASE. By Prof. A. B. Hart.

CHARLES FRANCIS ADAMS. By C. F. Adams.

CHARLES SUMNER. By Moorfield Storey.

THADDEUS STEVENS. By Samuel W. McCall.

CRITICAL NOTICES.

FRANKLIN. He has managed to condense the whole mass of matter gleaned from all sources into his volume without losing in a single sentence the freedom or lightness of his style or giving his book in any part the crowded look of an epitome. — *The Independent* (New York).

SAMUEL ADAMS. Thoroughly appreciative and sympathetic, yet fair and critical. . . . This biography is a piece of good work — a clear and simple presentation of a noble man and pure patriot; it is written in a spirit of candor and humanity. — *Worcester Spy.*

HENRY. Professor Tyler has not only made one of the best and most readable of American biographies; he may fairly be said to have reconstructed the life of Patrick Henry, and to have vindicated the memory of that great man from the unappreciative and injurious estimate which has been placed upon it. — *New York Evening Post.*

WASHINGTON. Mr. Lodge has written an admirable biography, and one which cannot but confirm the American people in the prevailing estimate concerning the Father of his Country. — *New York Tribune.*

JOHN ADAMS. A good piece of literary work. . . . It covers the ground thoroughly, and gives just the sort of simple and succinct account that is wanted. — *New York Evening Post.*

HAMILTON. Mr. Lodge has done his work with conscientious care, and the biography of Hamilton is a book which cannot have too many readers. It is more than a biography; it is a study in the science of government. — *St. Paul Pioneer Press.*

MORRIS. Mr. Roosevelt has produced an animated and intensely interesting biographical volume. . . . Mr. Roosevelt never loses sight of the picturesque background of politics, war-governments, and diplomacy. — *Magazine of American History* (New York).

JAY. It is an important addition to the admirable series of "American Statesmen," and elevates yet higher the character of a man whom all American patriots most delight to honor. — *New York Tribune.*

MARSHALL. Well done, with simplicity, clearness, precision, and judgment, and in a spirit of moderation and equity   A valuable addition to the series. — *New York Tribune.*

JEFFERSON. A singularly just, well-proportioned, and interesting sketch of the personal and political career of the author of the Declaration of Independence. — *Boston Journal.*

MADISON. The execution of the work deserves the highest praise. It is very readable, in a bright and vigorous style, and is marked by unity and consecutiveness of plan. — *The Nation* (New York).

GALLATIN. It is one of the most carefully prepared of these very valuable volumes, . . . abounding in information not so readily accessible as is that pertaining to men more often treated by the biographer. — *Boston Correspondent Hartford Courant.*

MONROE. President Gilman has made the most of his hero, without the least hero-worship, and has done full justice to Mr. Monroe's "relations to the public service during half a century." . . . The appendix is peculiarly valuable for its synopsis of Monroe's Presidential Messages, and its extensive Bibliography of Monroe and the Monroe Doctrine. — *N. Y. Christian Intelligencer.*

JOHN QUINCY ADAMS. That Mr. Morse's conclusions will in the main be those of posterity we have very little doubt, and he has set an admirable example to his coadjutors in respect of interesting narrative, just proportion, and judicial candor. — *New York Evening Post.*

RANDOLPH. The book has been to me intensely interesting. . . . It is rich in new facts and side lights, and is worthy of its place in the already brilliant series of monographs on American Statesmen. — Prof. MOSES COIT TYLER.

JACKSON. Professor Sumner has . . . all in all, made the justest long estimate of Jackson that has had itself put between the covers of a book. — *New York Times.*

VAN BUREN. This absorbing book. . . . To give any adequate idea of the personal interest of the book, or its intimate bearing on nearly the whole course of our political history, would be equivalent to quoting the larger part of it. — *Brooklyn Eagle.*

CLAY. We have in this life of Henry Clay a biography of one of the most distinguished of American statesmen, and a political history of the United States for the first half of the nineteenth century. Indeed, it is not too much to say that, for the period covered, we have no other book which equals or begins to equal this life of Henry Clay as an introduction to the study of American politics. — *Political Science Quarterly* (New York).

WEBSTER. It will be read by students of history; it will be invaluable as a work of reference; it will be an authority as regards matters of fact and criticism; it hits the keynote of Webster's durable and ever-growing fame; it is adequate, calm, impartial; it is admirable. — *Philadelphia Press.*

CALHOUN. Nothing can exceed the skill with which the political career of the great South Carolinian is portrayed in these pages. . . . The whole discussion in relation to Calhoun's position is eminently philosophical and just. — *The Dial* (Chicago).

BENTON. An interesting addition to our political literature, and will be of great service if it spread an admiration for that austere public morality which was one of the marked characteristics of its chief figure. — *The Epoch* (New York).

CASS. Professor McLaughlin has given us one of the most satisfactory volumes in this able and important series. . . . The early life of Cass was devoted to the Northwest, and in the transformation which overtook it the work of Cass was the work of a national statesman. — *New York Times.*

LINCOLN. As a life of Lincoln it has no competitors; as a political history of the Union side during the Civil War, it is the most comprehensive, and, in proportion to its range, the most compact. — *Harvard Graduates' Magazine.*

SEWARD. The public will be grateful for his conscientious efforts to write a popular vindication of one of the ablest, most brilliant, fascinating, energetic, ambitious, and patriotic men in American history. — *New York Evening Post.*

CHASE. His great career as anti-slavery leader, United States Senator, Governor of Ohio, Secretary of the Treasury, and Chief Justice of the United States, is described in an adequate and effective manner by Professor Hart.

CHARLES FRANCIS ADAMS. His wise statesmanship before the Civil War, and the masterly ability and consummate diplomatic skill displayed by him while Minister to Great Britain, are judiciously set forth by his eminent son.

SUMNER. The majestic devotion of Sumner to the highest political ideals before and during his long term of lofty service to freedom in the United States Senate is fittingly delineated by Mr. Storey.

STEVENS. Thaddeus Stevens was unquestionably one of the most conspicuous figures of his time. . . . The book shows him the eccentric, fiery, and masterful congressional leader that he was. — *City and State* (Philadelphia).

HOUGHTON, MIFFLIN & CO.

4 PARK ST., BOSTON ; 11 EAST 17TH ST., NEW YORK ;
378–388 WABASH AVE., CHICAGO.

DATE DUE

NOV 24 1972			
FEB 2 5 1981			
GAYLORD			PRINTED IN U.S.A.